To the Instructor

The third edition of *Commanding Sentences* retains those features from the first and second editions that have been successful in writing courses at the college or high school level. This program is intended for students who need a step-by-step descriptive study of language functions and characteristics and experience in writing a wide variety of sentences before or during a writing course. This revised edition also continues to lend itself to a variety of classroom situations. It is equally effective for individualized instruction in the classroom or writing lab, for modular scheduling, and for lecture-discussion classes. Its detailed index makes it a quick reference in writing courses.

Revised on the basis of comments and suggestions from instructors who have used the first and second editions in their classrooms, the third edition contains some additions. First, the revised opening units in this edition simplify the study of sentence patterns by concentrating on five of the usual eight patterns, focusing on those patterns that serve as a basis for pronoun usage and sentence combining. Second, more examples and exercises on choosing verb tenses, writing questions, and using articles have been included for students more familiar with their own dialect or foreign language. Third, more exercises that ask students to generate their own sentences and paragraphs have been added. Fourth, lessons on sentence combining and meanings of connectors have been expanded to show students how to evaluate their ideas and present them logically.

The Unit Practice Tests have been retained. In addition, the vocabulary and sentence structure in the first six units of the text continue to be carefully controlled to enable students to understand lessons, complete exercises, and write their own sentences easily. The remaining units, in which students develop longer, more complicated sentences, are necessarily written at a higher reading level.

Grammatical terminology throughout the text continues to be limited to those terms needed to discuss parts of the sentence. Students using these terms quickly become aware of the patterns in sentences and develop a strong foundation for combining sentences in later units. In addition, the order of the lessons has been carefully sequenced for students who lack the background to use handbooks or conventional texts.

Based on the mastery concept and learning objectives, *Commanding Sentences* consists of eleven units of sequential lessons, an appendix on spelling, exercises for each lesson to test application, answers at the end of the text for immediate feedback, and Unit Practice Tests to prepare students for the Unit Reviews. The test package, available for duplication, is included in the *Instructor's Manual*. It contains a Writing Pretest for placing students, Unit Reviews (Forms A, B, and C), a practice test for the Posttest, and three forms of the Posttest. Answers for the Unit Reviews are found in the *Instructor's Manual*, which also includes detailed suggestions for the ways you may use these materials and for administering tests and grading.

If you have any questions about the *Commanding Sentences* program, please write me at 3157 Oak Cliff Circle, Carmichael, CA 95608, or call me at (916) 487-6477.

Helen Mills

Contents

To the Student Writer   vi

Unit One
Basic Sentence Patterns   1

Lesson 1   Finding the Subject and Predicate   2
Lesson 2   Identifying Verbs   4
Lesson 3   Identifying Nouns   7
Lesson 4   Sentences with Action Verbs   11
Lesson 5   Sentences with Linking Verbs   17

Practice Test   22

Unit Two
Verbs and Adverbs   25

Lesson 6   Adding Adverbs to Sentences   26
Lesson 7   The Present Tense   29
Lesson 8   The Past Tense   34
Lesson 9   The Future Tense   39

Practice Test   43

Unit Three
More About Verbs   47

Lesson 10   The Perfect Tenses   50
Lesson 11   The Progressive Tenses   57
Lesson 12   Modal (One-Form) Verbs   64
Lesson 13   Negatives and Questions   67
Lesson 14   Troublesome Verbs   75

Practice Test   79

Unit Four
Nouns and Modifiers   83

Lesson 15   Nouns   84
Lesson 16   Determiners   87
Lesson 17   Possessives   94
Lesson 18   Adjectives   96
Lesson 19   Adverbs   102
Lesson 20   Prepositional Phrases   108

Practice Test   117

Unit Five
More Basic Sentence Patterns   123

Lesson 21   Sentences with Subject Complements   124
Lesson 22   Sentences with Indirect Objects   130
Lesson 23   Sentence Keys for All Sentence Patterns   133

Practice Test   140

Unit Six
Pronouns and Agreement   145

Lesson 24   Personal Pronouns   146
Lesson 25   Other Pronouns   152
Lesson 26   Pronoun Reference and Agreement   156
Lesson 27   Subject-Verb Agreement   166

Practice Test   170

COMMANDING SENTENCES

Third Edition

Helen Mills
Professor Emeritus of English
American River College

Sheffield Publishing Company

Salem, Wisconsin

Special thanks to

my family: LeRoy, Marilyn and David
my students and tutors, who have been my teachers

William McCrory
Shirley New
Nora Nishimoto
M. Melvin Gardner

Byron Patterson
Robert Allen
Marilyn Mills
Frank Adams
Darrell Eckersley
Robert G. Fountaine
Walter Graffin
Joan Kohman
Lynn Miller
Mary Beverly Moore
Jeanette Morgan
Shaheen Sayeed
Thomas C. Ware

Michael Anderson
Linda Peterson
Susan Strunk

Acknowledgments
Montgomery Gregory, "A Review of Cane" from *The Merrill Studies in Cane.* Columbus, Ohio: Charles C. Merrill Publishing Company, 1971, p. 134. Norman Mailer, *Of a Fire on the Moon.* Boston: Little, Brown and Company, 1970, p. 36. "Survival on Land– Tropics" from the *AOPA Handbook for Pilots.* Washington, D.C.: Aircraft Owners and Pilots Association, 1975, p. 117.

For information about this book, contact:
Sheffield Publishing Company
PO Box 359
Salem, Wisconsin 53168
Phone 262.843.2281
Fax 262.843.3683
E-mail: info@spcbooks.com

An Instructor's Manual, which includes the test package, to accompany *Commanding Sentences* is available from the publisher.

Copyright © 1983, 1979, 1974 by Helen Mills
1990, reissued by Sheffield Publishing Company

ISBN 0-88133-524-X
ISBN 978-0-88133-524-8

Printed in the United States of America

20 19 18 17

Unit Seven
Coordination *173*

Lesson 28 Compound Sentences *174*
Lesson 29 Transitional Expressions *179*
Lesson 30 Compound Subjects and
          Compound Predicates *187*
Lesson 31 Appositives *193*
Lesson 32 Sentence Combining
          Review *197*

Practice Test *200*

Unit Eight
Subordination: Dependent Clauses *205*

Lesson 33 Adverbial Clauses *206*
Lesson 34 Adjective Clauses *214*
Lesson 35 Noun Clauses *225*
Lesson 36 Clauses Within Clauses *231*
Lesson 37 Review of Phrases and
          Clauses *234*

Practice Test *238*

Practice Writing Test *242*

Unit Nine
Subordination: Verbal Phrases *243*

Lesson 38 The V-ing Verbal Phrase *244*
Lesson 39 Active and Passive Verbs *252*
Lesson 40 The V-ed Verbal Phrase *256*
Lesson 41 The Infinitive Verbal
          Phrase *260*
Lesson 42 Misplaced and Dangling
          Modifiers *265*
Lesson 43 Absolute Phrases *269*
Lesson 44 Combining Phrases and
          Clauses *271*
Lesson 45 Fragments: Nonsentences *276*

Practice Test *280*

Unit Ten
Punctuation and Capitalization *283*

Lesson 46 Punctuation to Separate *284*
Lesson 47 Punctuation to Enclose Extra
          Information *291*
Lesson 48 Conventional Uses of
          Punctuation *298*
Lesson 49 Capitalization *305*

Practice Test *308*

Unit Eleven
Refining Sentences *313*

Lesson 50 Point of View *314*
Lesson 51 The Appropriate Word *319*
Lesson 52 Comparison *326*
Lesson 53 Parallelism *330*
Lesson 54 Sentence Editing *334*

Practice Test *341*

Practice Writing Test *344*

Spelling Appendix *345*

Answer Key *347*

Index *377*

To the Student Writer

Writing effectively and fluently takes knowledge and practice, like any other skill you may want to acquire. *Commanding Sentences* offers you the information about language and the practice you need to write well-constructed, understandable sentences, which you will use later in writing essays and reports. The text consists of eleven study units that contain short lessons. Each lesson explains something you need to know about sentences. Exercises in each lesson test your understanding of the lessons. At the end of each study unit is a practice test you should complete to test your mastery of the unit and to prepare you for the Unit Review.

The beginning lessons may seem almost too easy, but they are very important lessons because they give you the background you need for the later lessons. If you skip over them, you may bring about unnecessary problems for yourself.

In the beginning lessons, you will learn to write very short sentences. They will be like the rough sketches that artists make before they paint a picture. Then you will gradually add more and more words, filling in details, just as artists fill in their paintings with lines and colors.

Whether you are using *Commanding Sentences* in a class, a writing lab, or on your own, you can complete this book successfully if you follow these steps:

1. Read each lesson carefully, and study the examples.
2. To test your ability to apply the information you have studied, complete the exercise following the explanation.
3. Before going on to the next part of the lesson, check your answers with the Answer Key in the back of the book. Show sentences you have written to your instructor or tutor.
4. Correct any errors by studying again the explanation given in the lesson, or ask your instructor or tutor for help. Write corrections above your original answers so that you can see where you had problems while you study for the Unit Review.
5. When you have completed all the lessons in a study unit, review the lessons and corrected exercises.
6. Take the practice test at the end of the study unit. Check your answers with the Answer Key.
7. Show your practice test to your instructor, who will give you a copy of the Unit Review. Although you should get 85 percent on the Unit Review before going on to the next study unit, a score of 60 or 70 percent tells you that you have learned most of the information but that you need to study a little more to receive 85 percent when you take Form B of the Unit Review.

Helen Mills

Unit One

Basic Sentence Patterns

When you write paragraphs or reports for college or business, you are supposed to express your ideas in a series of related sentences so that readers can easily understand the points you are making. After all, the purpose of writing your ideas down is to share your information with others. As a member of the world community, you are a part of the rapid, constant exchange of ideas going on as governments report their differences and agreements, businesses arrange contracts and write reports, and science shares new discoveries with almost everyone in the world. The speed of communication is increasing as computer networks connect people to one another all over the world, and the need to think clearly and present ideas in well-constructed sentences continues to be essential because computer programming and computer communication demand precise language and logical presentations.

To participate actively, you can prepare by studying and then practicing writing to develop fluency. Even if you understand your topic thoroughly, you may find expressing the ideas difficult because you may not be able to control your writing to put your ideas into well-constructed sentences. You can overcome your difficulties by studying sentences because the sentence is the key unit used to communicate ideas to readers. As a reader you are very much aware that poorly written sentences keep you from understanding what a writer has said.

In this text you begin your study with basic sentences, which you then expand by adding words and word groups to them. You also learn to combine two or more sentences with related ideas into a single sentence and to use connectors to show readers the relationship of these ideas. In this way you make your writing cohesive; in other words, it hangs together. As you practice writing sentences in the step-by-step exercises in the lessons that follow, you will gradually gain control and skill in expressing your ideas in writing. Unit One builds a foundation for the other lessons by introducing you to the three main sentence patterns in English.

Lesson 1

Finding the Subject and Predicate

To understand sentence patterns, you should know that sentences are made up of two parts: the **subject** and the **predicate.** The word groups below, for example, are all **sentences.** Each one has a subject and a predicate:

SENTENCE =	SUBJECT	PREDICATE
	Roy and Joan	opened a flower shop.
	Joan	arranges flowers.
	People	order flowers.
	Roy	delivers the flowers to homes and offices.

The subject and the predicate of a sentence are related in the following way: The subject tells who or what the sentence is about, and the predicate tells something about the subject. Both parts are required to make a sentence like those in the examples above.

The SUBJECT may be a **noun.** In the following sentences, the noun is labeled NS *(noun subject).* It tells *who* or *what* the sentence is about. The subject may also be a **pronoun,** a word like *I, you, he, she, it, we,* and *they,* because pronouns may take the place of nouns. Pronouns are also labeled NS.

Each PREDICATE must have a verb in it. In the following sentences, the verb is labeled V. It says (asks or commands) something about the subject.

SUBJECT	PREDICATE	
NS Snow	V falls.	V NS (*What* falls? *Snow*)
NS It	V glistens.	V NS (*What* glistens? *It*)
NS People	V shiver.	V NS (*Who* shiver? *People*)
NS They	V hurry.	V NS (*Who* hurry? *They*)

The subject may also be a group of words. For example, it may be two or more nouns joined by *and*. *And* is a connector called a **conjunction.** In the following sentence, the conjunction is labeled C:

SUBJECT	PREDICATE	
NS C NS	V	V NS
Stores and offices	close.	(*What* close? *Stores*
		NS
		and *offices)*

The predicate may also be a group of words, which must have at least one verb in it. For example, the predicate may be two or more verbs joined by *and:*

SUBJECT	PREDICATE	
NS	V C V	V V
People	slip and slide.	(*Who* slip and slide?
		NS
		People)

EXERCISE 1

1. Name the two parts of a sentence.

   a. _____   b. _____

2. Name two kinds of words that may be the subject in a sentence.

   a. _____   b. _____

3. Name the kind of word that must be in each predicate.

   a. _____

Check your answers with the Answer Key at the end of this book.

Lesson 2

Identifying Verbs

To tell whether a word group is a sentence, start by finding the verb. **The verb is the most important word in the sentence.** In the box below is a test to help you find the verb in any sentence. The first part of the test, using *I* or *they* before a word, is the easiest to remember and the easiest to use. The second and third parts of the test should help you spot words that may be verbs. Then you can decide whether they are verbs by using the first part of the test with them.

Verb Test

1. Place *I* or *they* before the word if it does not end in *-s:*

       V   V   V
   I call.   *They* answer.   *I* smile.

   Place *he* or *she* before the word if it ends in *-s:*

       V   V   V
   She calls.   *He* answers.   *She* helps.

2. Notice whether the word ends in the suffix *-ed.* A word ending in *-ed* may be a verb:

       V   V   V
   I inquir*ed.*   *They* respond*ed.*   *She* answer*ed.*

       V   V   V
   She call*ed* her friend this morning and smil*ed* when he answer*ed.*

3. Notice whether auxiliary (helping) verbs like *have, are, should,* and *would* are used before the verb. Auxiliary verbs are signals that the main verb follows. (You will study auxiliary verbs in Lessons 10, 11, and 12.)

       V—————   V—————
   He *has* arrived.   They *are* departing.

       V—————   V—————————
   She *should* call.   He *would have* answered.

Try applying Part 1 or Part 2 of the Verb Test to the following words:

        cabin   pilot   orders   heart   desks   helped

You can see that three of them—*pilot, orders,* and *helped*—can function as verbs with *I, they,* or *he,* but the other three cannot:

I pilot [a plane].	NOT: *I* cabin.
He orders [supplies].	NOT: *He* desks.
They helped.	NOT: *They* heart.

By applying the Verb Test to words in the following sentence, you will be able to find the verb:

Lee repaired the house.

For example, if you apply the Verb Test, placing *I* or *they* before the first word, you will discover that *Lee* is not a verb:

NOT: I Lee.　　　　　　NOT: They Lee.

When you look at *repaired,* the second word, you can see that it ends with the suffix *-ed,* and you can use *I* or *they* with it:

V　　　　　　　　　　　　V
I repaired . . .　　　　　　They repaired . . .

The word *repaired* is a verb in this sentence and should be labeled V:

V
Lee repaired the house.

In the next sentence you can use *he* or *she* with *paints,* which ends with the suffix *-s;* therefore, *paints* is a verb in this sentence:

V
Ellen paints the rooms.

EXERCISE 2A

Use the Verb Test to decide whether each of the following words can be used as a verb. If the word can be used as a verb, write V in the space at the right. If the word cannot be used as a verb, leave the space blank.

EXAMPLE:　rule　＿＿V＿＿　(*They* rule [the country].)

speech　＿＿＿＿　(NOT: *They* speech.)

1. cut ＿＿＿	4. played ＿＿＿	7. know ＿＿＿
2. see ＿＿＿	5. pretty ＿＿＿	8. enemy ＿＿＿
3. hides ＿＿＿	6. health ＿＿＿	9. container ＿＿＿

Check your answers with the Answer Key at the end of this book. If you missed more than two words, study the Verb Test, get help from your instructor or tutor, and then use the Verb Test with the following words:

10. library _____   13. life _____   16. happy _____

11. brings _____   14. family _____   17. protect _____

12. give _____   15. hunt _____   18. picked _____

Check your answers with the Answer Key. If you missed more than two words, talk with your instructor or tutor before you go on to the next exercise.

EXERCISE 2B

Write V above each verb in the following sentences. Be sure to use the Verb Test.

                                             V
EXAMPLE: The horse runs.   (*He* runs. *Runs* is the verb.)

1. The people arrive.

2. The game starts.

3. The player hits the ball.

4. The people cheer.

5. The game ends.

6. The team wins the game.

7. The people leave.

Check your answers with the Answer Key.

Lesson 3

Identifying Nouns

Nouns are also important words in sentences. They name persons, places, or things. Nouns may be singular (they name one person, place, or thing) or plural (more than one). Plural nouns usually end in -s or -es. Verbs and nouns together form the framework of sentences. Most sentences will have at least one noun; others may have two or more:

```
N    V      N        N     C   N     V          N
Ted wrote a song.   Steve and Mary played their guitars.
```

Noun Test

To find a noun, place *the* before the word:

```
     N             N              N             N
the call     the people     the families    the chance

     N                  N              N
The call came late.   The people left the party early.
```

NOTE: **Proper nouns,** words that name a specific person, place, or thing, and begin with a capital letter, cannot be identified by using the Noun Test because *the* usually cannot be placed before them. You can identify proper nouns by determining that they name specific persons, places, or things and noting the capital letter at the beginning:

```
N                   N
Mrs. Walker goes to Minneapolis often.
```

Other words that point to nouns are *a, an, any, our, your, her, his, their, several, two, John's,* and *child's,* but you can also use *the* to find the nouns:

```
      N                   N        N
John's answer brought a smile to her face.   (the answer, the smile, the face)
```

Sometimes nouns appear without *the* or any of the other words before them. However, you can still use *the* to find the nouns:

```
   N           N
People enjoy concerts.   (the people, the concerts)
```

EXERCISE 3A

Use the Noun Test to identify nouns in the list below. If, after using the Noun Test, you are still not sure whether the word is a noun, find the word in your dictionary. Most dictionaries use *n.* to label nouns. If the word can be used as a noun, write N in the space at the right. If the word cannot be used as a noun, leave the space blank.

EXAMPLE: company   __N__ (*the* company)

                remain   _____ (NOT: *the* remain)

1. silver _____
2. flowers _____
3. begin _____

4. seem _____
5. metal _____
6. hole _____

7. tell _____
8. history _____
9. born _____

Check your answers with the Answer Key. If you missed two or more, get help from your instructor or tutor, and then use the Noun Test on the following words:

10. city _____
11. room _____
12. salt _____

13. would _____
14. ask _____
15. dust _____

16. paths _____
17. happen _____
18. noise _____

Check your answers with the Answer Key. If you missed two or more, talk with your instructor or tutor before you go on to the next exercise.

EXERCISE 3B

Use the Noun Test to find the nouns in the following sentences. Write N above each noun.

            N   N
EXAMPLE: Linda fell off the ladder.

1. Linda hurt her arm.

2. A friend drove Linda to the hospital.

3. The doctor examined Linda's arm.

4. Linda had broken her arm.

5. The doctor put a cast on the arm.

NOUN OR VERB?

Words such as *plan, circle, walk,* and many others can be both nouns and verbs, depending on their function in the sentence. Nouns name. Verbs often tell what the subject is doing.

	VERB		NOUN

	V
The hikers **plan** a trip.	

	N
The **plan** satisfies everyone.	

	V
They **circle** the mountain.	

	N
They travel in a **circle**.	

	V
Some **walk** slowly.	

	N
The **walk** tires them.	

EXERCISE 3C

Use the Verb Test and the Noun Test on each of the following words. If the word can function as a verb, write V in the first blank. If it can function as a noun, write N in the second blank.

	V	N			V	N
1. head	_____	_____		5. cup	_____	_____
2. map	_____	_____		6. music	_____	_____
3. went	_____	_____		7. cap	_____	_____
4. bats	_____	_____		8. pick	_____	_____

EXERCISE 3D

Using the Verb Test and the Noun Test, determine whether the word in bold type functions as a noun or as a verb. Write N or V in the blank at the right.

EXAMPLE: Birds and bees **fly.**   (*they* fly)   V

The **fly** buzzed loudly.   (*the* fly)   N

1. The **lights** shine brightly.   _____

2. The clerks **check** the supplies.   _____

3. The **changes** pleased most people.   _____

4. Kathy liked Glenn's **answer.**   _____

5. Karen **lights** the furnace.   _____

6. Bob **changes** plans daily.   _____

7. Ted wrote a **check.**   _____

8. Tina and Jessie **answer** letters.   _____

EXERCISE 3E

Write short sentences using each of the following words either as a noun or as a verb.

1. ice (noun)

2. pick (verb)

3. hunt (verb)

4. bear (noun)

Show these sentences to your instructor or tutor.

EXERCISE 3F

Write V above each verb and N above each noun in the following sentences. Use the Verb Test and the Noun Test.

EXAMPLE:
$$\overset{N}{\text{Betty}} \text{ and } \overset{N}{\text{Ted}} \overset{V}{\text{ rented }} \text{a} \overset{N}{\text{ cabin.}}$$

1. Candles lighted the room.

2. Their friends heard the wind.

3. Betty served the drinks.

4. Ted cooked sausages.

5. Karen screamed.

6. She rubbed her leg.

7. A cat meowed.

8. Everyone laughed.

EXERCISE 3G

The sentences in Exercise 3F tell a story. Read all the sentences again. Then write complete sentences, **not** parts of sentences, in the following exercise to tell what happened.

1. Write a sentence telling what Ted did.

2. Write a sentence telling two things Karen did.

3. Write a sentence telling what everyone did when Karen screamed.

Show these sentences to your instructor or tutor.

Lesson 4

Sentences with Action Verbs

You have learned that a **subject** and **predicate** are the necessary parts of a **sentence.** In some of the sentences in the preceding lessons, the predicate contains only a verb or two or more verbs joined by *and.* In others, the predicate contains a verb and a noun. These combinations make up two of the three main sentence patterns in English.

FIRST SENTENCE PATTERN

The first sentence pattern consists of a noun or a pronoun and a verb. The noun or pronoun functions as the subject; the predicate is only the verb. When verbs stand alone as the predicate, they are called **intransitive** verbs. The label for these verbs is Vi, which means *verb intransitive.* This label appears in dictionaries following words that can function as intransitive verbs.

The first sentence pattern, then, is NS Vi. In the first sentence below, *day* is the subject; the sentence is about the day. The predicate is the verb *begins,* and it tells that the day begins. The second sentence is about Judy, the subject. The predicate is the verb *wakes* and *dresses,* and it tells what Judy does. *And* is a conjunction, labeled C:

SUBJECT	PREDICATE
NS The day	Vi begins.
NS Judy	Vi C Vi wakes and dresses.

SECOND SENTENCE PATTERN

The second sentence pattern has a predicate that consists of a verb and a noun. In the sentence, "Judy cooks cereal," Judy does something *(cooks)* to something *(cereal).* *Cooks* is a **transitive verb** (Vt) in this sentence because the noun *cereal* completes the verb. *Cereal* is a noun that functions as a **direct object** (Ndo) because it is directly affected by the subject *(Judy)* and the action of the verb *(cooks).* The direct object completes the predicate. The second sentence pattern is NS Vt Ndo:

SUBJECT	PREDICATE
NS Judy	Vt Ndo cooks cereal.
NS She	Vt Ndo C Vt Ndo toasts bread and fries eggs.

Transitive or Intransitive Verb?

The sentences about Judy show the difference between **intransitive** and **transitive** verbs:

> The **intransitive verb** can make up the predicate by itself.

> The **transitive verb,** however, always needs a direct object, a noun affected by the action of the verb, to complete the predicate. The direct object is different from the subject.

To identify intransitive and transitive verbs easily, use the following Sentence Keys **in the order given.**
 You must find the verb first because it is the most important word in a sentence. Then find the subject. Although the subject usually appears first in many sentences, **you cannot label the first noun you see as subject because the subject sometimes appears after the verb.** Therefore, if you find the verb first, you will then be able to locate the subject easily.

Sentence Keys

1. Find the verb by using the Verb Test. Write V above the verb:

           V   V
   Judy wakes. She and her friend eat breakfast.   (Verb Test: *she* wakes; *they* eat)

2. Ask *who* or *what,* and then say the verb. The word that answers the question is the subject. Label it NS:

               V
   Who or what wakes? Judy . . . *Judy* is the subject.

               V
   Who or what eat? She and her friend . . . *She* and *friend* are the subjects.

   NS V   NS   NS V
   Judy wakes. She and her friend eat breakfast.

3. Read the subject and verb together and ask *whom* or *what.*
   a. If the word that answers the question completes the verb and is different from the subject, it is the **direct object.** Write Ndo above it. The verb is **transitive.** Write Vt above the verb.

```
NS          NS   V
```
She and her friend eat whom or what? . . . breakfast.   *Breakfast* is the direct
                                                         object. The verb *eat* is
                                                         transitive.

```
NS          NS   Vt  Ndo
```
She and her friend eat breakfast.

b. If there is no answer to *whom* or *what,* the verb is **intransitive.** Write Vi above
the verb:

```
NS   V
```
Judy wakes what? No answer. The verb *wakes* is intransitive.

```
NS   Vi
```
Judy wakes.

EXERCISE 4A

Identify the sentence pattern in each of the following sentences by using the steps in
the Sentence Keys **in the order they are given.** Label the words either NS Vi   or
NS Vt Ndo. (You do not have to label *the, a,* or *his.*)

```
            NS      Vt    Ndo NS Vi      NS Vi
```
EXAMPLE: The carpenter owned land. He thought. He smiled.

1. The carpenter bought lumber.   5. He yelled.

2. He built a cabin.   6. He called his doctor.

3. He sawed the wood and hammered nails. 7. The doctor used a splint and bandages.

4. The carpenter smashed his thumb.   8. The carpenter rested.

Verbs That Can Be Either Transitive or Intransitive

Some verbs can be intransitive in one sentence and transitive in another sentence. For
example, *types* is transitive in the following sentence because *reports* completes the
verb:

```
NS   Vt    Ndo
```
Molly types reports.

But in the next sentence *types* is intransitive because it stands alone as the predicate:

```
NS   Vi
```
Steve types.

To decide whether a verb is transitive or intransitive use Step 3 of the Sentence Keys. If
a sentence contains a direct object, a word that answers *whom* or *what* after the verb,
the verb is transitive.

Use the Sentence Keys to determine whether the verbs in the following sentences are intransitive or transitive. Label the words in the sentences with NS Vi   or   NS Vt Ndo. Write the subject and the predicate in the blanks at the right.

	SUBJECT	PREDICATE
EXAMPLE: The dog watches. *(NS Vi)*	dog	watches
The dog watches the cat. *(NS Vt Ndo)*	dog	watches the cat

1. Lucy rides.

2. The engine runs.

3. The senator won the election.

4. Matt draws.

5. Lucy rides her bicycle.

6. Steve runs the engine.

7. The senator won.

WRITING SENTENCES

You are studying sentence patterns to help you express your ideas clearly and effectively. In writing sentences you usually think of the idea first and then write a sentence. If you sometimes have no ideas when you are supposed to write sentences for exercises in this book, you can use the following method even though it is not the usual way. By beginning with a single word, it will be easier to think of other words you can relate to it to write a sentence. Here are the steps:

1. Write a word that can function as a verb. Write V above it:

> V
> land

2. Ask *who* or *what,* and say the verb. The word that answers the question is the subject. Place it before the verb. Write NS above it:

> NS V   NS V
> Who or what land? The planes land. The pilots land.

3. Read the subject and verb together, and ask *whom* or *what.*
   a. If you give no answer, the verb is intransitive. Write Vi above the verb:

$$\overset{\text{NS}}{\text{The planes}} \overset{\text{Vi}}{\text{land.}}$$

   b. If you add a noun to tell *whom* or *what,* the verb is transitive, and the noun is a direct object. Write Vt above the verb and Ndo above the direct object:

$$\overset{\text{NS}}{\text{The pilots}} \overset{\text{Vt}}{\text{land}} \overset{\text{Ndo}}{\text{the planes.}}$$

NOTE: If you write a sentence like the following one, the name *Bill* is NOT the subject:

      NOT: Bill, land the plane.

Bill is the person spoken to. *Bill* is a noun of direct address, which is followed by a comma because it is NOT a part of the sentence. The sentence is a command. The subject is *you,* which is not written in the sentence, but it is understood:

$$\overset{\text{NS}}{\text{Bill, (you)}} \overset{\text{Vt}}{\text{land}} \overset{\text{Ndo}}{\text{the plane.}}$$

EXERCISE 4C

Use each of the following words as a transitive verb (Vt) in one sentence and as an intransitive verb (Vi) in another sentence. Write NS Vi   or   NS Vt Ndo above each sentence.

1. *call* or *called* (Vi)

   call or *called* (Vt)

2. *sail* or *sailed* (Vi)

   sail or *sailed* (Vt)

3. *sing* or *sang* (Vi)

   sing or *sang* (Vt)

4. *stop* or *stopped* (VI)

   stop or *stopped* (Vt)

Show these sentences to your instructor or tutor.

Lesson 5

Sentences with Linking Verbs

The transitive and intransitive verbs you studied in the last lesson generally indicate action. In this lesson, you will learn about **linking verbs,** which join the subject to a noun that renames the subject. The symbol for the linking verb is LV. The noun that renames the subject is called a **subject complement,** and the symbol for it is Nsc. The third basic sentence pattern, then, is NS LV Nsc.

The examples below contain linking verbs and subject complements. In the first sentence, for example, the linking verb *is* joins *Greg* and *musician,* two nouns that name the same person:

```
NS   LV   Nsc
Greg is a musician.              (Greg = musician)

     NS      LV  Nsc
His friends are artists.         (Friends = artists)

NS LV    Nsc
I  am a mechanic.                (I = mechanic)
```

If you compare the direct object with the subject complement, you will see that the direct object is usually **different** from the subject, and the subject complement is the same as the subject:

```
                 NS      Vt       Ndo
DIFFERENT:   Charlie chose a partner.     (Partner is NOT Charlie. It is
                                           another person.)


                 NS     LV     Nsc
SAME:        Charlie is Jon's partner.    (Charlie and partner are the
                                           same person.)
```

LINKING VERBS: *BE, BECOME, REMAIN*

Only a few words can function as linking verbs between two nouns that name the same person or thing. The most frequently used is the verb *be,* which indicates a state of being. It has eight forms: *am, is, are, be, was, were, been, being.* You will learn more about the verb *be* in later lessons. For the present, become familiar with the forms

given above so that you can recognize them in the exercises that follow. The verbs *become* and *remain,* which also function as linking verbs, show result. In the following examples, each verb links two nouns that name the same person:

SUBJECT	PREDICATE	
NS—————— Joe Morgan	LV Nsc was the principal.	(Joe Morgan = princi-pal)
NS He	LV Nsc became the superin-tendent)	(He = superintendent)
NS—————— Ted Thompson	LV remained Joe Nsc Morgan's assistant.	(Ted Thompson = assistant)

In Lesson 21 you will see that linking verbs can join the subject to other words besides nouns.

To analyze sentences with the linking verb, you can use the Sentence Keys you learned in the preceding lesson by making one change in the third step.

Sentence Keys

1. Find the verb by using the Verb Test. Write V above the verb:

       V   V   V
   Terry bought a car.   Terry celebrated.   Terry is the owner.

2. Ask *who* or *what,* and then say the verb. The word that answers the question is the subject. Label it NS:

                   V
   Who or what bought? Terry . . . *Terry* is the subject.

   NS V   NS V   NS V
   Terry bought a car. Terry celebrated. Terry is the owner.

3. Read the subject and verb together and ask *whom* or *what.*
   a. If the word that answers the question completes the verb and is different from the subject, it is the **direct object.** Write Ndo above it. The verb is **transitive.** Write Vt above the verb:

   NS V
   Terry bought whom or what? . . . a car. *Car* is the direct object. The verb *bought* is transitive.

   NS   Vt   Ndo
   Terry bought a car.

b. If there is no answer to *whom* or *what,* the verb is **intransitive.** Write Vi above the verb:

    NS   V
    Terry celebrated whom or what? No answer. The verb *celebrated* is intransitive.

    NS   Vi
    Terry celebrated.

c. If the word that answers the question completes the verb and renames the subject, the word is a **subject complement.** Write Nsc above it. The verb is a **linking verb.** Write LV above the verb:

    NS   V
    Terry is whom or what? . . . the owner.   *Terry* and *owner* are the same person.
    Owner is the subject complement.
    The verb *is* is a linking verb.

    NS   LV   Nsc
    Terry is the owner.

EXERCISE 5A

Write the sentence pattern above each of the following sentences by labeling the words with NS LV Nsc. Write the subject and predicate in the blanks at the right.

	SUBJECT	PREDICATE
EXAMPLE: NS LV Nsc Louise became a lawyer.	Louise	became a lawyer
1. The dog is a collie.		
2. Walt is a reporter and photographer.		
3. Mr. Watson is the teacher.		
4. Mary Ryan became the chairperson.		
5. He remained a supervisor.		
6. Three desserts are cake, ice cream, and pie.		
7. Tiger is a cat.		
8. Haynes Institute is a college.		

EXERCISE 5B

Write the sentence patterns above each of the following sentences by using the Sentence Keys. Label the words in the sentences with NS Vi, NS Vt Ndo, or NS LV Nsc.

1. Jean is an artist.

2. She designs greeting cards.

3. Her husband is Mike.

4. Jean and Mike moved.

5. Jean called the movers.

6. Mike packed the suitcases and boxes.

7. The movers carried the furniture.

8. The movers loaded the van.

9. Boxes and furniture filled the van.

10. Jean and Mike left the apartment.

11. They cleaned the house.

12. The van arrived.

13. The movers arranged the furniture.

14. Jean unpacked several boxes.

15. Mike found his tools.

16. Jean and Mike bought food.

17. They ate dinner.

18. They read the newspaper.

19. They watched television.

20. The day ended.

EXERCISE 5C

The sentences in Exercise 5B tell a story. Read the sentences again. Then write complete sentences, **not** parts of sentences, in the following exercise to tell what happened.

1. Write a sentence telling one thing that Mike and Jean did together.

2. Write a sentence telling one thing that the movers did.

3. Write a sentence telling one thing that Mike and Jean did in their new house.

Show these sentences to your instructor or tutor.

WRITING SENTENCES ABOUT ONE TOPIC

When you write a paragraph or a report, you write several sentences because you need more than one sentence to discuss a single topic. To help your readers understand your topic, these sentences should be related to each other. As you do the lessons in

this text, you will learn several techniques to show how ideas are related, and you will have a chance to use these techniques in your own writing.

In the beginning writing assignments try to keep your sentences short. Use the patterns that you are learning in lessons. Because the sentences are short, your writing may sound choppy. Do not be concerned, but pay special attention to the techniques so that you will gradually learn to make your sentences flow smoothly. As you apply these techniques, you will find that your writing will become fluent and cohesive (hang together).

The first technique you will try in the following writing assignment is using the same term as the subject in more than one sentence. For example, if you use *people* in one sentence, you can repeat it in another sentence to show that the next sentence is also about people. In this way you link your sentences together.

A second technique is using personal pronouns such as *he, she, it,* and *they* in place of subjects. *He, she,* and *it* can replace singular subjects; *they* can replace a plural subject.

In the following set of sentences *people* is the subject of two sentences, and *they,* which refers to *people,* is the subject of the other sentences:

> Most *people* enjoy food. *They* try several kinds. Some *people* like cooking. *They* prepare their meals. *They* choose fresh fruits, vegetables, and meats. *They* use spices and seasonings.

A warning: Always use a noun as the subject of your first sentence. If you use only pronouns, your readers will wonder who or what you are writing about. In the following example the names of two people—*Geri* and *Tom*—can replace *they,* or *bears* can replace *they:*

> NOT: *They* wander through the forest. *They* pick berries.
> BUT: *Geri* and *Tom* wander through the forest. *They* pick berries.
> OR: *Bears* wander through the forest. *They* pick berries.

EXERCISE 5D

Write five or more sentences about one topic on a sheet of notebook paper. Keep the sentences short. Repeat nouns, or use the pronouns *he, she, it,* and *they* to refer to and replace the nouns. Show these sentences to your instructor or tutor.

Unit One Review

Practice Test

SCORE PART I (Total—100 points) _____
SCORE PART II* (Total—100 points) _____
TOTAL _____
AVERAGE _____

*Average scores for Part I and Part II only if the Part I score is 85 percent or more.

PART I

A. Use the Verb Test and the Noun Test on each of these words. You may also use your dictionary. If the word can function as a verb, write V in the first blank. If it can function as a noun, write N in the second blank.
(8 points—1 point each)　　(Lessons 2, 3)　　　　　　　　Score _____

1. seat _____ _____　　5. went _____ _____

2. steam _____ _____　　6. use _____ _____

3. cry _____ _____　　7. feet _____ _____

4. watch _____ _____　　8. time _____ _____

B. Each sentence below follows one of these patterns: Ns Vi, NS Vt Ndo, or NS LV Nsc. Using the Sentence Keys, **label the words** in each sentence to find one of these patterns. Write the subject and the predicate in the blanks at the right. The predicate is the verb and the direct object (Ndo) or subject complement (Nsc).
(42 points—4 points for each pattern; 3 points for subject and predicate)
(Lessons 4, 5)　　　　　　　　　　　　　　　　　　　　Score _____

	SUBJECT	PREDICATE
1. The plane carried passengers and cargo.	_____	_____
2. The plane was a jumbo jet.	_____	_____
3. Darkness covered the land.	_____	_____

4. The stars and the moon shone. _____ _____

5. The plane passed Chicago and
   Milwaukee. _____ _____

6. Passengers saw the lights. _____ _____

C. The sentences in Exercise B tell a story. Read all the sentences again. Then write
   complete sentences, **not** parts of sentences, in the following exercise to tell what
   happened.
   (15 points—5 points each)   (Lessons 4, 5)   Score _____

   1. Write a sentence telling what covered the land.

   2. Write a sentence telling what cities the plane passed.

   3. Write a sentence telling what the passengers saw.

D. Write a sentence to match the sentence pattern following each number. **Label the
   words** in your sentences with the following patterns: NS Vi, Ns Vt Ndo, or
   NS LV Nsc.
   (35 points—7 points each)   (Lessons 4, 5)   Score _____

   1. NS Vt Ndo

   2. NS LV Nsc

   3. NS Vi

   4. NS and NS Vt Ndo

   5. NS Vi and Vi

   PART II

   Write ten sentences. Keep them short—three to seven words—like those you have
   been writing in Unit One. Use nouns as subjects of your sentences. Write about just
   one topic.
   (100 points—10 points each)   Score _____

   1.

2.

3.

4.

5.

6.

7.

8.

9.

10.

Unit Two

Verbs and Adverbs

Using the Sentence Keys to find the patterns in sentences helps you see the parts of sentences. The keys also help you decide whether a word group is a sentence. By understanding these details about sentences, you can increase your control of your written language. You will then be able to write a paragraph or a report that expresses your ideas clearly.

In Unit One you learned that sentences consist of a subject and a predicate. You also learned that the subject, a single word or a word group functioning as a noun, tells what the sentence is about and that the predicate, which consists of a verb alone or verbs and nouns, tells something about the subject.

You have learned to find verbs in sentences by using the Verb Test, and you may have noticed that some of the sentences were about something happening today—the present—and others about yesterday—the past. And you probably are aware that you can also write about tomorrow—the future—with particular verbs. We can draw a line to represent time and show these three periods of time. Notice how time is divided into two parts—the past and the future—by the present:

_____ X _____

Past   Present   Future

The way to indicate the past, present, or future is to use particular verb tenses. *Tense* refers to the time something happened and how long it went on. You will study the present, past, and future tenses in this unit. In addition, you will learn to add adverbs to sentences to indicate when something happened.

Lesson 6

Adding Adverbs to Sentences

When you write the sentence "The child screamed," you tell what the child did, but you can give a much clearer idea of what happened by adding **adverbs** to the sentence:

> The child screamed **loudly** *(how)* **during the night** *(when)* **because of his tooth-ache** *(why)*.

Adverbs are words or word groups that tell *when, where, why,* or *how.* They function as **modifiers,** words or word groups that change, limit, or extend the meaning of other words in the sentence. In the following sentences, the adverb is labeled Adv. Read the sentences below with and without the adverbs to see how they make the sentences specific. Notice that adverbs may come at the beginning, in the middle, or at the end of sentences:

	SUBJECT	PREDICATE
	NS A man	Vt Ndo selected his book
		Adv–where——— **in the library.**
	NS He	Vi Adv–where——— went **to the stairway.**
Adv–how **Suddenly**	NS he	Vi Adv–where——— fell **down the stairs.**
	NS The noise	Adv–how Vt **quickly brought**
		Ndo **several** people.
Adv–when **Soon**	NS an ambulance	Vi arrived.
	NS The attendants	Vt Ndo Adv–how lifted him **carefully.**

```
            NS                              Vt      Ndo
            They                            took the man

                                            Adv–where————
                                            to the hospital

                                            Adv————————————————
                                            because of his injuries.
```

To find adverbs in sentences, first use the Sentence Keys you learned in Unit One to identify the basic sentence patterns. Then use the following test to decide whether a word or a word group can function as an adverb.

Adverb Test

Read the subject, verb, and direct object (if there is one) together, and ask *when, where, why,* and *how.* The words that answer these questions are adverbs. Write Adv above the word or word group:

```
            NS      Vi                    NS  Vt   Ndo
On Sunday Marilyn went to the fair. She won prizes easily.
```

Marilyn went where? . . . to the fair. When? On Sunday. . .
She won prizes how? . . . easily. *On Sunday, to the fair,* and *easily* are adverbs.

```
Adv———————  NS      Vi   Adv———————  NS  Vt  Ndo     Adv
On Sunday Marilyn went to the fair. She won prizes easily.
```

EXERCISE 6A

Using the Sentence Keys, first identify the patterns (NS Vi or NS Vt Ndo) for each of the following sentences. Then use the Adverb Test to find the adverbs. Write Adv above each adverb. If the adverb is a word group, draw a line over the words in a group.

1. Joann and Tom spend their weekends at an open-air market.

2. During the week Joann finds rocks on the beach and in fields.

3. Later she carefully polishes the rocks and drills holes into them.

4. She sits outside under a tree and makes jewelry.

5. Tom skillfully shapes clay into plates, jars, and bowls.

6. Next, he carefully places them into a furnace and bakes them hard.

7. Sometimes he paints the plates, bowls, and jars and bakes them again.

8. People eagerly buy the pottery and jewelry at the market.

The following sentences are made up of nouns and verbs. Add one or more adverbs to each of the sentences. Remember to use words or word groups that tell *when, where, why,* or *how.* You may place adverbs at the beginning, in the middle, or at the end of sentences. Write Adv above each adverb.

EXAMPLE: The **sun rose.**

Adv–when————   NS   Vi   Adv–where————
At six o'clock the **sun rose** over the city.

1. Keri received a camera.

2. She studied photography.

3. She took photographs.

4. She photographed an automobile accident.

5. Two cars crashed.

6. Each driver blamed the other one.

7. Keri developed the film.

8. The police needed the pictures.

9. The pictures identified the victim.

Show these sentences to your instructor or tutor.

EXERCISE 6C

Write five sentences that contain adverbs. **Label the words** in your sentences.

1.

2.

3.

4.

5.

Show these sentences to your instructor or tutor.

Lesson 7

The Present Tense

The sentences below tell that something is happening now—today:

> People **cheer.** The president **waves** at the crowd.

The verbs *cheer* and *waves* in the sentences above are in the present tense. If you refer to the chart on page 30, you will notice that two parts of the verb are used to form the present tense. *Cheer* is Part 1, the base, and *waves* is Part 2, formed by adding *-s* to the base. The ways to use Part 1 and Part 2 of the verb are explained below.

PART 1 (BASE)

Part 1 (Base) of the verb is used with plural subjects and with the pronouns *I* and *you* to tell about something happening now. *Plural* means *more than one.*

1. The subject may be a plural noun such as *students* or *friends:*

>   NS   Vt   Ndo   NS   Vt   Ndo
> The **students** design clothes. Their **friends** model them.

2. The subject may also be two or more nouns joined by *and:*

>   NS   NS   Vt   Ndo   Adv———
> **Van** and **Akiko** sell the clothes to stores.

3. The subject may be a plural pronoun like *we, you,* or *they* or the pronoun *I:*

>   NS   Vt   Ndo   Adv———
> **They** make money for the group.

Notice that the verb *be,* which you studied briefly in Lesson 5, has three forms for Part 1: *am, are,* and *be.*

Am is always used in written language with the pronoun *I:*

>   NS LV   Nsc   NS LV   Nsc
> I **am** a pilot. I **am** the instructor.

Are is used in written language with plural nouns and pronouns:

>   NS LV Nsc   NS   LV Nsc   NS   NS   LV Nsc
> **We are** students. **They are** teachers.   The teachers and students **are** friends.

Be is used for commands. The subject *you* is understood:

      (NS)   LV   NSC   (NS)   LV   Nsc
      (You) **be** an actor. (You) **be** a tree.

PART 2 (BASE + *S*)

Part 2 (Base + *s*) of most verbs is formed by adding -*s* to Part 1 (Base). Part 2 is used with singular subjects to tell about something happening now. *Singular* means *one*.

1. The subject may be a singular noun like *instructor*:

      NS   Vt   Ndo
      The **instructor** praises the students.

2. The subject may be a singular pronoun like *he, she,* or *it*:

      NS Vt   Ndo Adv
      She helps them constantly.

NOTE: While Part 2 of the verb is generally formed by adding -*s* to Part 1 (Base), there are some exceptions. If a word ends in *y* preceded by a consonant, change the *y* to *i* and add *es: study/studies.* If a word ends in *y* preceded by a vowel, add -*s: pay/pays.* If a word ends in *ch, sh, s, x, z,* or *o,* add -*es: wish/wishes, catch/catches, fix/fixes, buzz/buzzes.* Exception: *quiz/quizzes.*

Part 1 (Base)	Part 2 (Base + *s*)
laugh	laughs
paint	paints
have	has
do	does
study	studies
pay	pays
wish	wishes
miss	misses
am, are, be	is

SUBJECT-VERB AGREEMENT

You can say that the subject and verb agree (or are in harmony with each other) when you use Part 1 of the verb with plural subjects and the pronouns *I* and *you* and Part 2 of the verb with singular subjects. If you do not use Part 1 and 2 in the ways discussed in this lesson, you may have subject-verb agreement problems in your writing. The correction symbol SV Agr is used to indicate subject-verb agreement problems. You can eliminate these problems by being sure that you use Part 1 with plural subjects and the pronouns *I* and *you* and Part 2 with singular nouns and pronouns.

EXERCISE 7A

Write NS above each subject and V above each verb in each of the following sentences. Decide whether the subject of each sentence is singular or plural. Write S (singular) or P (plural) in the blanks at the right.

1. Kara and John own a motor home. _____

2. They plan trips every summer. _____

3. A friend sometimes goes with them. _____

4. Their children enjoy the outdoors. _____

5. Even the dog and the cat like traveling. _____

6. They explore new territory. _____

7. Cooking sometimes creates problems. _____

8. Sleeping bags and blankets protect the children at night. _____

EXERCISE 7B

Part 1 of a verb is given in parentheses before each of the following sentences. Read the sentence. Then decide whether you need Part 1 or Part 2 to make the subject and verb agree. Write the correct form in the blank.

1. (occupy) Each bird _____ a territory.

2. (live) A robin, a sparrow, and an oriole _____ in the same area.

3. (need) Each one _____ different food.

4. (live) Two robins _____ in separate territories.

5. (warn) Each male _____ other males with his song.

6. (keep) He _____ other males away.

7. (attract) He also _____ a female with his song.

8. (build) The male and female _____ a nest.

9. (feed) They _____ their babies.

10. (fly) Later they _____ to a warm climate.

OTHER USES OF THE PRESENT TENSE

You learned earlier that Part 1 and Part 2 of verbs are used for the present tense to tell about things happening now. They can also be used for the present tense to tell about

something happening over and over again when adverbs like *every day, every week, each month, frequently, sometimes, often, usually,* and *never* are added to sentences:

```
NS    C   NS———— Adv          Vi    Adv————
Jerry and Susan Blake frequently **travel** to Europe.
```

```
NS———— Vi    Adv   Adv————————
Jerry Blake **travels** alone from time to time.
```

When you express a fact that is true all the time, you use the present tense:

```
NS———— LV  Nsc      Adv————————————
Mt. Whitney **is** a mountain in the United States.
```

```
     NS   Vi       Adv————————
The earth **revolves** around the sun.
```

Commands are always expressed in the present tense with Part 1 because the subject is *you,* which is understood:

```
Vi  Adv   Adv   Vt       Ndo
**Go** home now. **Lock** the door.
```

```
(NS)  Vi  Adv   Adv  (NS)  Vt      Ndo
(You) **Go** home now. (You) **Lock** the door.
```

EXERCISE 7C

In the following sentences write V above each verb and Adv above each adverb that tells that something happens over and over.

1. Stewart travels to Miami every week.

2. He usually has business appointments in the morning.

3. Once a month he buys new clothes or books.

4. Stewart and his friends frequently have dinner together.

5. Sometimes he stays in Miami for the weekend.

EXERCISE 7D

Use Sentence Keys 1 and 2 to identify the verb and the subject in each of the following sentences. Write V above each verb and NS above each subject. The verb forms in these sentences are **not** the ones used in Standard English. Write the correct forms in the blanks at the right.

```
                    NS      V
EXAMPLE:   Three couples goes to a camp each summer.        _____go_____
```

1. Susan reserve three cabins each year.   _____

2. She usually make reservations in January.   _____

3. Jerry and Bob buys beer and soft drinks.   _____

4. Each couple bring pillows and sheets.   _____

5. Betty are the leader.   _____

6. She make plans for the group every day.   _____

7. One day they hikes in the woods.   _____

8. Another day they swims in the river.   _____

9. Each evening they eats dinner together outside.   _____

10. Afterwards they sings songs and tells stories around
the campfire.   _____

INFINITIVES: *TO* + PART 1 (BASE)

When you read the sentence "Diane tries to work carefully," you may think that *work* is
the verb in the sentence. Actually the verb is *tries,* and *to work* is an **infinitive,** which is
made up of *to* and Part 1 (Base) of the verb. **The infinitive cannot function as the verb
in a sentence:**

      NOT: Buyers **to prefer** small cars.

A verb must appear in each predicate, either alone or with an infinitive:

             NS   V
      BUT: Buyers **prefer** small cars.

             NS   V   Inf_____
      OR: Buyers **seem to prefer** small cars.

You will learn more about infinitives when you study verbals in Unit Nine in this text.
For the present, learn to recognize infinitives, and do not label them as verbs. Write Inf
above each infinitive.

Lesson 8

The Past Tense

The following sentences tell about something that happened at a definite time in the past:

The restaurant **opened** yesterday. Many people **bought** lunches and dinners.

The verbs *opened* and *bought* in the sentences above are in the past tense. The two verbs indicate that a single action took place at a stated or implied time in the past.

The past tense may also indicate repeated or habitual actions, just as the present tense can, when used with adverbs such as *sometimes, often, usually, never, frequently, every day, every week,* and *each month.*

NS   Vi   NS   Vt

Teodor jogged **every morning** before breakfast. He **frequently** met two neighbors.

The past tense is expressed by Part 3 (Past) of verbs. These verbs may be regular or irregular (not regular).

PART 3 (PAST): REGULAR VERBS

Part 3 is used with both singular and plural subjects (except the verb *be,* which has two forms: *was* and *were*). Part 3 of most verbs is formed by adding the suffix (ending) *-ed* to Part 1 (Base). For example, *cook* becomes *cooked, bake* becomes *baked,* and *wash* becomes *washed.* Verbs adding *-ed* are called **regular verbs.** They can be used with singular and plural subjects, like those in the following sentences:

NS   Vt   Ndo   NS   Vt   Ndo   NS   Vt

Kevin **cooked** the meat. Sheri **washed** the vegetables. Their guests **enjoyed**

Ndo

the meal.

When you add *-ed* to some regular verbs such as *trim* or *beg,* you must double the final consonant: *trimmed, begged.* Some verbs such as *try* or *study* change the *y* to *i* before adding *-ed: tried, studied.* (See your dictionary.)

PART 3 (PAST): IRREGULAR VERBS

Some verbs are **irregular** in their Part 3 (Past) forms because they do not add *-ed* to Part 1. They may be irregular in the following ways.

1. Part 3 may be the same as Part 1:

Water pipes sometimes **burst** suddenly.
Last week the water pipes **burst** without warning.

2. Sometimes only one letter in the Part 1 form changes to make Part 3:

The students now **come** for reading every day.
Last year they **came** for reading only twice a week.

3. The Part 3 form of other verbs is almost entirely different from the Part 1 form because of spelling changes:

Lucy and Don **buy** something almost every week.
Last week they **bought** a television set.

The following list gives the Part 1 and Part 3 forms for some common verbs. (The forms for these and other irregular verbs are given on pages 76–78.)

Part 1 (Base)	Part 3 (Past)	Part 1 (Base)	Part 3 (Past)
bring	brought	have	had
catch	caught	say	said
do	did	teach	taught
fight	fought	think	thought
find	found	am, are, be	was, were

Notice that the verb *be* has two forms for Part 3: *was* and *were. Was* is used with singular subjects and the pronoun *I,* and *were* is used with plural nouns and pronouns:

NS————— LV   Nsc   NS   C   NS   LV   Nsc
Beth Jones **was** the director. Two men and a woman **were** her assistants.

If you are not sure whether a verb is regular or irregular, find Part I (Base) in the dictionary. If the verb is regular, you will usually find only Part 1 in many dictionaries. Part 2 is not given because you add *-s* or *-es* to most verbs. Add *-ed* to form Part 3 for the past tense:

flash (flash) *vt., vi.,* flashed

If the verb is regular but undergoes a spelling change before *-ed* to form Part 3 (Past), you may find Part 3 given in the dictionary. For example, in *drag* the final *g* is doubled:

drag (drag) *vt., vi.,* dragged, drag′ging

In *glide* the final *e* is dropped:

glide (glīd) *vi.,* glid′ed, glid′ing

In *cry* the *y* changes to *i* after the consonant *r:*

cry (krī) *vi.,* cried, cry′ing

If the verb is irregular, the dictionary will give you Part 3 (Past) after Part 1:

buy (bī) *vt.,* bought, buy'ing
draw (drô) *vt.,* drew, drawn, draw'ing
shut (shut) *vt.,* shut, shut'ting

EXERCISE 8A

Determine whether the following verbs are regular or irregular by finding each one in a dictionary. Write R (regular) or I (irregular) in the first blank. Then write the Part 3 (Past) form in the second blank.

EXAMPLE: occupy ___R___ ____occupied____   stop ___R___ ____stopped____

____I____ ____sang____   win ___I___ ____won____

1. drag _____ _____   6. reply _____ _____

2. reward _____ _____   7. shake _____ _____

3. accept _____ _____   8. build _____ _____

4. sink _____ _____   9. swim _____ _____

5. forget _____ _____   10. drink _____ _____

EXERCISE 8B

Read each of the following sentences. Then write the Part 3 (Past) form of the verb given in parentheses in the blank. Use a dictionary to find Part 3 of irregular verbs.

EXAMPLE: *(drive)* Wayne and Lisa _____drove_____ through the mountains.

(travel) They _____traveled_____ to California.

1. *(leave)* They _____ home on Saturday.

2. *(visit)* They _____ friends along the way.

3. *(stop)* Wayne and Lisa _____ in Indianapolis and Denver.

4. *(see)* They _____ Mary Ellen first and then Ken.

5. *(be)* Ken _____ a college classmate.

6. *(live)* Mary Ellen _____ near Lisa for many years.

7. *(drive)* Wayne _____ the car in the mountains.

8. *(wind)* The road _____ back and forth.

9. *(stall)* Suddenly the car _____.

10. *(need)* The car _____ gasoline.

EXERCISE 8C

Read each of the following sentences. Write Adv above each adverb that indicates when something happens or happened. Next, write *Present* or *Past* in the blank at the right.

1. Last year Rita sold jeans and tops. _____

2. She made a profit each week. _____

3. In June she hired Mark and Megan. _____

4. Now she has a successful business. _____

5. Once a month they travel to buyers' meetings. _____

EXERCISE 8D

Read each of the following sentences. Label adverbs that indicate when something happens or happened. Then write Part 1 (Base), Part 2 (Base + *s*), or Part 3 (Past) of the verb in the blank.

1. *(race)*   Last year Ray _____ his horse.

2. *(win)*   The horse _____ prizes frequently.

3. *(exercise)*   Ray and a friend _____ the horse every day.

4. *(feed)*   Ray _____ the horse every day.

5. *(brush)*   Once a day the friend _____ the horse's coat and mane.

EXERCISE 8E

The following paragraph is written in the past tense. Draw a line through each verb in the past tense, and write the present tense form, either Part 1 (Base) or Part 2 (Base + *s*), above it.

are
EXAMPLE: Jennifer and Steve ~~were~~ friends.

Jennifer and Steve wrote magazine articles. Jennifer interviewed famous people.

One was a baseball player. Two people were novelists. She told about their lives and

their interests. Steve discussed photography. He took photographs. He made drawings.

Jennifer and Steve sometimes worked together. She interviewed people. Steve photo-

graphed them.

EXERCISE 8F

Even though you do not usually write sentences according to patterns, you will gradually learn how language works by writing sentences to match the patterns given below.
Write all the verbs in the past tense. If you cannot think of a verb to use, look in a dictionary to find words that can be used as verbs.

1. NS Vi (Adv)

2. NS Vt Ndo (Adv)

3. NS and NS Vt Ndo (Adv)

4. NS Vi and Vi

5. NS Vt Ndo (Adv)

6. NS LV Nsc

Show these sentences to your instructor or tutor.

Lesson 9

The Future Tense

The sentences below tell about events that will happen in the future:

> The tourists **will go** to the city. They **are going to take** the train. They **leave** in the morning.

Although all three sentences are about future happenings, they each have a different verb form to indicate the future. The first two contain the verb phrases *will go* and *are going to take;* the third one has Part 1 of the verb *leave* and the adverbial phrase *in the morning.* Details about each of these ways to indicate the future follow.

WILL OR *SHALL* AND PART 1 (BASE)

You may use *will* or *shall,* two auxiliary (helping) verbs, with Part 1 to form the future tense. The auxiliary verb and the main verb together form a unit. *Will* or *shall* and Part 1 of the verb can be used with singular and plural subjects:

```
        NS       Vi————— Adv————— Adv
The tourists will arrive in the city tomorrow.

        NS      Vt—————  Ndo    Adv
Gloria will meet her friends there.
```

BE + *GOING TO* AND PART 1 (BASE)

Another way to write about the future is to use a Part 1 form of the verb *be (am, is, are)* with *going to* and Part 1 of a verb. In this text, we consider *be* + *going to* + Part 1 as a unit and label it as the verb in the sentence because the whole phrase is needed to express the future tense:

```
        NS       Vt—————————— Ndo  Adv——————
The tourists are going to have a party on Wednesday.

NS     Vt—————————— Ndo
John is going to invite Gloria.
```

PART 1 (BASE) AND AN ADVERB TELLING *WHEN*

Still another way you may show future time is by using Part 1 (Base) of the verb and an adverb telling *when,* such as *next week, later, in a few days, tomorrow:*

NS   Vi   Adv———— Adv Adv NS Vi   Adv

The tourists **arrive** in the city later today. John **arrives** tomorrow.

SUMMARY OF VERB FORMS
EXPRESSING THE FUTURE

SUBJECT	AUXILIARY VERB	MAIN VERB	NDO	ADV
The tourists	will	go		to the city.
They	are going to	take	the train.	
They		leave		in the morning.
They	will	arrive		tomorrow.
They	are going to	have	a party	on Wednesday.

EXERCISE 9A

Write NS above the subject and V above the verb or verb phrase in each of the following sentences. Then write the subject in the first blank, the auxiliary (helping) verbs, if there are any, in the second blank, and the main verb in the third blank.

EXAMPLE:	SUBJECT	AUXILIARY	MAIN VERB
NS NS V———— Linda and Steve are going to ———— switch roles.	Linda and Steve	are going to	switch
NS V———— The children will go to school V and help Steve.	The children	will	go, help
1. Linda begins working next week.	_____	_____	_____
2. Steve will stay home.	_____	_____	_____
3. He will be a "househusband."	_____	_____	_____
4. He will clean the house and wash clothes.	_____	_____	_____
5. Linda will buy groceries and help in the kitchen.	_____	_____	_____

6. The children will clean their
rooms.

_____ _____ _____

7. The family is going to try the
experiment for a year.

_____ _____ _____

8. Other families are going to
try the experiment also.

_____ _____ _____

EXERCISE 9B

Read each of the following sentences. Then write the appropriate form of the verb in parentheses in the blank. Use Part 1 or Part 2 of the verb given.

1. *(ride)* Neil _____ his bicycle everywhere.

2. *(travel)* The bicycle _____ slowly.

3. *(need)* Neil _____ a car.

4. *(will + have)* Neil _____ a job next week.

5. *(will + earn)* He _____ money.

6. *(be + going to + spend)* He _____ some money for a car.

7. *(will + buy)* He _____ clothes.

8. *(be + going to + entertain)* He and Marianne _____ their
friends.

9. *(will + enjoy)* They _____ themselves.

EXERCISE 9C

Write sentences telling about something that will happen in the future. Use the words in parentheses as auxiliary and main verbs. You may add adverbs. **Label the words in your sentences.**

1. *(will + choose)*

2. *(leave)* Adv

3. *(be + going to + try)*

4. *(receive)* Adv

5. *(will + give)*

Show these sentences to your instructor or tutor.

Unit Two Review

Practice Test

PART I

A. Add one or more adverbs to each of the following sentences. Use words or word groups that tell *when*, *where*, *why*, or *how*. Write Adv above each adverb.
(10 points—2 points each)   (Lesson 6)   Score _____

1. The supervisor wrote a letter.

2. The supervisor sent the letter to the president of the company.

3. The president sent a reply.

4. He ordered changes.

5. He thanked the supervisor.

B. Decide whether each of the following verbs is regular or irregular. Write R (regular) or I (irregular) in the first blank. Then write the Part 3 (Past) form in the second blank. Use a dictionary if you need help.
(20 points—2 points each)   (Lesson 8)   Score _____

1. study _____ _____   6. cling _____ _____

2. roll _____ _____   7. drop _____ _____

3. chase _____ _____   8. go _____ _____

4. bear _____ _____   9. freeze _____ _____

5. bend _____ _____   10. know _____ _____

C. Write V above the verb and NS above the subject in each of the following sentences. Be sure to extend a line over the auxiliary verb, if there is one, as well as over the main verb. The verb forms given are **not** the ones used in Standard English. Write the preferred verb forms in the blanks at the right. Be sure to keep the verb in the same tense as that given in the sentence.
(20 points—2 points each)   (Lessons 7, 8, 9)   Score _____

1. Seagulls circles over the water.   _____

2. Charlie are the tutor.   _____

3. The tiger catched a snake.   _____

4. Maggie buyed towels and sheets.   _____

5. The fence are going to keep the animals out of the yard.   _____

6. Three squirrels runned up and down the tree.   _____

7. The tire bursted without warning.   _____

8. The dog snuck into the house.   _____

9. Bells ringed every hour.   _____

10. Swans swimmed in the lake.   _____

D. Write NS above the subject and V above the verb or verb phrase in each of the following sentences. Then write the subject in the first blank, the auxiliary (helping) verbs, if there are any, in the second blank, and the main verb in the third blank. If the subject is understood, write *(you)* in the first blank.
(30 points—6 points each)   (Lessons 7, 8, 9)   Score _____

	SUBJECT	AUXILIARY	MAIN VERB
1. Donna is going to buy film for the camera.	_____	_____	_____
2. Amy and Ted will work late today.	_____	_____	_____
3. Sit down in the chair.	_____	_____	_____
4. The rain fell hard for several hours.	_____	_____	_____
5. Don Johnson is a boxer.	_____	_____	_____

E. Write a form of the verb in parentheses to complete each sentence. In some sentences you may use Part 1, Part 2, or Part 3 alone; in others you may use Part 1 and auxiliary verbs. Adverbs telling *when* should help you decide which form to use.
(20 points—4 points each)   (Lessons 6, 7, 8, 9)   Score _____

1. *(examine)*   The doctor _____ several people yesterday.

2. *(plant)*   The farmers _____ tomatoes tomorrow.

3. *(swim)*   Jim _____ long distances every day.

4. *(win)*   Last week the lawyer _____ the case.

5. *(fly)*   Helicopters _____ over the park once a week.

PART II

A. Write sentences of your own, using the verb forms indicated in the parentheses. You may choose one of your own verbs or use any of these words as verbs: *discover, collect, ride, imagine, turn, wear, divide, point, push, visit.*
(40 points—8 points each)   Score _____

   1. (Part 1–Base)

   2. (Part 3–Past)

   3. (Part 2–Base + *s*)

   4. (*be going to* + Part 1–Base)

   5. (*will* + Part 1–Base)

B. Write sentences of your own to match the following patterns. Use the Sentence Keys to **label the words in each sentence.**
(40 points—8 points each   Score _____

   1. NS Vi and Vi (Adv)

   2. NS LV Nsc

3. NS and NS Vt Ndo (Adv)

4. NS Vt Ndo (Adv)

5. NS VI (Adv)

C. Write five sentences of your own about **one** topic. Tell the verb tense by writing *Present* or *Past* in the blank at the right.
(20 points—4 points each)   Score _____

1.   _____

2.   _____

3.   _____

4.   _____

5.   _____

Unit Three

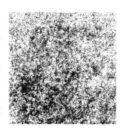

More About Verbs

Although we divide time into three parts—past, present, and future—we have more than three verb tenses to cover the three periods of time. These tenses allow a writer to be more precise about events happening at different times in the past, present, and future.

Recorded history, for example, goes back at least three thousand years. To tell about each event that happened, you learned that you can use the past tense:

> James Watt **invented** the steam engine around 1770.

> In 1807 Robert Fulton **traveled** in the first successful steamboat from New York to Albany.

If you wish to say one event happened before another, you can use a verb phrase like *had constructed:*

> The Roberts brothers **had constructed** the first hydrogen balloon in 1783.
> The next year they developed the first airship.

Or you can show that action continues for a time:

> People **are** constantly **improving** and **refining** machinery and tools.

Details about the verb tenses shown in the examples above and others are given in this unit. In addition, you will learn about modal (one-form) verbs that make it possible to express wishes, give permission, and show repeated action.

VERB TENSES

The following summary is an overview of the verb tenses you studied in Unit Two and those you will study in Unit Three.

The tenses are formed by using the five parts of the verb shown in the chart on page 48. They are arranged in this order because you will find the parts of the verb *begin,* for example, in this way in many dictionaries.

Part 1 (Base)	Part 2 (Base + s)	Part 3 (Past)	Part 4 (V-ed)	Part 5 (V-ing)
begin	begins	began	begun	beginning
arrive	arrives	arrived	arrived	arriving

TIME LINE

Below is a time line that shows the simple and perfect verb tenses and the relationship of the tenses to the times that the tenses express. You studied the past, present and future in Unit Two, and you will study the perfect tenses in Unit Three. Refer to this time line to help you understand the relationships of the tenses:

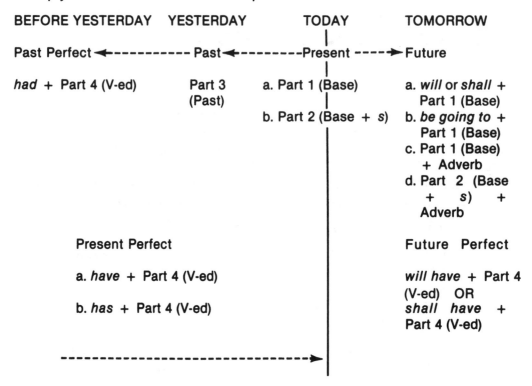

REGULAR AND IRREGULAR VERBS

	Part 1 Base	Part 2 Base + s	Part 3 Base + ed	Part 4 V-ed	Part 5 V-ing
Regular	talk	talks	talked	talked	talking
Irregular	break	breaks	broke	broken	breaking

EXAMPLES:

Past	Anita **bought** a Firebird in 1973.
Past Perfect	She **had owned** a Barracuda before that.
Present Perfect—b	She **has thought** about a new car for the past few months.
Present Perfect—a	Her friends **have talked** about the car with her.
Present—b	Anita **wants** a fast car.
Present—a	Her friends **tell** her about their cars.
Future—a	Anita **will decide** soon.
Future—b	She **is going to borrow** half the money.

Future—c		New cars **arrive** early next week.
Future—d		Anita's car **arrives** with the others next week.
Future Perfect		By this time next month Anita **will have driven** a new car for at least a week.

The simple and perfect tenses discussed above indicate completion of an activity, but the progressive tenses show an activity in progress or continuing for a time:

PROGRESSIVE TENSES

PAST	Past perfect	The swimmers **had been training** for the contest.
	Past	The swimmers **were training** for the contest.
	Present perfect	The swimmers **have been training** for the contest.
PRESENT	Present	The swimmers **are training** for the contest. The swimmer **is training** for the contest.
FUTURE	Future	The swimmers **will be training** for the contest.
	Future perfect	The swimmers **will have been training** for the contest.

As you study the lessons about verbs and do the exercises, you will be expected to write and use the verb tenses correctly, but you do not have to remember the names of all the tenses. The adverbs you use will often help you determine the tense to use in a particular sentence.

Lesson 10

The Perfect Tenses

The five parts of the verb, presented briefly in the introduction to Unit Three, give us the flexibility to discuss events happening at different times in the past, present, and future. You have learned, for example, that Part 3 (Past) of the verb is used by itself to talk or write about an event that was completed some time in the past:

> Ms. Winters **held** the job for five years.

In other words, Ms. Winters held her job for a five-year period some time in the past. It could have ended yesterday, a year ago, or ten years ago.

The verb in the next sentence indicates that Ms. Winters began her job in the past and was working to the present:

> Ms. Winters **has held** her job for five years.

The next sentence below shows that Ms. Winters became general manager at a time in the past, but before that time in the past when she received her promotion, she had worked five years:

> Ms. Winters **had held** her job for five years. Then she **became** general manager of the real estate company.

And the verb in the following sentence indicates completion of an activity in the future:

> By this time next year Ms. Winters **will have spent** ten years with the company.

Each of the verbs (with *have, has,* or *had* as auxiliary verbs) in the sentences above represents one of the perfect tenses which allows you to show how the times when events happened are related to one another in the past and future. To form the perfect tenses, you use the verb **have** as an auxiliary verb and Part 4 (V-ed) for the main verb. You will study the three perfect tenses in this lesson after learning something about Part 4.

PART 4 (V-ED): REGULAR AND IRREGULAR VERBS

Like Part 3 (Past), Part 4 (V-ed) may be regular or irregular. Part 4 of some verbs adds -*ed* to Part 1, but others may show spelling changes. Here are some regular and irregular verbs:*

*You will find an alphabetical list of irregular verbs on pages 76–78.

	Part 1 (Base)	Part 2 (Base + s)	Part 3 (Past)	Part 4 (V-ed)
REGULAR VERBS	happen	happens	happened	happened
	talk	talks	talked	talked
IRREGULAR VERBS	set	sets	set	set
	sit	sits	sat	sat
	ride	rides	rode	ridden
	choose	chooses	chose	chosen
	have	has	had	had

If you cannot decide whether a verb is regular or irregular while you are writing, look up the base word in a dictionary. If the verb is regular, only Part 1 will appear. If the Part 3 and Part 4 forms are spelled the same, dictionaries usually list the word once. If Part 4 is spelled differently from Part 3, the dictionary will give you Part 4 after Parts 1 and 3. For example, if you look up the verbs *begin* and *buy* you will find the following forms:

begin   began, begun
buy   bought

HAVE: MAIN VERB AND AUXILIARY VERB

The last verb shown in the list of irregular verbs is *have* and its Part 2, Part 3, and Part 4 forms. *Have,* unlike most other verbs, may function as a main verb or an auxiliary verb. When *have* functions as a main verb, it means *possess* or *contain.* The following examples show Parts 1, 2, and 3 functioning as the main verbs in sentences:

PLURAL SUBJECT   The students **have** books.
SINGULAR SUBJECT   The book **has** information.
SINGULAR OR PLURAL SUBJECT   Joan **had** her own book.
                                 Ken and Bonnie **had** their own books.

Have, has, and *had* function as auxiliary verbs when they are combined with Part 4 of a verb to form the perfect tenses:

The students **have taken** a test.   Joan **has passed.**   She **had studied** hard.

EXERCISE 10A

Read each of the following sentences. In the blanks at the right write *Main* if *have, has,* and *had* function as the main verb and *Aux* if *have, has,* and *had* function as auxiliary verbs.

1. The cook has prepared the meal.   _____

2. Museums have many works of art.   _____

3. The pioneers had strength and courage.   _____

4. The runners have eaten the pizza.   _____

5. The car had a flat tire.   _____

6. Laura had visited her family last month.   _____

The Present Perfect Tense (*Have* or *Has* + Part 4)

The present perfect tense indicates an action that took place at an indefinite time in the past or over a period of time that may extend from the past to the present. The present perfect tense is formed by using *have* or *has* with Part 4 (V-ed) of a verb. *Have* is used with plural subjects and the pronouns *I* and *you*, and *has* is used with singular subjects.

The past tense, which you studied in Lesson 8, indicates a definite time in the past. It is Part 3 (Past) of a verb:

PRESENT PERFECT	PAST
(Indefinite time in the past continuing to the present with adverbial phrases beginning with *for* and *since*)	(Definite time in the past with adverbs such as *last year, two years ago, at six o'clock, on Friday,* and *yesterday*)
	Ted and Jim Fisher **bought** the grocery store ten years ago.
Ted and Jim Fisher **have owned** the grocery store for ten years.	Ted and Jim Fisher **owned** the grocery store for ten years (in the past). (They no longer own it.)
(Indefinite time before moment of speaking, sometimes with *recently, just, yet,* and *already*.)	
Jim Fisher **has enjoyed** the experience.	Last year Ted **took** a leave of absence.
The two brothers **have** recently **sold** the store.	They **sold** the store last week.

Other adverbial expressions that might indicate present perfect tense are the following: *often, many times, all day, lately, frequently, finally, just, never, ever, yet, Sunday morning, within the past year (month, week), during this time (week, month, year).*

EXERCISE 10B

The following sentences contain verbs in the present and past tense. Rewrite each sentence in the space below by changing the verb to the present perfect tense and adding adverbs such as *often, many times, all day, lately, frequently,* etc.

1. Jason and Linda ride bicycles to work.

2. They save money.

3. They used the money for a vacation.

4. They went to England.

5. They hiked and camped in the countryside.

The Past Perfect Tense (*Had* + Part 4)

The past perfect tense indicates a time in the past before a definite time in the past. It is formed by using *had* + Part 4 of a verb. In the following example the first sentence indicates that Ted and Jim Fisher sold their store at a definite time in the past. The second sentence tells that they had bought the store before they sold it:

PAST: Ted and Jim Fisher **sold** the grocery store last week.
PAST PERFECT: They **had owned** the store for ten years (before they sold it last week).

When you are writing about events that happen at different times, carefully choose Part 3 (Past), *have/has* with Part 4 (V-ed), or *had* with Part 4 (V-ed) to show the relationship of events clearly.

EXERCISE 10C

Read ALL the following sentences. Write *Adv* above each adverb. Then fill in the blank with the Part 3 (Past), *have/has* + Part 4 (V-ed), or *had* + Part 4 (V-ed) form of the verb given in parentheses.

1. *(learn)*   In recent years people _____ about the energy crisis.

2. *(try)*   They _____ to use less natural gas.

3. *(receive)*   Before the energy crisis people _____ reduced rates for using large quantities of natural gas.

4. *(heat)*   Homeowners _____ their houses to 80 degrees with gas.

5. *(encourage)*   Gas companies _____ people to buy gas dryers and gas ranges.

6. *(change)*   But for the past few years the gas companies _____ _____ their advertising campaigns.

7. *(show)*   They _____ _____ people ways to save gas.

The Future Perfect Tense (*Will Have* or *Shall Have* + Part 4)

The auxiliary verbs *will have* or *shall have* together with a main verb form **the future perfect tense, which indicates the completion of an activity in the future.**

> By this time next year Peter and Paul Fox **will have completed** a trip around the world.

TWO OR MORE VERBS IN THE PREDICATE

If you write a sentence with one subject and two or more verbs, you do not have to repeat the auxiliary verb. In the following sentence the verbs are *has received* and *has placed*, but *has* is written just once:

```
NS       Vt————————   Ndo        Vt    Ndo  Adv—————————
```
Lindsay **has received** the supplies and **placed** them on the shelves.

EXERCISE 10D

Use Sentence Keys 1 and 2 to identify the verbs and the subject in the following sentences. Write V above each verb or verb phrase and NS above each subject. Be sure to extend a line over the auxiliary verb as well as the main verb. The verb forms given are **not** the ones used in Standard English. Write the correct forms in the blanks at the right. Use a dictionary to find Part 3 and Part 4 of irregular verbs.

1. The ship have sailed for six weeks.   _____

2. Nancy has drove all night.   _____

3. Bob had drank the hot tea and burned his lips. _____

4. Mark seen his girlfriend yesterday.   _____

5. The people has discuss the problem several times. _____

6. Fred done nothing for a week.   _____

7. The plumber have bought a new car.   _____

8. David had choosed a cereal for breakfast.   _____

9. Susan Miller has wrote the contract.   _____

10. The choir had sang in seven states.   _____

EXERCISE 10E

Write sentences using the verbs in parentheses. Use the parts of verbs indicated. Write NS above each subject and V above each verb or verb phrase. Be sure to draw a line over the auxiliary verb as well as the main verb.

1. (*drag:* Part 3)

2. (*drug:* Part 1)

3. (*swim:* Part 4)

4. (*sneak:* Part 3)

5. (*drink:* Part 4)

6. (*go:* Part 2)

7. (*see:* Part 4)

8. (*grow:* Part 2)

9. (*buy:* Part 4)

10. (*shake:* Part 3)

Show these sentences to your instructor or tutor.

EXERCISE 10F

Read ALL of the sentences in the exercise below before filling in the blanks. The sentences are about events taking place at different times. First, write Adv above the adverbs that tell you when each event happened. Then fill in the blank by using a form of the verb given in parentheses as the main verb and adding auxiliary verbs if they are needed. Look at the examples below and those given in this lesson if you need help.

EXAMPLE:	(*buy*)	Mike ____bought____ a coat last year.		PAST TENSE
	(*buy*)	He ____had bought____ a suit the year before.		PAST PERFECT
	(*need*)	Now Mike ____needs____ more clothes.		PRESENT TENSE
	(*buy*)	He ____has bought____ one shirt so far.		PRESENT PERFECT
	(*have*)	He ____will have____ money next week for more clothes.		FUTURE

1. (cause) An earthquake _____ deaths, injuries, and destruction in a town last week.

2. (need) The people _____ help badly.

3. (organize) Fortunately doctors, nurses, and many people _____ a plan for emergencies two years before.

4. (meet) They _____ several times the year before.

5. (organize) At the meetings they _____ rescue teams.

6. (buy) In addition, they _____ supplies.

7. (hold) They _____ _____ practice drills four times during the year.

8. (help) After the earthquake the teams quickly _____ the people.

9. (make) Since the earthquake the teams _____ new plans.

10. (buy) They _____ more supplies.

11. (train) Next week they _____ more people.

12. (prepare) By this time next month they _____ for a new emergency.

EXERCISE 10G

Read all the sentences in Exercise 10F again because they serve as an example of how to use verb tenses to show when one event happened in relation to another event. Then write ten sentences of your own on another sheet of paper about events that happened over a period of time. Use any of the simple or perfect tenses you have studied in Lessons 7–10 and adverbs to show the relationship of the events to one another. Keep your sentences short and simple. Show these sentences to your instructor or tutor.

Lesson 11

The Progressive Tenses

The verb tenses you have studied to this point have indicated that something happens, has been completed, or will take place at another time. You can also show something continuing for a short or a long period of time by using one of the progressive tenses as in the first and last sentences below:

The cat **was sleeping.**   (something in progress)
The telephone **rang.**   (a completed event)
The cat **meowed.**   (a completed event)
The noise **was disturbing** her. (something in progress)

The progressive tenses allow you to show how events in progress are related to one another in the past and future. To form progressive tenses, you use the verb *be* as an auxiliary verb and Part 5 (V-ing) for the main verb. Before you study the progressive tenses in this lesson, you will learn something about Part 5.

PART 5 (V-ING)

Part 5 of verbs is formed by adding the suffix *-ing* to Part 1 (Base). For example, *walk* becomes *walking, sing* becomes *singing,* and *study* becomes *studying.* When you add *-ing* to some verbs such as *begin* or *occur,* you must double the final consonant: *beginning, occurring.* Some verbs such as *write* or *bake* drop the final *e* before adding *-ing: writing, baking.*

The *-ing* form of a word must be used with an auxiliary verb in order to function as a verb. Another function of *-ing* words will be discussed later in this lesson.

BE: MAIN VERB AND AUXILIARY VERB

The following review of the verb *be* as a main verb and the chart showing its several forms should be helpful to you in recognizing and using the progressive tenses.

Be as a Main Verb

When *be* functions as a main verb, it is always a linking verb. You learned in Lesson 5 that it links the subject to a noun that renames the subject:

NS————— LV   Nsc   Adv——— Adv——— NS————— LV   Nsc

Mr. Warren is my instructor this year. Last year Ms. Brown **was** my instructor.

NS LV————— Nsc   Adv—————

She had been my instructor for two years.

Be + Part 5

When *be* appears with Part 5 (V-ing) of a verb, it functions as an auxiliary verb in a verb phrase:

Adv   NS   Vt————— Ndo

Today the tourists are packing their clothes.

Adv   NS   Vi————————— Adv———

Tomorrow they will be leaving for Alaska.

The verb *be* has more forms than any other verb—a total of eight: *be, am, is, are, was were, been, being.* The chart below shows all the forms in all the tenses when it functions as a main verb or as an auxiliary verb:

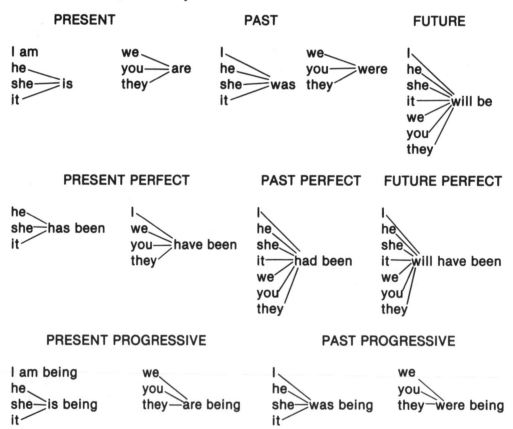

You found examples of the past progressive tense in the sentences about the cat being disturbed by the telephone. Now here are examples of the remaining progressive tenses:

PRESENT PROGRESSIVE	NS	C	NS	Vt———— Ndo

PRESENT PROGRESSIVE

NS   C   NS   Vt——————   Ndo

Ted and Lisa **are buying** a condominium.

PRESENT PERFECT
PROGRESSIVE

NS   Vt————————   Ndo

They **have been saving** their money.

NS   Vt————————   Ndo

Lisa **has been comparing** prices.

PAST PERFECT
PROGRESSIVE

NS   Vt————————   Ndo   Adv————

They **had been planning** the purchase for a year.

FUTURE PROGRESSIVE

NS   Vt——————   Ndo   Adv

They **will be making** the payment tomorrow.

TWO OR MORE VERBS IN THE PREDICATE

If you write a sentence with one subject and two or more verbs, you do not need to repeat the auxiliary verb because it is understood. In the following sentence the verbs are *is leaving* and *(is) arriving*:

NS   Vi———— Adv——— C   VI   Adv————

The plane **is leaving** at 2 P.M. and **arriving** at 6 P.M.

However, if you write a sentence with two subjects and one is singular and one is plural, each auxiliary verb must be stated:

NS   Vi———— C   NS   Vi————

The company **is failing,** and the workers **are striking.**

EXERCISE 11A

Use Sentence Keys 1 and 2 to identify the verbs and the subject in each of the following sentences. Write V above each verb or verb phrase and NS above each subject. Then write the subject in the first blank, the auxiliary verbs, if there are any, in the second blank, and the main verb in the third blank.

	SUBJECT	AUXILIARY	MAIN VERB
EXAMPLE: NS V———— The clouds had been ———— gathering in the sky.	clouds	had been	gathering
1. A storm was coming.	_____	_____	_____
2. Suddenly rain was pounding the earth.	_____	_____	_____
3. Without warning the dam had cracked and released water.	_____	_____	_____

4. Water was rushing into the town. _____ _____ _____

5. People were running and scream-

   ing. _____ _____ _____

6. The water flooded the streets

   and crushed houses. _____ _____ _____

7. Mud was covering everything. _____ _____ _____

8. Water hid the town. _____ _____ _____

EXERCISE 11B

Read the following sentences. Then write the appropriate form of the verb phrase given in parentheses in the blank, using one of the progressive tenses.

1. *(be + work)* Ed and Al _____ on the building at the moment.

2. *(have + be + study)* They _____ the plans for several days.

3. *(will + be + fly)* Next week Doris and Lou _____ to Rio.

4. *(be + run)* Before the event Martha _____ on the track.

5. *(be + help)* I _____ now with the revision.

6. *(be + walk)* Leslie _____ the dog at this hour.

7. *(have + be + enjoy)* Until now the hitchhiker _____ the ride.

8. *(have + be + write)* The class _____ better sentences since last week.

9. *(be + stop)* The shuttle buses _____ at the stadium this past Sunday.

10. *(be + ride)* Presently Fran _____ on a horse.

11. *(will + be + tape)* Desmond _____ the concert next Thursday.

EXERCISE 11C

In the following exercise the base of verbs is given. In the four blanks following each verb, write the remaining parts. If you need help, find Part 1 in the list of irregular verbs on pages 76–78 or in a dictionary. Then in the sentences that follow use the form of the verb requested by the number in parentheses. Add auxiliary verbs if they are needed.

	Base Part 1	Base + s Part 2	Past Part 3	V-ed Part 4	V-ing Part 5
EXAMPLE:	enjoy	enjoys	enjoyed	enjoyed	enjoying

(Part 1)   Brian and his friends _____ enjoy _____ skiing once a week.

1. sit _____ _____ _____ _____

(Part 1)   Afterwards they _____ before a fire in the lodge.

2. play _____ _____ _____ _____

(Part 2)   Brian _____ his guitar and sings.

3. ride _____ _____ _____ _____

(Part 3)   One day Brian and his friends _____ a ski lift up the mountain.

4. ski _____ _____ _____ _____

(Part 3)   Brian and his friends _____ down the slope several times.

(*had* + *be* + Part 5)   They _____ _____ _____ for several hours.

5. hit _____ _____ _____ _____

(Part 3)   Brian _____ a tree.

6. hurt _____ _____ _____ _____

(Part 3)   His leg _____ badly.

7. carry _____ _____ _____ _____

(Part 3)   His friends _____ him down the hill to the hospital.

8. break _____ _____ _____ _____

(Part 4)   Brian _____ _____ his leg.

9. plan _____ _____ _____ _____

(*had* + *be* + Part 5)   He _____ _____ _____ a trip to New York.

10. change _____ _____ _____ _____

(Part 3)   He quickly _____ his plans.

11. entertain _____ _____ _____ _____

   (Part 5) His friends _____ _____ him.

12. sign _____ _____ _____ _____

   (Part 3) They _____ his cast.

13. visit _____ _____ _____ _____

   (Part 3) They _____ him every day.

EXERCISE 11D

Read the sentences in Exercise 11C. Write five or more sentences telling what happened to Brian and what his friends did. Be careful to use appropriate tenses to show the order in which events took place.

Show these sentences to your instructor or tutor.

PART 5 (V-ING) AS A NOUN

You have learned that a word ending in -ing cannot be called a verb unless an auxiliary verb comes before it. In other words, the following phrases can be called verbs because a form of the verb be comes before the Part 5 form:

    NS Vt———— Ndo   NS C NS Vt————Ndo
    Joe **is reading** a newspaper. Joe and Mike **are studying** algebra.

When a word ending in -ing is used alone, it sometimes functions as a noun:

    NS   Vt   Ndo NS Vt   Ndo
    Studying takes time. Joe enjoys **reading.**

Notice that the noun may be either a subject or a direct object.

Use the Sentence Keys to identify the patterns in each of the following sentences. Label the words in the sentences. If the verb consists of auxiliary verbs and a main verb, be sure to draw a line over the entire phrase. Decide whether the word ending in *-ing* is a noun or a verb.

             NS   C   NS   Vt———— Ndo Adv————————

EXAMPLE: Sarah and Ruth are taking jobs in a summer camp.

             NS   Vt   Ndo   Adv————

            They enjoy riding on a train.

1. Sarah and Ruth pack their suitcases.

2. They are taking blouses, jeans, and swimsuits.

3. They are going to Door County, Wisconsin.

4. Working and relaxing please them.

5. The train leaves the station.

6. Passengers are waving their hands.

7. They smile at their friends.

8. Sarah and Ruth are enjoying the ride.

9. They like looking out the window.

10. Traveling is a wonderful experience.

Lesson 12

Modal (One-Form) Verbs

Will and *shall,* used to form the future tense (Lesson 9), are two of several verbs called *modal* or *one-form* verbs. They function as auxiliary verbs in a verb phrase. They help express mood or attitude toward something. The mood or attitude they express is shown in the following examples:

1. *may, can*:* permitted or allowed

    NS Vi——— Adv——————   NS Vi——— Adv——————
    You **may go** to the game. You **can go** to the game.

    *Some people believe that *may* is the only word to use to ask for permission; they consider using *can* impolite.

2. *can, could:* able or capable

    NS Vt———   Ndo   NS Vt——————   Ndo
    He **can lift** the motorcycle. He **could have won** the race.

3. *must, have to, had to:* necessary

    NS Vt————   Ndo Adv   NS Vt——————   Ndo
    She **must return** the book tomorrow. She **has to complete** the assignment

    Adv
    today.

4. *may, might, could, should:* possible or probable

    NS   Vt———   Ndo   Adv   NS   Vt———   Ndo   Adv
    They **may try** the equipment today. They **might try** the equipment today.

    NS   Vt————   Ndo   Adv——— NS   Vt————   Ndo
    They **could reach** a decision next week. They **should reach** a decision

    Adv———
    next week.

5. *should, ought to:* responsible

    NS   Vt————   Ndo Adv   NS   Vt——————   Ndo Adv
    She **should take** the test now. She **ought to take** the test now.

6. *would, used to:* usual or repeated

NS   Vi├──────── Adv────────Adv────────   NS   Vt──── Ndo
The family **used to drive** in the country every Sunday.   They **would eat** lunch

Adv────────
under a tree.

FUNCTION OF MODAL AUXILIARIES

The modal auxiliaries must be used with another verb or verbs:

    NOT: They **may** in the ocean.

             NS   Vi────── Adv────────
    BUT: They **may swim** in the ocean.

They may be used with *have* and Part 4 of a verb or *be* and Part 5 of a verb:

    NS   Vi──────────── Adv────────   NS   Vi──────────── Adv────────
    They **may have swum** in the ocean.   They **may be swimming** in the ocean.

In addition, the modal auxiliaries do not have an infinitive form. In other words, you cannot place *to* before any of them:

    NOT: to may   to should   to ought to

Modals do not have Part 2, Part 4 (V-ed), or Part 5 (V-ing) forms:

    Part 2   NOT: mays   musts
    Part 4   NOT: (has) mayed   (have) musted
    Part 5   NOT: (is) maying   (were) musting

THE VERBS *DO, HAVE,* AND *BE*

In contrast, the verbs *do, have,* and *be* may function as main verbs in some sentences and as auxiliary verbs in other sentences. When these words are auxiliaries, *do* is used to emphasize something, *have* is used with the perfect tenses (Lesson 10), and *be* (Lesson 11) is used with progressive tenses. Their forms are summarized below:

Part 1 (Base)	Part 2 (Base + s)	Part 3 (Past)	Part 4 (V-ed)	Part 5 (V-ing)
do	does	did	done	doing
have	has	had	had	having
am, are, be	is	was, were	been	being

The following examples show each of the verbs used as main verbs in sentences on the left and as auxiliary verbs on the right:

                      MAIN VERB   AUXILIARY VERB

NS   LV   Nsc   NS   Vt──────── Ndo
Max **is** an artist.   He **is designing** a house.

NS   Vt   Ndo   NS   Vt──────── Ndo   Adv
He **has** many ideas.   He **has used** them frequently.

```
Ns  Vt        Ndo        Adv                    Vt   Vt——————   Ndo
He does his planning daily.                    He does enjoy his work.
```

EXERCISE 12A

Use the Sentence Keys to identify the patterns in the following sentences. Label the patterns NS Vi (Adv), NS Vt Ndo (Adv), or NS LV Nsc.

1. Jim is an attorney.

2. He may spend a holiday at home.

3. He would prefer a trip to San

   Francisco.

4. He should be mowing the lawn and

   painting the fence.

5. He might work in the morning and rest

   in the afternoon.

6. He could also play tennis in the after-

   noon.

7. He does enjoy the game.

8. He will make plans early next time.

EXERCISE 12B

Write sentences using the parts of verbs in parentheses. You may use words like *yell, hear, type, prefer, gather, invite,* or any others you choose as the main verbs.

1. (*can* + Part 1)

2. (*would* + Part 1)

3. (*must* + *be* + Part 5)

4. (*used to* + Part 1)

5. (*may* + *be* + Part 5)

Show these sentences to your instructor or tutor.

Lesson 13

Negatives and Questions

The sentences you have been studying and writing to this point have all been *positive* statements; they have all given information about something that happens, has been completed, or will take place at another time:

```
                NS Vt——— Ndo Adv        NS Vt——————— Ndo
POSITIVE:  I  will visit you tomorrow.  We should discuss the contract.
```

If you want to explain that something did not happen, you can add the word *not* to the sentence. The word *not* makes the statement *negative.* Because *not* qualifies the verb, it is an adverb. Remember that *not is not a part of the verb phrase* even though it stands between the auxiliary verb and the main verb. In the following example, *not* comes between *will,* the auxiliary verb, and *visit,* the main verb:

```
                NS Vt  Adv Vt   Ndo Adv       NS  Vt    Adv Vt
NEGATIVE:  I  will not visit you tomorrow.  We should not discuss the

                                            Ndo
                                            contract.
```

If the verb in a positive statement is a single word, in most cases you must use an auxiliary verb, like a form of the verb *do,* before the word *not* and then place Part 1 after *not.* The auxiliary verb, instead of the main verb, shows the tense. In the following examples *began* shows the past tense in the positive statement, and *did* in the phrase *did begin* shows the past tense in the negative statement. *Types* in the second positive sentence and *use* in the third positive sentence indicate the present tense; *does* and *do* indicate the present tense in the negative second and third sentences:

POSITIVE   NEGATIVE

```
         NS  Vt                    NS   Vt  Adv Vt        Ndo
PAST:    Kim began a new           Kim did not begin a new business.
         Ndo
         business.

         NS  Vt    Ndo             NS  Vt   Adv Vt  Ndo    Adv———
PRESENT: She types letters         She does not type letters for people.
         Adv———
         for people.

              NS    Vt                  NS    Vt  Adv Vt
PRESENT: Many people use her       Many people do not use her
         Ndo                       Ndo
         services.                 services.
```

The verb *be,* however, may be used alone with *not:*

POSITIVE	NEGATIVE
NS LV Nsc	NS LV Adv Nsc
Jerome **is** a scientist.	Jerome **is** not a scientist.

EXERCISE 13A

Make each of the following sentences negative by using *not.* Use a form of auxiliary verb *do* with each verb in the negative statement.

EXAMPLE: POSITIVE: The window cracks.   The storm continued.
             NEGATIVE: The window does not crack.   The storm did not continue.

1. Snow falls.

2. Tree branches break.

3. Animals hide.

4. The car skids.

5. The car crashes.

6. The driver escapes.

7. The baby crawled.

8. Her brother ran.

9. The dog barked.

10. The cat hid.

Another way to make a sentence negative is to use the word *never* instead of *not.* Notice that you do not have to add an auxiliary in the first negative statement:

                 NS   Vt   Ndo
POSITIVE: She **called** Leo.

```
               NS   Adv   Vt      Ndo
NEGATIVE:  She never called Leo.

               NS   Vt————  Ndo
Positive:  She has called Leo.

               NS   Vt  Adv   Vt     Ndo
NEGATIVE:  She has never called Leo.
```

EXERCISE 13B

Use the word in parentheses to make each of the following sentences negative. Write Adv above *not* or *never*. In some cases you will have to add an auxiliary verb. Label the words in the sentences.

EXAMPLE: *(not)* The rock group came to town.

```
                       NS      Vi  Adv Vi    Adv————
            The rock group did not come to town.
```

1. *(not)* The singer is Tana Lee.

2. *(never)* She has performed in many concerts.

3. *(not)* Sometimes she wears unusual costumes.

4. *(not)* She uses heavy makeup on her face.

5. *(never)* Her performances please her audiences.

CONTRACTIONS

Another way to write a negative statement is to use a contraction like *can't* or *don't*:

I **can't visit** you tomorrow. I **don't have** time.

Can't is made up of the word *cannot* with the letters *no* removed and the apostrophe (') inserted to show that letters have been omitted. *Don't* is a contraction of the words *do not:*

cann∅t   can't   do n∅t   don't

Other contractions which may be used to make sentences negative are:

isn't	aren't	wasn't	weren't
doesn't	didn't	hasn't	haven't
won't*	wouldn't	shouldn't	couldn't

Won't is a contraction of the words *will not.*

Contractions like *can't* and *don't* fit smoothly into spoken language. Sometimes, however, speakers forget they have made a sentence negative by using the contraction and add another negative word like *never* or *hardly* to their sentences. It is preferable in speaking and writing to use only one negative in sentences like these:

NOT: Manuel can**not never** agree with Rick.

        NS Vi Adv Adv Vi Adv————
BUT: Manuel can**not ever** agree with Rick.

        NS Vi Adv Vi Adv————
MORE USUAL: Manuel **can** never **agree** with Rick.

NOT: Phil **can't hardly** hear the bell.

BUT: Phil **can hardly** hear the bell.

NOTE: Sometimes a pronoun and a verb will combine to form positive contractions. Here is a list of some of these contractions and their complete forms:

I'm/I am   I've/I have we'll/we will you'd/you would
he's/he is OR he has   it's/it is   they're/they are

Although contractions appear in all kinds of prose, they are found most often in informal writing. As a result, if you are writing formal essays or business reports, you probably should not use contractions.

EXERCISE 13C

Write the full forms of the following contractions.

EXAMPLE: they're _____ they are _____ don't _____ do not _____

1. shouldn't _____ 5. he's _____

2. can't _____ 6. I'll _____

3. won't _____ 7. they'd _____

4. didn't _____ 8. you've _____

EXERCISE 13D

The sentences below contain two negative expressions. Rewrite each sentence, omitting one of the negative words.

EXAMPLE: The trees can't never grow without water.

REWRITTEN: The trees can never grow without water.
OR: The trees can't ever grow without water.

1. Animals can't hardly live without water.

2. The rocket wouldn't hardly fly without fuel.

3. Mary won't never leave home.

4. She doesn't never want freedom.

QUESTIONS

You may write questions in three ways. One kind of question asks for *yes* or *no* as the answer: *Did that woman ask for me?* A second kind, beginning with words such as *who, which,* and *what,* asks for some information: *Who is she?* The third kind expects a person to choose one of two or three choices: *Does she want to look at me or talk with me?*

1. *YES–NO* Questions

   The usual order of a sentence is subject first, followed by the verb:

        NS   Vt   Ndo
   The plumber **installed** the shower.

To write the sentence as a question, use an auxiliary verb at the beginning of the question, place the subject next, follow it with the main verb (Part 1), and end it with a question mark:

            Vt   NS   Vt   Ndo
   NOT: **Did** the plumber **installed** the shower?

            Vt   NS   Vt   Ndo
   BUT: **Did** the plumber **install** the shower?

            Vt   NS   Vt   Ndo
   Does the plumber **install** showers?

            Vt NS   Vt   Ndo
   Do plumbers **install** showers?

If the verb consists of an auxiliary verb and a main verb, use the auxiliary verb at the beginning of the question:

                   NS   Vt————   Ndo
   STATEMENT: The plumber **will repair** the faucet.

                 Vt   NS   Vt   Ndo
   QUESTION: **Will** the plumber **repair** the faucet?

Sometimes the question begins with an auxiliary verb and *not:*

            Vt Adv   NS   Vt   Ndo
   Didn't the plumber **install** the shower?

Vt   Adv NS Vt   Ndo
Won't he repair the faucet?

Vt   Adv   NS   Vt   Ndo
Doesn't the plumber **install** the shower?

EXERCISE 13E

Rewrite each of the following statements as a *yes–no* question. Use forms of the auxiliary verb *do* with the main verb.

EXAMPLE: Statement: The sun shines.   Plants grow.
           Question: Does the sun shine?   Do plants grow?

1. Rick drives race cars.

2. He owns three cars.

3. His friends attend the races.

4. They cheer loudly.

5. Rick wins.

6. Maggie bought a novel.

7. She enjoyed the story.

8. Betty also read the novel.

9. She liked the hero.

2. *WH*-Questions

Questions may begin with *WH*-question words such as *who*, *which*, and *what*, which can function as the subject or direct object in the sentence:

NS   LV Nsc——————   Ndo   Vt   NS Vt   Adv——————
Who is Blaine Peters?   **What** can we learn about him?

Questions may also begin with words such as *when, where, why,* and *how,* all of which function as adverbs. The auxiliary verb, if one is used, appears before the subject, and the main verb comes after it:

Adv Vi NS————————Vi   Adv   Adv   Adv Vi NS
Why has Blaine Peters come here? **How** long will he stay?

To change statements to questions, use the *WH*-word in place of one of the words in the statement. In the first example *What* replaces *The campfire:*

STATEMENT ~~The campfire~~ burned brightly.
QUESTION: **What** burned brightly?

In the next example *who* may replace *hikers,* or *what* may replace *their hands:*

~~The hikers~~ warmed their hands.   **Who** warmed their hands?
The hikers warmed ~~their hands.~~   **What** did the hikers warm?

In the last two examples *where* replaces *on the ground,* and *how long* replaces *an hour:*

The hikers sat ~~on the ground.~~   **Where** did the hikers sit?
They rested ~~an hour.~~   **How long** did they rest?

EXERCISE 13F

Rewrite each of the following sentences in two ways to make them questions.

a. Write the sentences as a *yes-no* question by beginning it with a verb. In some sentences you may want to use contractions.

b. Write the sentences as a *WH*-question, using the words in parentheses.

EXAMPLE: Kites have served several purposes.
          a. Have kites served several purposes?
          b. *(what)* What have served several purposes?

1. Children and adults fly kites for fun.

a.

b. *(who)*

2. Kite builders usually use colorful paper and thin wood for kites.

a.

b. *(what)*

3. They build the kites carefully.

a.

b. *(how)*

4. Workers once took a line across Niagara Falls with a kite.

a.

b. *(where)*

5. First, they carried a thin line with the kite.

a.

b. *(what)*

6. Then they pulled a rope across the Falls with the thin line.

a.

b. *(how)*

7. Finally, they pulled a cable across with the rope.

a.

b. *(what)*

Lesson 14

Troublesome Verbs

If you have a hard time deciding whether to use the verbs *sit* or *set*, *lie* or *lay*, *rise* or *raise*, try to remember that *sit*, *lie*, and *rise* are all intransitive verbs; in other words, they do not need a noun to complete the predicate. Notice that the letter *i* is the second letter in each of these Part 1 forms and that the word *intransitive* begins with *i*:

NS   Vi   Adv———   Adv   Ns   Vi   Adv   NS   Vi
Diane **sits** in the chair. Later she **lies** down. She **rises** early.

The words *set*, *lay*, and *raise*, on the other hand, are transitive verbs; they need a direct object to complete the predicate:

NS   Vt   Ndo   Adv———   NS   Vt   Ndo   Adv   NS
Russ **sets** the glass on the table. He **lays** the book down. He

Vt   Ndo
raises the window.

The following chart shows the parts for each of these verbs:

	INTRANSITIVE					TRANSITIVE			
1	2	3	4	5	1	2	3	4	5
sit	sits	sat	sat	sitting	set	sets	set††	set	setting
lie*	lies	lay†	lain	lying	lay†	lays	laid	laid	laying
rise	rises	rose	risen	rising	raise	raises	raised	raised	raising

EXERCISE 14

Use the Sentence Keys to identify the patterns in each of the following sentences. Look at the verb chart on pages 76–78 to check the verb form given. If the form given in the sentence should be changed, write the appropriate form in the blank and label it Vi or Vt. If the form is acceptable, write A in the blank.

*The principal parts of the verb *to lie*, meaning to tell an untruth, are *lie, lied, lied*. The word *lye* names an alkaline solution made from wood ashes.

†Notice that *lay* is a form for both the intransitive and the transitive verb, but one form is used to talk about the past and the other is used to talk about the present. We may confuse these because we have difficulty hearing whether the speaker is saying *lay* or *laid*. They sound similar.

††*Set* may be intransitive in sentences like these:

NS   Vi   NS   Vi   Adv———
The sun set.   The hen set on eggs.

EXAMPLE: The plumber s̶e̶t̶ the pipe on the ground.   _____set(Vt)_____

                    NS   Vi   Adv─────────
            The dog l̶a̶i̶d̶ on the sidewalk.   _____lay (VI)_____

1. The seasick sailor laid in his bunk all day.   _____

2. The sun had rose at six o'clock.   _____

3. Squashes and pumpkins lay in the field.   _____

4. Set the suitcase on the rack.   _____

5. The exhausted man had laid there for two hours.   _____

6. Bob had set down in the broken rocker.   _____

7. Lie the baby in her crib.   _____

8. Divers raised the sunken treasure.   _____

9. The fishing net had risen to the surface.   _____

10. The cat lay on the soft pillow in the sun.   _____

ALPHABETICAL LIST OF IRREGULAR VERBS

Part 1 (Base)	Part 2 (Base + s)	Part 3 (Past)	Part 4 (V-ed)	Part 5 (V-ing)
arise	arises	arose	arisen	arising
awake	awakes	awoke	awaken	awaking
be, am, are	is	was, were	been	being
bear (bring forth)	bears	bore	born	bearing
bear (carry)	bears	bore	borne	bearing
beat	beats	beat	beaten	beating
become	becomes	became	become	becoming
begin	begins	began	begun	beginning
bend	bends	bent	bent	bending
bet	bets	bet	bet	betting
bid (command)	bids	bade	bid	bidding
bid (money)	bids	bid	bidden, bid	bidding
bind	binds	bound	bound	binding
bite	bites	bit	bitten	biting
bleed	bleeds	bled	bled	bleeding
blow	blows	blew	blown	blowing
break	breaks	broke	broken	breaking
bring	brings	brought	brought	bringing
build	builds	built, builded	built, builded	building
burst	bursts	burst	burst	bursting
buy	buys	bought	bought	buying
cast	casts	cast	cast	casting
catch	catches	caught	caught	catching
choose	chooses	chose	chosen	choosing
cling	clings	clung	clung	clinging

come	comes	came	come	coming
cost	costs	cost	cost	costing
creep	creeps	crept	crept	creeping
cut	cuts	cut	cut	cutting
deal	deals	dealt	dealt	dealing
dig	digs	dug	dug	digging
dive	dives	dived, dove	dived	diving
do	does	did	done	doing
draw	draws	drew	drawn	drawing
drink	drinks	drank	drunk	drinking
drive	drives	drove	driven	driving
eat	eats	ate	eaten	eating
fall	falls	fell	fallen	falling
feed	feeds	fed	fed	feeding
feel	feels	felt	felt	feeling
fight	fights	fought	fought	fighting
find	finds	found	found	finding
flee	flees	fled	fled	fleeing
fling	flings	flung	flung	flinging
fly	flies	flew	flown	flying
forget	forgets	forgot	forgotten	forgetting
freeze	freezes	froze	frozen	freezing
get	gets	got	got, gotten	getting
give	gives	gave	given	giving
go	goes	went	gone	going
grind	grinds	ground	ground	grinding
grow	grows	grew	grown	growing
hang (suspend)	hangs	hung	hung	hanging
hang (execute)	hangs	hanged	hanged	hanged
have	has	had	had	having
hear	hears	heard	heard	hearing
hide	hides	hid	hidden	hiding
hit	hits	hit	hit	hitting
hurt	hurts	hurt	hurt	hurting
hold	holds	held	held	holding
keep	keeps	kept	kept	keeping
knit	knits	knitted, knit	knitted, knit	knitting
know	knows	knew	known	knowing
lay	lays	laid	laid	laying
lead	leads	led	led	leading
leave	leaves	left	left	leaving
let	lets	let	let	letting
lie (position)	lies	lay	lain	lying
lie (falsehood)	lies	lied	lied	lying
light	lights	lit (lighted)	lit (lighted)	lighting
lose	loses	lost	lost	losing
make	makes	made	made	making
mean	means	meant	meant	meaning
meet	meets	met	met	meeting
pay	pays	paid	paid	paying
put	puts	put	put	putting
quit	quits	quitted, quit	quitted, quit	quitting
read	reads	read	read	reading
ride	rides	rode	ridden	riding
ring	rings	rang	rung	ringing
rise	rises	rose	risen	rising
run	runs	ran	run	running
say	says	said	said	saying
see	sees	saw	seen	seeing
sell	sells	sold	sold	selling
send	sends	sent	sent	sending
sew	sews	sewed	sewed, sewn	sewing
shake	shakes	shook	shaken	shaking
shine	shines	shone	shone	shining
show	shows	showed	shown, showed	showing

shrink	shrinks	shrank, shrunk	shrunk	shrinking
shoot	shoots	shot	shot	shooting
shut	shuts	shut	shut	shutting
sing	sings	sang	sung	singing
sink	sinks	sank, sunk	sunk	sinking
sit	sits	sat	sat	sitting
slay	slays	slew	slain	slaying
sleep	sleeps	slept	slept	sleeping
slide	slides	slid	slid	sliding
sling	slings	slung	slung	slinging
slit	slits	slit	slit	slitting
speak	speaks	spoke	spoken	speaking
spin	spins	spun	spun	spinning
spread	spreads	spread	spread	spreading
spring	springs	sprang	sprung	springing
stand	stands	stood	stood	standing
steal	steals	stole	stolen	stealing
strike	strikes	struck	struck, stricken	striking
string	strings	strung	strung	stringing
stick	sticks	stuck	stuck	sticking
sting	stings	stung	stung	stinging
swear	swears	swore	sworn	swearing
sweep	sweeps	swept	swept	sweeping
swim	swims	swam	swum	swimming
swing	swings	swung	swung	swinging
take	takes	took	taken	taking
teach	teaches	taught	taught	teaching
tear	tears	tore	torn	tearing
tell	tells	told	told	telling
think	thinks	thought	thought	thinking
throw	throws	threw	threw	throwing
wake	wakes	woke, waked	woke, waked, woken	waking
wear	wears	wore	worn	wearing
weave	weaves	wove	woven	weaving
win	wins	won	won	winning
write	writes	wrote	written	writing

Unit Three Review

Practice Test

SCORE PART I (Total—100 points) _____
SCORE PART II* (Total—100 points) _____
TOTAL _____
AVERAGE _____

*Average scores for Part I and Part II only if the Part I score is 85 percent or more.

PART I

A. In this exercise Part 1 of the verbs is given. In the four blanks following each verb, write Parts 2, 3, 4, and 5. If you need help, find Part 1 in a dictionary. Then in the sentences that follow fill in the blanks with a form of the verb in parentheses. Add auxiliary verbs if they are needed.
(30 points—1 point each part; 2 points for sentence)
(Lessons 7, 8, 9, 10, 11)   Score _____

Part 1 (Base)	Part 2 (Base + s)	Part 3 (Past)	Part 4 (V-ed)	Part 5 (V-ing)
1. drag	_____	_____	_____	_____

(Part 3) The horse _____ the log to the clearing.

| 2. fall | _____ | _____ | _____ | _____ |

(Part 1) In autumn the leaves _____ to the ground.

| 3. travel | _____ | _____ | _____ | _____ |

(Part 5) This year salespeople _____ _____ in Europe.

| 4. speak | _____ | _____ | _____ | _____ |

(Part 4) Joe _____ _____ about the problem.

| 5. swim | _____ | _____ | _____ | _____ |

(Part 2) The salmon _____ upstream.

B. Use the word in parentheses to make each of the following sentences negative. In some cases you will have to add an auxiliary verb. Then write NS above each subject, V above each verb or verb phrase, and Adv above *not* or *never*.
(6 points—2 points each)   (Lesson 13)   Score _____

1. *(never)*   The student had to write an essay.

2. *(not)*   He selected a topic easily.

3. *(not)*   He wrote the essay carefully.

C. Underline the contractions in the following sentences. Write the complete form in the blanks at the right.
(8 points—2 points each)   (Lesson 13)   Score _____

1. Barb can't complete the assignment.   _____

2. Mr. Farrell won't admit the error.   _____

3. They're having a difficult time.   _____

4. He's calling the taxpayers.   _____

D. Rewrite each of the following sentences in two ways to make them questions.
   a. Write the sentence as a *yes-no* question by beginning it with a verb. In some sentences you may want to use contractions.
   b. Write the sentence as a *WH*-question, using the words in parentheses.
(18 points—3 points each)   (Lesson 13)   Score _____

1. The flight lasted five hours.

   a.

   b. *(what)*

2. The travelers arrived in Hawaii.

   a.

   b. *(who)*

3. Friends met them in the terminal.

   a.

   b. *(where)*

E. Read ALL of the sentences in the following exercise before filling in the blanks. The sentences are about events taking place at different times. The adverbs help tell you when each event happened. Fill in the blanks by using the verb in parentheses as the main verb and adding auxiliary verbs if they are needed.
(20 points—4 points each)   (Lessons 7, 8, 9, 10, 11)   Score _____

1. *(build)*   A contractor _____ a house for the Johnsons two years ago.

2. *(want)*   They _____ a new house for at least four years.

3. *(need)*   Now they _____ a family room and another bedroom.

4. *(build)*   The same contractor _____ the addition next month.

5. *(decorate)*   By this time next year they _____ the new rooms.

F. Write Parts 2, 3, 4, and 5 of each of the verbs given below. Then fill in the blank in each sentence with the part in parentheses.
(18 points—1 point each part; 2 points for sentence)   (Lesson 14) Score _____

1. lie   _____   _____   _____   _____

   (Part 5)   Leaves _____ _____ on the street for several weeks.

2. raise   _____   _____   _____   _____

   (Part 3)   The boy _____ his head off the pillow.

3. set   _____   _____   _____   _____

   (Part 4)   The jeweler _____ _____ the rubies in the ring.

PART II

A. In this exercise Part 1 of the verbs is given. In the four blanks following each verb, write Parts 2, 3, 4, and 5. If you need help, find Part 1 in a dictionary. Then write sentences of your own, using the part of the verb in parentheses.
(50 points—1 point for each part; 6 points for each sentence)
(Lessons 7, 8, 9, 10, 11)   Score _____

Part 1 (Base)	Part 2 (Base + *s*)	Part 3 (Past)	Part 4 (V-ed)	Part 5 (V-ing)
1. stand	_____	_____	_____	_____

   (Part 3) _____

2. run _____ _____ _____ _____

(Part 2) _____

3. say _____ _____ _____ _____

(Part 5) _____

4. turn _____ _____ _____ _____

(Part 1) _____

5. speak _____ _____ _____ _____

(Part 4) _____

B. Read all the sentences in Part 1, E once again because they serve as an example of how to use verb tenses to show when one event happened in relation to another event. Then write five sentences of your own about events that happened over a period of time. Use any of the simple tenses, perfect tenses, or progressive tenses you have studied in Lessons 7 through 12 and adverbs to show the relationship of the events to one another. You may write about events in the news that happen over a period of time or about your experiences or plans in the past, present, and future. Keep your sentences short and simple.
(50 points—10 points each)   Score _____

1.

2.

3.

4.

5.

Unit Four

Nouns and Modifiers

The sentence patterns you have been studying consist of verbs and nouns: NS Vi, NS Vt Ndo, and NS LV Nsc. And the sentences themselves have been mainly verbs and nouns.

You studied verbs in some detail in Units Two and Three. In the first part of this unit you will learn more about nouns—singular and plural forms, general and specific nouns, and common and proper nouns. (See also the Spelling Appendix for a discussion of noun plurals.)

Then you will learn to add modifiers to the sentences. **Modifiers** are words or word groups that change, extend, or limit the meaning of other words or word groups in the sentence. You already know something about adverbs, one kind of modifier. You know, for example, that they tell *when, where, why,* or *how:*

Adv-how   Adv-when—————————
The audience **quickly** left the theater **during the performance**

Adv-why————————————— Adv-where—————
because of the earthquake and ran **into the street.**

In addition, you will study the forms of adverbs and learn more about their function in sentences.

The other kind of modifier you will study is adjectives, words that describe nouns and give additional information about them. For example, if you describe a knife as *shiny* and *sharp,* it will look very different from one that is *dull* and *rusty:*

  sharp, shiny knife   dull, rusty knife

You will also learn how to identify adjectives and where to place them in sentences.

Lesson 15

Nouns

In the exercises you have been doing up to this point, you have been using *the* as the Noun Test to identify nouns. Now you will learn more about the characteristics of nouns. You will learn, for example, how to make nouns plural. You will also learn that nouns may be general or specific. Knowing these characteristics and others will help you use nouns accurately.

Nouns name persons, places, things, actions, and concepts:

N   N   N

The witness told the truth about the accident.

Nouns may function as subjects, objects, and complements in sentences:

NS   Vt   Ndo   Vt   Ndo   NS   LV Nsc————

The **clerk** took **orders** and delivered **messages**. The **clerk** is **John Warren**.

NUMBER: SINGULAR AND PLURAL NOUNS

Most nouns can be singular or plural. *Singular* means *one,* and *plural* means *more than one.* For example, *flower* is a singular noun because it represents one flower. To make it plural, simply add the suffix *-s* to the singular form. It becomes *flowers.*

Not all nouns form plurals by adding only *-s.* For example, the plural suffix for nouns ending in *ch, sh, s, x,* and *z* is *-es:*

watch / watches   Davis / Davises   box / boxes   dish / dishes

Whenever you are not sure about how a word forms a plural, find it in a dictionary. If a noun plural form is not given, you can usually add *-s* or *-es* to the word:

car / cars   bush / bushes   sex / sexes

For a more detailed discussion about how nouns form their plurals, see the Spelling Appendix.

EXERCISE 15A

Use the Noun Test to find two nouns in each of the following sentences. Write N above each noun. Then write the plural form of the noun in the blanks at the right.

           N

EXAMPLE: The scientist tried the

           N

           experiment.   _scientists_   _experiments_

1. The fire destroyed the apartment.   _____   _____

2. The boss opened the window.   _____   _____

3. The boy fed the fish.   _____   _____

4. The traveler explored the valley.   _____   _____

5. The grandmother bought a toy.   _____   _____

COMMON NOUNS AND PROPER NOUNS

Common nouns are general terms, words like *building, bread, teeth, dog,* and *office,* which begin with small letters. **Proper nouns,** on the other hand, are the specific names that begin with capital letters:

COMMON NOUNS	PROPER NOUNS
person	Richard Halliburton, Georgina, Donald
place	Chicago, California, United States
month	January, April, June
day	Monday, Wednesday, Friday
street	Fifth Avenue, College Oak Drive

ABSTRACT NOUNS AND CONCRETE NOUNS

Concrete nouns name objects that can be seen or touched: *train, apple, toy, building, stairs, calendar.*

Abstract nouns name qualities or ideas that cannot be seen or touched: *joy, holiday, relief, sadness, thought, opinion.*

GENERAL NOUNS AND SPECIFIC NOUNS

Nouns can be general or specific in relation to other nouns. For example, the word *food* is a noun that can represent many kinds of food:

GENERAL	SPECIFIC
food	meat, cereal, vegetables, fruit

The word *food,* then, is general in relation to the specific term *fruit,* which is one kind of food. However, the word *fruit* in relation to different kinds of fruit can be general:

GENERAL	SPECIFIC
fruit	apple, pear, peach, banana

The word *apple,* in turn, can be a general term in relation to the names of particular varieties of apples:

GENERAL	SPECIFIC
apple	Delicious, Rome Beauty, Gravenstein

Nouns that name qualities, thoughts, or opinions (abstract ideas that cannot be seen or touched) may also be general or specific:

GENERAL	SPECIFIC
activity	running, jumping, swimming, diving

EXERCISE 15B

Listed below are a number of specific words related to the general terms given in the column on the left. Match the specific terms to the general terms by writing the specific terms in the blanks.

Specific terms: Chicago, bread, car, pine, Atlanta, shoes, box, maple, meat, bottle, poplar, sofa, Cleveland, fruit, cup, Massachusetts, socks, telephone, fir, shirt, bag, vegetables, Boston, blouse, window

GENERAL TERMS   SPECIFIC TERMS

1. food   _____ _____ _____ _____

2. container   _____ _____ _____ _____

3. tree   _____ _____ _____ _____

4. city   _____ _____ _____ _____

5. clothing   _____ _____ _____ _____

EXERCISE 15C

Think of a general term for each group of specific terms given below. Write the general term in the blank.

GENERAL TERMS   SPECIFIC TERMS

1. _____   bed, chair, table, sofa

2. _____   Ohio, Oregon, Hawaii, New York

3. _____   Buick, Chevrolet, Plymouth, Dodge

4. _____   pansy, daisy, tulip, rose

5. _____   pork, beef, lamb, chicken

Lesson 16

Determiners

In using the Noun Test you have been placing *the* before words to decide whether the words can function as nouns:

the picture   **the** test   **the** story   **the** paper   **the** chance

In addition to using *the,* you may also use words such as *a, an, some, two, Roy's,* and *every* to identify many nouns. These words are called **determiners** because they "determine" or point to nouns. Determiners are labeled Adj in this text because they tell *which one* just as adjectives do. To identify determiners you can use the Adjective Test: ask *which one* or *how many* and say the noun.

    You can find determiners in this way. First, use Sentence Keys to label the basic sentence pattern:

      NS   Vt   Ndo   NS   Vt   Ndo
The clerk sold five shirts. Dave's brother bought them.

The only words not labeled in the sentences above are *the, five,* and *Dave's.* Next, use the Adjective Test to identify these three words. Each word tells which one or how many:

Which clerk? **The** clerk   How many shirts? **Five** shirts
Which (or whose) brother?   **Dave's** brother

Finally, write Adj above *the, five,* and *Dave's:*

Adj NS   Vt   Adj Ndo   Adj   NS   Vt   Ndo
The clerk sold five shirts. Dave's brother bought them.

Another test is substituting *the* for the word you think is a determiner:

Sara's brother owns *two* restaurants.   (**The** brother owns **the** restaurants.)

Her brother likes **this** restaurant, not **that.**   (**The** brother likes **the** restaurant, not *the.*)

In the second sentence above, you can see that *her* and *this* are determiners, but the word *that* is not.

    The following words may function as determiners. In some cases, they may function in a noun position.

1. These words always function as determiners:

the   a   an   my   our   your   its   their   every

Adj NS   Vt   Adj Ndo   Adj   NS   Vt   Adj Ndo
The manager called **my** parents. **Every** child wants a pet.

2. Possessives like *Pat's, his*, and *her* may function as determiners or they may stand by themselves in noun positions:

                         Adj   NS   Adv   Vt   Ndo

DETERMINERS: **Michael's** sister always helped him.

                         Adj NS   V   Adj   Ndo

                         Her willingness pleased **their** mother.

                         NS Adv   Vt   Ndo Adv

NOUN POSITION: He always helped **her** too.

3. These words may function as determiners, or they may stand by themselves in noun positions:

two	half	thirty-one	first
this	that	these	those
all	both	each	other
any	either	neither	no
more	most	much	many
various	several	some	few

    DETERMINER   **NOUN**

    NS   Vt   Adj   Ndo   NS Vt   Ndo

    Michael needed **some** money.   He needed **some.**

    Adj   NS   Vi Adv   NS   Vt   Ndo

    These shirts fit well.   **Both** have pockets.

Sometimes more than one determiner may be used to point to the same noun:

    Adj Adj NS   Vi   Adj Adj NS   Vi   Adv————————

    Both the tanks exploded. **A few** people went to the hospital.

EXERCISE 16A

Write the sentence pattern above each of the following sentences. Then look at each word in bold type. If the word functions as a determiner (Adj), write Adj in the blank at the right. If it functions in a noun position, write N in the blank.

               Adj   NS   Vt———————— Adj   Ndo   Adv

EXAMPLE: **Several** people have opened pastry shops recently.   _____**Adj**_____

              N   Vt———————— Ndo

             Those have attracted attention.   _____**N**_____

1. Joan and Evelyn opened **their** shop on Friday the thirteenth.   _____

2. **Joan's** specialty is puff pastry.   _____

3. **Half** the pastry has a cream filling.   _____

4. Evelyn bakes and decorates cakes. **Those** sell quickly.   _____

5. **Suzanne's** shop specializes in wedding cakes. _____

6. Suzanne uses fresh fruit and fruit glazes instead of **the** usual buttercream or sugar icings. _____

7. A **fourth** woman makes fruit pies with flaky crusts in her shop. _____

8. **All** the women omit preservatives and artificial flavors and coloring from the food. _____

USING DETERMINERS WITH NOUNS

The following chart lists words in the first column that can function as determiners before nouns. The other columns show which determiners can be used with singular count nouns, plural count nouns, and uncountable nouns.

Count nouns include everything that can be counted. You can write, for example, *one pencil, two pencils, many pencils* or *one opportunity, two opportunities, many opportunities*. Count nouns such as *pencil* and *opportunity* have both a singular and a plural form: *pencil/pencils; opportunity/opportunities.*

Uncountable (mass) nouns include everything that cannot be counted; as a result, they often do not have a plural form. For example, you cannot write *two relaxations* or *several advices.*

Some words, such as *meat* in the fourth column below, can be both uncountable and count nouns, depending on how they are used. You can use *many, few,* or *fewer* with a plural count noun to indicate number, but you must use *much, (a) little* or *less* with an uncountable noun to indicate amount:

COUNT NOUN: The restaurant includes only a *few meats* in its menu.

UNCOUNTABLE NOUN: The restaurant includes only a *little meat* in its menu.

DETERMINER	SINGULAR COUNT NOUN	PLURAL COUNT NOUN	UNCOUNTABLE NOUN
the	the tiger	the tigers	the meat
a/an	a tiger, an elephant		
some	some tiger	some tigers	some meat
any	any tiger	any tigers	any meat
no	no tiger	no tigers	no meat
each	each tiger		
every	every tiger		
either	either tiger		
neither	neither tiger		
one	one tiger		
two		two tigers	
this	this tiger		this meat
that	that tiger		that meat
these		these tigers	
those		those tigers	

DETERMINER	SINGULAR COUNT NOUN	PLURAL COUNT NOUN	UNCOUNTABLE NOUN
NO ARTICLE		tigers	meat
enough		enough tigers	enough meat
all		all tigers	all meat
most		most tigers	most meat
many		many tigers	
much			much meat
(a) few		(a) few tigers	
fewer		fewer tigers	
(a) little			(a) little meat
less			less
both		both tigers	
several		several tigers	
POSSESSIVES			
my/our/your	our tiger	my tigers	your meat
his/her/its	his tiger	her tigers	its meat
their	their tiger	their tigers	their meat

EXERCISE 16B

In the following sentences, circle the determiner that can be used before each noun. If no determiner can be used with the noun, circle NO DETERMINER. Then write the completed sentence.

EXAMPLE: ((The) Both Many) boy bought (those several (NO DETERMINER)) gum.

The boy bought gum.

1. (NO DETERMINER   A   Five) candy filled (a   the   this) jars.

_____

2. (An   That   Those) woman took (some   both   many) candy.

_____

3. (This   These   A) kind pleases (both   a   that) people.

_____

4. (All   That   First   A) employees offered (an   their   those) assistance.

_____

5. (The   An   These) information pleased (several   that   one) people.

_____

6. (Five   An   Each) elephants carried (an   NO DETERMINER   any) equipment.

_____

ARTICLES: *THE, A, AN*

You have learned that *the, a,* and *an* are determiners that point to nouns. They are also called articles. *The* is a definite article. It is definite because it points to a particular member or particular members of a group. It can occur with singular and plural count nouns and with mass nouns:

COUNT: **The** students passed **the** exam.
MASS: Joe needs **the** information. He appreciates **the** help.

The may also be used in the following ways:

1. To make an indefinite term such as *a meeting* specific:

Geri attended **a** meeting of tax experts. **The** meeting was held last night.

2. With a common noun followed by a proper noun:

Several hundred people saw **the** play **Hamlet** last night.
The actor Charles Lambert greeted friends afterwards.

3. With general terms that give more information about specific terms:

Jessie Hunter, **the** history teacher, organized a field trip.
Students visited Virginia City, **the** old mining town in Nevada.

4. With the names of professions or occupations when the person's name is not mentioned:

Dr. Perkins will address the graduating class. **The** doctor was a student here fifteen years ago.

5. With the names of geographical locations and the names of trains, ships, or airplanes:

The *Queen Mary* sailed **the** Atlantic for many years.
The Mississippi, **the** Nile, and **the** Rhine are well-known rivers.

6. With the names of geographical locations that are plural or consist of an adjective and a noun:

The tour of **the** British Isles and **the** Netherlands took three weeks.
Some travelers visited **the** Republic of Panama.

7. With the names of musical instruments:

Sandy plays **the** piano but prefers guitar music.

The does not appear when the noun is used in a general sense:

GENERAL	SPECIFIC
Tea and soft drinks are refreshing.	The tea is too strong, and the soft drinks are not chilled.
Work can sometimes be boring.	The work in the office is tiring.
People usually enjoy sports.	The people down the street enjoy the winter sports.

The words *a* and *an* are indefinite articles. They refer to any member of a group, and they can occur with singular count nouns but not with mass nouns:

COUNT: a student   an exam
NOT: an information   a help

Notice that *a* is used before words beginning with consonants, and *an* is used before words beginning with vowels:

> CONSONANTS: a rock   a schedule
> VOWELS: an explanation   an apple

The indefinite article *a* or *an* is used in the following ways:

1. Before a singular count noun when it means *one:*

> John told **a** lie. He had **an** excuse.

2. With words such as *dozen, gross, hundred, thousand* to mean *one:*

> **A** hundred geese flew overhead this morning.
> Ellen gave **a** million reasons for her decision.

3. With names of a nationality, religion, profession, or trade:

> Spiros is **a** Greek. He is **an** aeronautical engineer. His wife is **a** Protestant.

4. With words that state a unit of measurement:

> Patricia paid five dollars **a** yard for the fabric.
> The dressmaker earns ten dollars **an** hour.

Comparison of *the* and *a/an*

The definite and indefinite articles both point to a member of a group. For example, one group may be *doctors* and another may be *patients*. In the following sentence the definite article *the* indicates a particular doctor in a group of doctors and a particular patient in a group of patients:

> **The** doctor examined **the** patient.

The indefinite articles *(a, an)* refer to any doctor in a group of doctors or any patient in a group of patients:

> **A** doctor examined **a** patient.

If the articles do not occur, the nouns refer to the whole group, not to individual members:

> Doctors examine patients.

EXERCISE 16C

Read ALL the sentences in the following paragraph before you fill in the spaces. You will find spaces before all the nouns in each of the sentences. Some of the nouns may refer in general to a group, person, or product. Other nouns may refer specifically to a group, person, or product. In some cases you may be able to consider the noun general *or* specific, depending on how you interpret the sentence. Write *the, a,* or *an* before the

nouns that you believe need determiners. Write X in the space if you believe the noun does not need a determiner.

EXAMPLE: Nikki has an appointment with _____X_____ Professor Jones, but _____the_____ professor is not in his office.

_____ Electronics manufacturers organized _____ convention. _____

Members set _____ date for early in _____ November. Two members sent

_____ invitations to _____ business representatives in _____ United

States, _____ British Isles, _____ Japan, _____ China, _____ Philip

pines, and _____ Netherlands. _____ president Thomas Wilson offered

_____ prize of _____ hundred dollars for _____ well-designed program.

_____ meeting place was _____ Convention Center in _____ Los Angeles.

On _____ last day _____ manufacturers met for _____ dinner in _____

hotel banquet room. _____ dinner included _____ appetizers, _____ steak,

_____ vegetables, _____ dessert, and _____ tea, or _____ coffee.

_____ coffee was imported from _____ Brazil. Sheri Patton, _____ singer,

provided _____ entertainment after _____ dinner.

Lesson 17

Possessives

You learned in Lesson 16 that **possessives** such as *his, her, their,* and *Dave's* function as determiners because they point to nouns. In this lesson you will learn to change nouns to the possessive form. Because possessives modify nouns and tell *which one,* they are labeled Adj.

Although nouns referring to people and some animals (and sometimes things) can be made into possessives, these words no longer function as nouns when they come before and modify other nouns. In the examples below notice that *guests* and *cat* are nouns but that *guests'* and *cat's* are adjectives that modify *coats* and *paw:*

    Adj N   Adj N   Adj Adj   N
The **guests** arrived at the party. The hostess took the **guests'** coats.

    Adj N   Adj N   Adj
Her **cat** walked in front of a guest. The guest accidentally stepped on the

    Adj   N
cat's paw.

The possessives *cat's* and *guests'* in the sentence above are another way of writing *of the cat* and *of the guests.* To change a word group beginning with *of* to a possessive, complete these steps:

1. Cross out *the* before the first noun and *of* following it:

    ~~the~~ paw ~~of~~ the cat   ~~the~~ coats ~~of~~ the guests

2. Add *-'s* to *cat* because it does not end in *-s,* and place *cat's* before *paw:*

    paw   the cat's   the cat's paw

Add only an apostrophe to *guests* because it ends in *-s,* and place *guests* before *coats:*

    coats   the guests'   the guests' coats

Here are other examples:

    ~~the~~ house ~~of~~ the neighbor   the neighbor's house
    ~~the~~ news ~~of~~ today   today's news
    ~~the~~ agreements ~~of~~ the countries   the countries' agreements
    ~~the~~ benefits ~~of~~ the employees   the employees' benefits

PLACING THE APOSTROPHE (')

Notice that in some instances you need to add an apostrophe only. Given below are directions for using the suffixes -'s and -' in writing possessives.

1. Add -'s to words not ending in -s:

> boy's   women's   kitten's   Frank's

2. Add only the apostrophe to words ending in -s:

> boys'   coaches'   Charles'   Jones'

3. Add -'s to the end of nouns with hyphens in them:

> sister-in-law's   passers-by's   fathers-in-law's

4. Add -'s to the second noun only when two nouns joined by *and* show joint ownership:

> Jane and Jill's parents   (Jane and Jill have the same parents.)
>
> BUT: Jane's and Jill's parents   (The girls have different parents.)

EXERCISE 17

Rewrite each of the phrases in bold type as a possessive modifier of the noun. Be sure to use the apostrophe (') in the right place.

EXAMPLE: The office **of the doctor** is closed.   _____the doctor's office_____

1. The sister **of Jay** and the brother **of Susan** are engaged.   _____

2. The house **of Bert Jones** is newly painted.   _____

3. The store **of Burton and Washborn** opened this week.   _____

4. Ghosts, goblins, and demons fill the dreams **of many children.**   _____

5. The response **of the editor** was brief.   _____

6. Dick borrowed the boat **of his father-in-law.**   _____

7. The conference **of the professors** was canceled.   _____

Lesson 18

Adjectives

When you see the word *light,* you may think of daylight or a source of light such as a lamp. Another person may picture another kind of light such as sunshine. The reason that two people do not think of the same kind of light immediately is that *light* is a general term that has more than one meaning. To make *light* specific, you can use descriptive words before it:

bright light	**dim** light	**yellow** light	**electric** light	**traffic** light
guiding light	**one** light	**every** light	**their** light	

These descriptive words function as **adjectives,** words or word groups that modify nouns and pronouns. Adjectives qualify, limit, or extend the meaning of a noun.

You cannot tell that some words function as adjectives when they stand alone. You must see them in relation to other words in a sentence. For example, *yellow* and *traffic,* used as adjectives in the example above, can also function as nouns:

```
NS      LV          Nsc      Adj    NS     Vt        Ndo
```
Yellow is a cheerful color. The **yellow** blanket covers the bed.

```
   NS     Vt    Ndo       NS    Vt         Adj    Ndo
```
The accident slowed **traffic.** The driver ignored the **traffic** light.

EXERCISE 18A

Given below are several terms. Write a word that can function as an adjective before each general term to make the general term specific. Then write a sentence using the adjective-noun combination. **Label the words in your sentences.**

```
                                    Adj  Adj      NS    Vt         Adj  Ndo
```
EXAMPLE: computer_____ game   The computer **game** challenges the players.

```
                                    Adv———— NS    Vt    Adj   Ndo
```
wild_____ game   Each year Dan hunts **wild** game.

1. _____ music

2. _____ plant

3. _____ boat

4. _____ company

5. _____ building.

Show these sentences to your instructor or tutor.

Often only a single adjective before a noun will not be enough to make the noun as specific as you wish. As a result, you probably will use more than one adjective before a noun. In the following example the nouns *storm* and *windows* are each preceded by three adjectives:

Adj Adj   Adj   NS   Vt   Adj   Adj   Adj   Ndo
The violent wind storm smashed several plate glass windows.

To identify adjectives, follow the same steps you used to find determiners in Lesson 16. First, use Sentence Keys to label the basic sentence pattern. Then use the Adjective Test to identify the adjectives.

Adjective Test

Find the nouns in the sentence, and ask *which one* or *how many*. The words that answer these questions are adjectives. Write Adj above the word:

           NS   Vt   Ndo
The high stone walls surrounded three large brick houses.

Which walls? The high walls . . . stone walls . . .
Which houses? The large houses . . . brick houses . . .
How many houses? . . . three houses

Adj   Adj   Adj   NS   Vt   Adj   Adj   Adj   Ndo
The high stone walls surrounded **three large brick** houses.

In addition to the Adjective Test, you can sometimes recognize adjectives by their position. Adjectives may appear between a determiner and the noun:

Adj Adj   Adj   NS   C   Adj Adj   NS   Vi   Adv————
A **long, white** envelope and **five sharpened** pencils lay on the desk.

Another way to identify adjectives is to notice whether they end in *-er* or *-est* or appear with the words *more, most, less, least*. Words that show comparison in one of these two ways may function as adjectives:

the **high** mountain	the **higher** mountain	the **highest** mountain
a **current** report	a *more* **current** report	the *most* **current** report

You will study more about comparison in Lesson 52.

EXERCISE 18B

Identify the sentence pattern in each of the following sentences. Then use the Adjective Test to identify the adjectives. Write the adjectives that tell *how many* in the first blank and *which one* in the second blank. There may be more than two adjectives in each sentence.

	HOW MANY	WHICH ONE
NS Vt EXAMPLE: Many thrilled people saw		
Ndo the five science exhibits.	many, five	thrilled, science

1. Several pine trees circled the old cabin. _____ _____

2. The smiling baby clapped its tiny hands. _____ _____

3. Ten red feathers decorated the smallest cap. _____ _____

4. The black-and-white dog chased twenty-five running sheep. _____ _____

5. Three frightened men opened the creaking cabin door. _____ _____

KINDS OF ADJECTIVE MODIFIERS

In addition to determiners and possessives, which you studied in Lessons 16 and 17, the following kinds of words function as adjectival modifiers.

1. **Descriptive adjectives** are words that answer the question *which one.* They can usually show comparison, and they may appear before or after the noun:

       Adj   Adj   NS   Adj   C   Adj   Vi   Adv—————
   Several **bright** costumes, **attractive** and **decorative,** lay on the table.

2. **Nominal adjectives** are words that usually function as nouns, but they may modify a noun to make it specific. They also answer the question *which one:*

       Adj Adj   NS   Vt   ·Ndo   Adv——————————
   The **gypsy** costumes added excitement to the performance.

       Adj NS   Vi   Adv
   The **gypsy** danced first.

3. *V-ed* and *V-ing* words, which you studied in Lessons 10 and 11, function as verbs only when auxiliary verbs appear with them. They may function by themselves as adjectives, answering the question *which one,* and may come before or after the noun. Compare the following sentences:

       Adj NS   Vi——————————— Adv——————————
   The costumes **had been decorated** with beads and ribbons.

       Adj Adj   NS   Vt   Adj Ndo
   The **decorated** costumes pleased the performers.

```
Adj  NS    Vi──────────── C  Vi        Adv────────────
```
The beads **were glistening** and **sparkling** in the bright light.

```
Adj  NS    Adj      C  Adj    Vt    Adj  Ndo
```
The beads, **glistening** and **sparkling,** showed many colors.

POSITION OF ADJECTIVES

In writing a sentence you sometimes use more than one adjective to modify a noun. The following chart shows the order of the various adjectives before nouns:

Determiner/ Number	Possessive	Descriptive	V-ed/V-ing	Nominal	Noun
A		windy			day
An	officer's	blue		wool	uniform
The		red		brick	building
Two			marching		bands
Several	players'	gaudy		baseball	uniforms
The first	winner's		unexpected		prize
The	performer's	bright,	glittering	gypsy	costume

PUNCTUATION WITH ADJECTIVES

If two or more descriptive adjectives come before the noun and they modify the noun equally, the conjunction *and* can appear between them:

large and heavy suitcase   **loud and frightening** noise

However, you may omit *and* and use a comma instead between the adjectives:

large, heavy suitcase   **loud, frightening** noise

If you cannot place *and* between the adjectives, do not separate them with a comma:

NOT: sparkling and diamond ring   broken and glass bottle
BUT: **sparkling diamond** ring   **broken glass** bottle

If two adjectives follow the noun they modify, place a comma before and a comma after the adjectives. You must use both commas to enclose the adjectives:

```
Adj  Adj      NS      Adj    C  Adj        Vt  Adj  Ndo
```
The children's bedroom, **pleasant** and **comfortable,** had two beds

```
C    Adj  Ndo
```
and two dressers.

EXERCISE 18C

Arrange the modifiers given below into a meaningful order before or after the noun in bold type. Include commas or the word *and* if needed.

EXAMPLE: cheerful yellow **paint** house bright
cheerful, bright yellow house **paint**
OR: yellow house **paint,** bright and cheerful

1. **drivers** five muscular truck

2. snow-covered the fir magnificent **trees**

3. **town** peaceful small American quiet

4. Hawaiian inviting warm secluded **beach** a sunny

EXERCISE 18D

Identify the sentence patterns in each of the following sentences. Then find the adjective modifiers by using the Adjective Test. Write Adj above each adjective. Insert commas only where they are needed in each sentence.

EXAMPLE:

<pre>
         NS   Vt   Adj Adj   Adj Ndo
EXAMPLE: Sally sang a   beautiful, sad, song.

         Adj Adj   Adj NS Vt   Adj Ndo
         The blooming cherry tree brightened the yard.
</pre>

1. Peggy bought an old-fashioned sewing machine.

2. The group praised the dedicated reliable teacher.

3. The young witness upset and nervous described the automobile accident.

4. Three small children hungry frightened and crying sat on the step.

5. The brilliant flashing street sign attracted attention.

EXERCISE 18E

Rewrite the following sentences by adding one or more adjectival modifiers for each of the nouns:

EXAMPLE: The dog chased the cat.

NS Vt   Ndo

The **black, short-haired** dog chased the **Persian** cat.

1. The man carried a package.

2. The car hit the tree.

3. The messenger delivered the letter.

4. The woman combed her hair.

5. Coins filled the chest.

Show these sentences to your instructor or tutor.

EXERCISE 18F

Write five sentences about a single topic. Be sure to use adjectives before nouns wherever the adjectives are needed to give specific information.

1.

2.

3.

4.

5.

Show these sentences to your instructor or tutor.

Lesson 19

Adverbs

Adverbs, like adjectives, are modifiers. When you studied them briefly in Lesson 6, you learned that they may be single words or word groups that change, limit, or extend the meaning of other words in the sentence. They modify verbs, adjectives, or other adverbs. In this lesson you will learn more about adverbs and their relationship to the words they modify.

To find adverbs in sentences, first use the Sentence Keys you learned in Unit One to identify the basic sentence patterns. Then use the following test to help you decide if a word or word group can function as an adverb.

Adverb Test

Read the subject, the verb, and the direct object (if there is one) together, and ask *when, where, why,* and *how.* The word or word group that answers any of these questions is an adverb. Write Adv above the word or word group:

> NS Vt Ndo NS Vi
> Last year the directors carefully chose the library site. Construction began
> there for the new building.

> The directors chose the site when? Last year . . . How? . . . carefully.
> Construction began where? . . . there. Why? . . . for the new building.

> Adv———— Adj NS Adv Vt Adj Adj Ndo NS
> **Last year** the directors **carefully** chose the library site. Construction

> Vi Adv Adv————————
> began **there for the new building.**

In addition to the Adverb Test, you can sometimes recognize adverbs by their form. Many of them end in *-ly:*

> Adj NS Vi Adv-how
> The engine runs **quietly.**

> Adj Adv-how Adj Adj NS Vt Adj Ndo
> The **remarkably** active old man chased the dog.

However, not all words ending in *-ly* are adverbs:

V	Adj	Adj
rely on him	holy city	friendly dog

A few words ending in -*ly*, such as *weekly*, *hourly*, and *monthly*, can function as both adjectives and adverbs:

Adj Adj NS Vi Adv
The daily paper arrives daily.

The following words frequently function as adverbs. Notice that they do not end in -*ly*:

almost	forth	more	seldom
already	here	much	soon
also	home	never	still
back	how	not	then
better	instead	now	there
even	least	quite	too
ever	less	rather	very

EXERCISE 19A

Identify the sentence patterns in each of the following sentences. Then find the adverbs by using the Adverb Test. Write Adv and *when, where, why,* or *how* above each adverb and adverbial phrase.

1. Yesterday Paul began a new job.

2. In the morning he attended two classes.

3. He listened closely and took notes constantly.

4. After lunch he carefully read company rules.

5. That evening he went home and studied his notes thoroughly.

6. He had prepared himself well.

7. The next day he understood the lectures easily.

8. Other new employees had not studied their notes completely.

9. Paul willingly helped two others after class.

10. They greatly appreciated his help.

USING ADVERBIAL MODIFIERS

When you understand the relationship of adverbs to the words they modify, you should be able to identify and use them comfortably. Adverbs can modify verbs, adjectives, and other adverbs. The examples on the next page show how adverbs are used in sentences.

1. Adverbs may modify verbs. The adverbs tell *when, where, why,* and *how:*

<pre>
NS   Vt————Adj Adj Ndo Adv———— NS Vt Adv   Vt   Ndo
</pre>
Burt will buy a new car next year. He is **gradually** saving money.

(Burt *will buy* a new car *when?* . . . next year. He *is saving* money *how?* . . .
gradually.)

2. Adverbs may modify adjectives. The adverbs tell *how:*

<pre>
NS Vt   Adj Adv   Adj Ndo NS Vt   Adj Adv Adj   Ndo
</pre>
He has an **extremely** good job. He wants a **very** expensive car.

(*How good* is the job? . . . extremely good. *How expensive* is the car? . . .
very expensive.)

3. Adverbs may modify other adverbs. The adverbs tell *how:*

<pre>
Adj Adj   NS   Vi————— Adv Adv   Adj NS Vi Adv Vi   Adv
</pre>
His savings account is growing **very** slowly. Next year cannot come soon
<pre>
Adv
</pre>
enough.*

(*How slowly* is the account growing? . . . very slowly. *How soon?* . . . soon
enough.)

  *Notice that the adverb *enough* follows the adjective or adverb it modifies.

4. Adverbs may modify sentences. They usually appear at the beginning of the sentence, but they may be shifted to the end of the sentence. They usually tell *how* or
when:

<pre>
Adv   NS   Vt   Ndo   Adv   NS Vi Adv—————
</pre>
Quickly the friends left the stadium. **Later** they met in a restaurant.   OR

<pre>
       NS   Vt   Ndo   Adv   NS Vi Adv————— Adv
</pre>
The friends left the stadium **quickly.** They met in a restaurant **later.**

An adverb that functions as a part of the predicate cannot appear at the
beginning of the sentence:

NOT: The taxi arrived. **Outside** John went.
BUT: The taxi arrived. John went **outside.**

EXERCISE 19B

Add an adverbial modifier to each of the words in bold type. Write the adverb in the
blank. Use words that answer the question *how.*

EXAMPLE: The **raging** wind fanned the roaring fire.   _____violently_____
          The **violently raging** wind fanned the roaring fire.

1. The child remained **quiet** in the doctor's office.   _____

2. The wind howled **loudly** during the storm.   _____

3. The **fragrant** white flowers grow in the spring.   _____

4. The inspector **explained** the building code.　　　　　_____

5. The bullet hit the **moving** target.　　　　　_____

Show these sentences to your instructor or tutor.

ADVERBS BEFORE AND AFTER VERBS

Adverbs that tell how often something happens appear before all verbs in the present and past tenses except *be.* The adverbs include *always, often, usually, seldom, never, hardly, sometimes, scarcely, ever, frequently,* and others:

	ADVERB	VERB	
The newspaper	**usually**	arrives	late.
Kathy	**seldom**	reads	it.
The old friends	**never**	missed	their annual picnic.
They	**always**	met	near the stream.

The adverb follows the verb *be:*

Harry is **seldom** home.

The adverbs appear between the auxiliary verb and the main verb:

	VERB	ADVERB	VERB
Carol	can	**hardly**	wait for graduation day.
Pat	has	**never**	offered help.

Adverbs that tell *where, how,* and *when* usually appear in the following order:

SUBJECT	ADV HOW	VERB	HOW	WHERE	HOW OFTEN	WHEN
Tom and Alene		run		in the park	every morning	at 6 A.M.
Alene		exercises	vigorously.			
Tom	lazily	relaxes		on the grass		after running.

EXERCISE 19C

Write three basic sentences with only nouns and verbs. Then add two or more adverbs or adverbial phrases to each sentence. Write Adv above each adverb or adverbial phrase.

1.

2.

3.

Ask your instructor or tutor to read your sentences.

MISUSED MODIFIERS

You have learned that adjectives modify nouns and pronouns and that adverbs modify verbs, adjectives, and other adverbs. In other words, an adjective does not modify another adjective.

In the examples below the adjective *real* cannot modify the adjective *good,* and the adjective *sure* cannot modify the verb *gave.* Although you may find this usage in informal speech, it is not acceptable in written Standard English. You must use an adverb to modify adjectives:

           NS   LV   Adj Adj   Nsc
NOT: Steve is a **real** good friend.

           NS   LV   Adv   Adj   Nsc
BUT: Steve is a **really** good friend.
OR: Steve is a **very**   good friend.

         NS Adj Vt   Adj   Ndo
NOT: He **sure** gave a successful party.

         NS Adv   Vt   Adj   Ndo
BUT: He **surely**   gave a successful party.
OR: He **certainly** gave a successful party.

Words like *good, bad,* and *fine* are adjectives and should not be used to modify verbs:

NOT: The students did **fine** on the test.

         NS   Vi Adv Adv———
BUT: The students did **well** on the test.

NOT: The father treated the children **bad.**

         NS   Vt   Ndo   Adv
BUT: The father treated the children **badly.**

EXERCISE 19D

The following sentences contain misused modifiers. Underline the word or words which are misused and write the preferred form in the blank at the right.

1. Linda bought a real expensive stereo.   _____

2. The motorcycle runs real good.   _____

3. The group did fine on the experiment.   _____

4. The boxer was sure fast on his feet.   _____

5. They sure have a large house.   _____

6. The mechanics talked bad about all the labor trouble.   _____

7. Last week Jane's friend hurt her feelings bad.   _____

8. The committee worked good together.   _____

Lesson 20

Prepositional Phrases

In the preceding lessons in this unit you learned to use adjectives and adverbs as modifiers to extend the meaning of other words and to relate general terms to one another. The adjectives and adverbs were mainly single words, but word groups such as *next year, earlier that month,* and *last week,* which show a time relationship, can function as adverbs. They show when each event happened and provide connections between sentences as in the following example:

> Science students must complete their projects **this week. Next week** the students will exhibit the projects at the science fair.

In this lesson you will learn about the prepositional phrase that functions as a modifier. You learned about one kind of prepositional phrase in Lesson 6 when you identified *in the library* and *down the stairs* as adverbs:

> NS   Vt   Ndo   Adv-where———   NS   Vi   Adv-where———
> A man selected his book **in the library.** He fell **down the stairs.**

You will also study prepositional phrases that may function as adjectives because they modify nouns.

The prepositional phrase consists of a preposition, such as *to, in, out,* or *down,* and a noun that functions as the object of the preposition:

> PREPOSITIONAL PHRASE: Preposition + Noun Object with Modifiers
>
> before   dawn
> in   a long, black car
> toward   the quiet town

These phrases can be added to the following basic sentence: Five men drove.

Each preposition acts as a connector; it connects the noun following it to the sentence. Pr is the label for prepositions in this text, and Nop stands for *noun object of the preposition:*

> Pr   Nop   Pr   Nop   Pr   Nop
> **Before dawn** five men **in a long, black car** drove **toward the quiet town.**

Most of the prepositions are listed on the next page. Notice that they are mainly single words, but a few are phrases:

aboard*	below*	in*	per
about*	beneath*	in addition to	round*
above*	beside*	in place of	since*
according to	besides*	in spite of	than
across*	between*	inside*	through*
after*	beyond*	into	throughout*
against	but	like	to
along*	by*	near*	toward
along with	concerning	next*	under*
amid	contrary to	of	underneath*
among	despite	off*	until
around*	down*	on*	up*
as	due to	opposite*	upon
at	during	out*	via
because of	except	outside*	with
before*	for	over*	within*
behind*	from	past*	without*

*These words may also be used alone as adverbs.

Finding prepositional phrases in a sentence is actually quite simple.

1. First use the Sentence Keys to identify the basic sentence patterns:

NS   VI
On Saturday ten neighbors on Oak Street went to a party.

Then examine the remaining words. In many sentences you will find prepositions followed by noun objects. These word groups are prepositional phrases:

Pr Nop   Adj NS   Pr Nop————— VI   Pr   Nop
On Saturday ten neighbors **on Oak Street** went **to a party.**

2. You can also identify prepositional phrases by recognizing the prepositions first and then finding the noun that follows each one—*at + midnight:*

Pr Nop   Pr Nop   Pr   Nop
At midnight all **of them** returned **to their homes.**

Among the remaining words you should find the basic sentence pattern:

Pr Nop   NS Pr Nop Vi   Pr Adj Nop
At midnight all **of them** returned **to their homes.**

Notice that prepositional phrases may appear at the beginning, in the middle, or at the end of sentences. Sometimes if a sentence begins with a prepositional phrase, you may find that the verb comes before the subject:

Pr   Nop Vi NS C NS————
Into the house went Jack and Susan Adams.

PREPOSITION OR ADVERB?

Many of the prepositions given in the list on this page can also be used by themselves as adverbs in sentences. They are marked with an asterisk. Compare the pairs of sentences on page 110:

ADVERB	PREPOSITION

Adj NS Vi Adv	———— Adv ———— Adj NS Vi Pr Adj Nop
The sailor came **out.**	The sailor came **out the door.**
NS Vi Adv	————Adv——— NS Vi Pr Adj Nop
He went **aboard.**	He went **aboard the ship.**
NS Vi Adv	———— Adv ———— NS Vi Pr Adj Nop
He fell **off.**	He fell **off the ladder.**

Those words not marked with an asterisk cannot function alone:

> NOT: Henri walked into.
> NOT: Jan climbed to.

EXERCISE 20A

Underline each prepositional phrase in the following sentences. Write Adv above words that appear to be prepositions but function alone as adverbs.

EXAMPLE: The visitors went <u>Pr   Nop
into the house</u>. The others stayed ^{Adv}outside.

1. The cat climbed up the tree.

2. Into the lake leaped the dog.

3. The lamp suddenly fell down.

4. Dale succeeds in spite of her prob-

   lems.

5. Their grandparents arrived home after

   dark.

6. How can you study in the family

   room?

7. The baby looks like him.

8. I will meet you at the drive-in.

9. Come to my house tonight.

10. I never saw him before.

RELATIONSHIPS EXPRESSED
BY ADVERBIAL PREPOSITIONAL PHRASES

The following prepositional phrases function as adverbial modifiers in sentences; therefore, NO commas separate them from the rest of the sentence. They express the following relationships:

1. Time—The prepositions *on, since, before, by, after,* and others can indicate when something happened or will happen:

                    Adv-when———— Adv-when————
The stranger arrived **on Saturday before noon.**

2. Cause—*Because of, on account of, from,* and others tell why something happened or is so:

                      Adv-why————————————————————
He worried townspeople **because of his mysterious actions.**

3. Manner—*With, like,* and *in* can tell how:

                    Adv-how————————
The stranger spoke **in a low, monotone voice.**

4. Purpose—*For* may express *in order to,* or it may show intended destination:

                 Adv-why——————————————
He had come **for a real estate auction.**

5. Position—The prepositions *in, on, at, near, above, below,* and others can tell where someone or something is with verbs such as *be, sit,* and *eat:*

                  Adv-where—————————   Adv-where————
The stranger ate **in the town's restaurant.** He sat **near the door.**

6. Movement—*Into, over, behind, below, toward, past,* and others can indicate movement from one place to another with verbs that show action:

                      Adv-where————————
The stranger looked **behind himself** several times. Then he went

Adv-where————   Adv-how————————
to the airport. He left **in his own plane.**

Adverbial prepositional phrases may function as transitions ("bridges") between sentences. They are usually enclosed in commas:

> The townspeople continued to worry. **Despite their concern,** they could not keep the stranger from returning.

EXERCISE 20B

Write Adv and *when, where, why,* or *how* above each prepositional phrase in the following sentences. In the blank write the word that the prepositional phrase modifies.

              NS Vi   Adv-where————
EXAMPLE: Each winter ice forms on the lake.   _____forms_____

1. Late Friday the temperature dropped suddenly to zero.   _____

2. Snow fell during the night.   _____

3. The lake froze within a few hours.   _____

4. The next day skaters glided over the lake.   _____

5. Three people built a huge fire near the lake.   _____

6. Some went into the warm lodge.   _____

7. They sat around the fireplace.   _____

8. Outside the lodge more snow fell.   _____

PREPOSITIONAL PHRASES AS ADJECTIVES

Some prepositional phrases may function as adjectives, telling *which one.* In the following sentences, each prepositional phrase modifies a noun or a pronoun because it comes immediately after a noun and tells *which one:*

Adj NS Adj——————— Vi   Adv
The girl **with the long hair** studies constantly. (Which girl? The girl **with the long hair . . .**)

NS Vt   Ndo Adj——— Adv———————
She spends all **of her time** in the library. (Which all? All **of her time . . .**)

NS   LV Nsc Adj——————— Adj————————————
She is one **of the women in my sociology class.** (Which one? One **of the women . . .** Which women? The women **in my sociology class . . .**)

Notice that the noun or pronoun that a prepositional phrase modifies might be the object of another prepositional phrase. In the sentence above, *of the women* modifies the pronoun *one* because it tells which one, and *in my sociology class* modifies *women* because it tells which women.

In the following sentence, *in the room* is an adverb that tells where the class meets, *at the top* is an adjective that tells which room, and *of the stairs* is an adjective that tells which top:

Adj NS   Vi   Adv——————— Adj———— Adj—————
Our class meets **in the room at the top of the stairs.** (Which room? The room **at the top . . .** Which top? The top **of the stairs . . .**)

EXERCISE 20C

Write Adj above each prepositional phrase that modifies a noun or pronoun. In the blank write the word each phrase modifies.

Adv——————— Adj———— NS——————— Vt   Adj Adj   Ndo
EXAMPLE: At the edge of town Sam Ward built a large house.   _____edge_____

1. He painted the outside of the house.   _____

2. Two of his sons painted the inside.   _____

3. Another son and his daughter wallpapered all of the rooms.   _____

4. A cheerful room on the third floor was Sam's bedroom.   _____

5. Each of his children had a second-floor bedroom.   _____

6. A small room off the kitchen was the breakfast room.   _____

7. They had the rest of their meals in the dining room.   _____

8. A stone fireplace filled one wall of the living room.   _____

9. Each evening Sam and his children enjoyed a cup of hot

   chocolate before the crackling fire.   _____

10. Later Sam spent an hour alone in his room at the top.   _____

ADVERBIAL PHRASE OR ADJECTIVE PHRASE?

Sometimes the same word group can be an adjective phrase in one sentence and an adverbial phrase in another sentence, depending on which word it modifies. In the sentence below, *near the door* tells which woman; therefore, the prepositional phrase is an adjective because it modifies the noun subject:

        Adj NS   Adj——————— Vi   Adv
        The woman **near the door** stood still.

In the next sentence, *near the door* is an adverb because it tells where the woman stood:

        Adj NS   Vi   Adv Adv———————
        The woman stood still **near the door.**

Here are more sentences in which the same word group is an adjective phrase in one sentence and an adverbial phrase in the other. Notice the differences in meaning:

ADJECTIVE (which one)   ADVERB (when, where, why, how)

        Adj-which man   Adv-how———
The man **with a cane** walked slowly.   The man walked slowly **with a cane.**

        Adj-which robin   Adv-where
The robin **in the nest** has three   The robin has three babies **in the**

babies.   **nest.**

        Adj-which class   Adv-when———
The class **after lunch** seems long.   The class seems long **after lunch.**

In sentences with several prepositional phrases, you may wonder how to decide whether each prepositional phrase is an adjective or an adverb. You should have no

problem if you write Adj above the phrases that tell *which one* and Adv above those that tell *when, where, why,* or *how.* Examine the following sentence carefully.

    Adv-when   Adj-which day————   NS   Vi   Adv-where   Adj-which store
On the day before Christmas, Dean rushed **to the store at the edge**

    Adj-which edge————   C   Vt   Ndo   Adj-which several Adj-which gifts
of the small town and bought several **of the gifts**   **on his long list.**

EXERCISE 20D

Read the following sentences. Write Adj above each adjectival prepositional phrase, and Adv and *when, where, why,* or *how* above each adverbial prepositional phrase.

              Adj————————   Adv-how————
EXAMPLE: All of the picnic tables were piled high with food.

1. The girl with the dog fell down.

2. The girl fell down with the dog.

3. Tom backed his car down the steep driveway and ran into the fence.

4. Two of the chairs in the kitchen needed a coat of paint.

5. By nightfall most of the hunters had returned to camp.

6. The flock of geese flew in formation over the quiet forest.

7. Tons of concrete filled the forms for the bridge pillars.

8. Dana waited anxiously at home for a telephone call.

9. At the end of the play the actors greeted members of the audience.

10. Dave moved the piano from one corner of the room to the other.

PLACING PREPOSITIONAL PHRASES

Prepositional phrases are modifiers; therefore, they must be placed close to the words they modify. If they are placed in another part of the sentence, readers may get the wrong meaning or become confused.

    Adjectival prepositional phrases must be placed immediately after the noun or pronoun they modify. They can only follow nouns and pronouns. They cannot come before them:

        NOT: The window needs paint **in the bedroom.**

               Adj NS   Adj————————Vt   Ndo
        BUT: The window **in the bedroom** needs paint.

Adverbial prepositional phrases must be placed near the verb, adjective, or adverb that they modify to keep the meaning clear:

NOT: The car skidded and smashed the store windows **in the middle of the street.**

BUT:
Adj NS Vi   Adv——————— Adj————— C Vt   Adj
The car skidded **in the middle of the street** and smashed the

Adj   Ndo
store windows.

EXERCISE 20E

In each of the following sentences a prepositional phrase is in the wrong place. Find and underline each of these phrases. Then write the word the prepositional phrase should follow in the blank at the right.

1. Last week Dick fell and injured himself on the back porch. _____

2. I wrote a letter while riding to Dallas on a scrap of paper. _____

3. A violent storm broke and quickly filled rivers and streams

   with great fury. _____

4. Becky was transferred to the island where the hotel was

   situated in a small boat. _____

5. A piano was offered for sale by a man going to the Orient with

   carved legs. _____

6. Some people think that my walnut chair is an antique with a

   knowledge of furniture. _____

7. Barbara will sell this old table before she moves with one

   broken leg. _____

EXERCISE 20F

Write prepositional phrases by adding a noun with modifiers after the prepositions given.

EXAMPLE: in _____the sky_____

1. to _____   4. below _____

2. by _____   5. above _____

3. of _____   6. for _____

Now write sentences using each of the prepositional phrases you wrote above. Use some phrases as adjectives and others as adverbs. **Label the phrases.**

1.

2.

3.

4.

5.

6.

Show these sentences to your instructor or tutor.

Unit Four Review

Practice Test

PART I

A. Underline two nouns in each of the following sentences. Then write the plural forms in the blanks at the right.
(10 points—2 points each)   (Lesson 15)   Score _____

1. The teacher planned a lesson.   _____   _____

2. His father bought a new car.   _____   _____

3. The chief carried a gun.   _____   _____

4. The monkey lived in the jungle.   _____   _____

5. The girl bought a white blouse.   _____   _____

B. Underline two nouns in each of the following sentences. Then decide if they are common nouns or proper nouns. Write C (common noun) or P (proper noun) in the blanks at the right.
(4 points—2 points each)   (Lesson 15)   Score _____

1. The students traveled throughout Europe.   _____   _____

2. Sara and her mother will arrive tomorrow.   _____   _____

C. Listed on the next page are a number of words that are general or specific in relation to one another. List words that are general in the column on the left. Then write the *matching* terms in the column on the right.
(10 points—2 points each)   (Lesson 15)   Score _____

EXAMPLE: General—furniture   Specific—chair

GENERAL AND SPECIFIC TERMS: rose, city, coin, food, robin, penny, Paris, flower
apple, bird

GENERAL	SPECIFIC
1. _____	_____
2. _____	_____
3. _____	_____
4. _____	_____
5. _____	_____

D. Indicate the function of each word in bold type by writing one of these symbols in the blank at the right: N (Noun or Pronoun), Adj (Adjective), Adv (Adverb).
(8 points—1 point each)   (Lessons 16, 17, 18, 19)   Score _____

1. **That** ship travels across the Atlantic.   _____

2. The **red** balloon floated in water.   _____

3. **Nan's** father changed jobs.   _____

4. He likes these shirts. **Those** do not please him.   _____

5. The girl dived into **the** water.   _____

6. Harold **carefully** prepared the assignment.   _____

7. **Their** tennis racquets needed new strings.   _____

8. Lynn bought a striped jacket **today.**   _____

E. Change each of the phrases in bold type to a possessive modifier of the noun. Add the apostrophe (') and -s in the proper order for each word.
(10 points—2 points each)   (Lesson 17)   Score _____

1. the signals **of the guards**   _____

2. the radio **of the driver**   _____

3. the toothbrush **of the child**   _____

4. the parents **of the boys**   _____

5. the team **of the women**   _____

F. Add modifiers to each of the nouns in the following sentences. First, write the nouns in Column II. Then think of appropriate adjective modifiers and write them in Column I.
(12 points—4 points each)   (Lesson 18)   Score _____

	ADJECTIVES	NOUNS
1. The captain sounded the alarm.	_____	_____
	_____	_____
2. The story pleased many readers.	_____	_____
	_____	_____
3. Waves hit the shore.	_____	_____
	_____	_____

G. Place a comma between adjectives where *and* has been omitted.
   (10 points—2 points each)   (Lesson 18)   Score _____

1. damp foggy day   4. powerful muscular football player

2. tall narrow cupboard   5. soft flowered paper towel

3. green metal table

H. Add an adverbial modifier to each of the words in bold type by writing the modifier
   in the blank at the right. Select adverbs that answer *how*.
   (10 points—2 points each)   (Lesson 19)   Score _____

1. Tania **planned** the sales meeting.   _____

2. The **large** basket contained bread and cheese.   _____

3. Marilyn **opened** the door.   _____

4. The guests enjoyed the **appetizing** food.   _____

5. The senator read the new contract **slowly.**   _____

I. Underline the misused modifiers in the following sentences and write the preferred
   forms in the blanks at the right.
   (6 points—2 points each)   (Lesson 19)   Score _____

1. The new television set works good.   _____

2. He bought a real valuable piece of property.   _____

3. The plumber hurt his hand bad.   _____

J. Underline each prepositional phrase in the following sentences, and write the words
   it modifies in the blank at the right. If you do not find a prepositional phrase in the
   sentence, place X in the blank.
   (14 points—2 points each)   (Lesson 20)   Score _____

1. The rooster on the fence crowed loudly.   _____

2. Into the burning hotel ran the firefighters. _____

3. Jack sat down. _____

4. The man with the red beard chewed his food rapidly. _____

5. The picture on the T-shirt attracted everyone's attention. _____

6. Adults and teenagers stayed outside. _____

7. Divers found black pearls in the water. _____

K. Revise each of the following sentences by placing modifiers in proper relationship to the words they modify.
(6 points—3 points each)   (Lesson 20)   Score _____

1. During the heavy rainstorm a man fed the hungry pig in a plastic raincoat and boots.

2. A young man slipped on some oil and was severely injured in his garage.

PART II

A. Write five prepositional phrases.
(15 points—3 points each)   (Lesson 20)   Score _____

1.

2.

3.

4.

5.

B. Write five sentences using each of the above prepositional phrases in a sentence. Write at least two sentences with adjective phrases. **Write Adj and Adv above each phrase.**
(35 points—7 points each)   (Lesson 20)   Score _____

1.

2.

3.

4.

5.

C. Write five sentences about **one** topic. Use adjectives and adjectival prepositional phrases in the sentences to make general terms specific and to give more information about nouns. Use adverbs and adverbial prepositional phrases to modify verbs, adjectives, and adverbs.
(50 points—10 points each)   (Lessons 15–20)   Score _____

1.

2.

3.

4.

5.

Unit Five

More Basic Sentence Patterns

Up to this point you have been working with sentences that have three basic patterns: NS Vi, NS Vt Ndo, and NS LV Nsc. You have also learned to add modifiers—adjectives and adverbs—to the basic sentence patterns. Study the following pairs of sentences.

BASIC SENTENCES

NS————— LV Nsc
Terry Harris is a golfer.

NS   Vt   Ndo
The woman plays golf.

NS Vi   C   Vi
She practices and wins.

SENTENCES WITH MODIFIERS

NS————— LV Adj Adj
Terry Harris is a   well-known,
Adj   Nsc
outstanding golfer.

Adj Adj   Adj NS   Vt
The energetic young woman plays
Ndo Adv_____ Adv_____
golf in tournaments all over the
_____
United States.

NS Vi   Adv_____
She practices several hours a day
C   Vi   Adv
and wins frequently.

By the time you finish this unit, you will have learned two more basic patterns for writing sentences in English.

Lesson 21

Sentences with Subject Complements

In Lesson 5 you learned that a linking verb can join a subject with a noun that renames the subject:

    Adj Adj   NS   LV——— Adj Adj   Nsc Adv———
    The college senior had been a riverboat pilot for three years.

In this lesson you will look again at sentences with noun subject complements. You will also look at sentences in which the linking verb joins the subject to an adjective that describes the subject. It is called an adjective complement, and the symbol for it is Adj-c:

    NS LV Adj-c   C Adv   Adj-c
    He was experienced and highly skilled.

NOUNS AS SUBJECT COMPLEMENTS

A noun that renames the subject is a subject complement. The linking verb connects the two nouns that name the same person or thing. The sentence pattern is NS LV Nsc:

    NS   LV   Adj Adj   Nsc
    Stuart became a furniture designer.   (Stuart = designer)

    NS LV———   Adj Nsc
    He had been a sign painter.   (He = painter)

    NS LV   Adj   Nsc
    He remained Charlie's assistant.   (He = assistant)

The nouns *designer, painter,* and *assistant* are all subject complements because they rename the subject *Stuart* or *he* in each of the sentences above. The nouns are joined to the subject by the linking verbs *be, become,* and *remain.*
    The direct object, on the other hand, is different from the subject:

    NS   Vt   Ndo
    Stuart painted signs.   *Stuart* and *signs* are different.

ADJECTIVES AS SUBJECT COMPLEMENTS

An adjective following a linking verb describes the subject. It is called an adjective complement. The sentence pattern is NS LV Adj-c:

```
            NS        LV  Adj-c
         The ground is damp.                    (damp ground)

            NS   LV       Adj-c
         The trees became wet.                  (wet trees)

            NS   LV       Adj-c
         The grass remained dry.                (dry grass)
```

You can tell that the words following the verbs in the above sentences are adjective complements because they describe the subjects when you put them in front of the subject of each sentence.

LINKING VERBS

A number of verbs can function as linking verbs. In the following examples the verbs are followed by subject complements or adjective complements. You can tell that they are linking verbs because the adjective following the verb describes the subject or the noun following the verb renames the subject.

1. The verb *be* is always a linking verb when it is used alone:*

```
    NS  LV  Nsc  NS LV————— Adj-c    C   Adj-c
    Don is a clerk. He has been reliable and efficient.
```

2. The verbs of the senses, such as *look, sound, smell, taste,* and *feel,* may be linking verbs:

```
        NS       LV    Adj-c  C   Adj-c
     The guests sound happy and excited.      (happy and excited guests)

        NS    C   NS     LV   Adj-c
     The food and drinks taste good.          (good food and drinks)

        NS LV   Adj-c
     The air feels warm.                      (warm air)
```

3. Verbs such as *become, remain, get, keep, prove, turn, fall, stand, appear, seem, run,* and *grow* may function as linking verbs:

```
     NS  LV         Nsc
     Joe became a baker.                      (Joe = baker)

     Adj  NS      LV    Adj-c
     His pastries proved popular.             (popular pastries)

     NS  LV   Adj-c C   Adj-c
     Joe grew fat  and rich.                  (fat and rich Joe)
```

Adverbs may follow the subject complement and the adjective complement:

```
     Adj  NS          LV   Adj-c  Adv—————————
     The contestants were happy with the results.
```

*Remember that the verb *be* has eight forms: *am, is, are, be, was, were, been,* and *being.*

```
  NS      LS           Nsc        Adv————— NS   LV        Adj-c  Adv—————
```
John became a counselor last year. John remains calm in a crisis.

Remember that the adjective or noun following the verb functions as a complement. If the adjective or noun does not describe or rename the subject, the verb is not a linking verb. It is functioning as a transitive or an intransitive verb:

```
     NS      Vt          Ndo      NS   LV       Adj-c
```
The visitor sounded the bell. The bell sounded loud.   (loud bell)

```
     NS     Vi        Adv————— NS   LV        Adj-c
```
The butler appeared at the door. He appeared angry.   (angry he)

To analyze sentences with the linking verb, you can use the Sentence Keys you learned in Unit One by making the following additions in the third step.

Sentence Keys

1 and 2. Follow the steps on pages 12–13 to find the verb and the subject:

```
     NS    V                NS    V             NS    V
```
Carol became a dancer. Carol feels happy. Carol is on the stage.

3. Read the subject and verb together and ask *who(m)* or *what.*
   c. If the word that answers the question renames the subject, the word is a **subject** complement. Write Nsc above it. The verb is a **linking verb.** Write LV above the verb:

```
     NS   LV        Nsc
```
Carol became a dancer.   (Carol = dancer)

   d. If the word describes the subject, the word is an **adjective complement.** Write Adj-c above it. The verb is a **linking verb.** Write LV above the verb:

```
     NS   LV    Adj-c
```
Carol feels happy.   (happy Carol)

EXERCISE 21A

Using the Sentence Keys, identify the pattern in each of the following sentences. Label the words with one of these patterns: NS LV Nsc or NS LV Adj-c.

1. Dale was the leader of the band.

2. The music sounds pleasant tonight.

3. The fabric feels soft and warm.

4. The three bottles are plastic containers.

5. Ted and Richard became volunteer firefighters.

6. Burt has been active in the ski club.

7. Tom and Margery are pianists.

8. The sky looks threatening in the west.

9. Mrs. Wilson remained the director of the company.

10. The story proved false.

EXERCISE 21B

Using the Sentence Keys, identify the pattern in each of the following sentences. Label the words with one of these pattersn: NS Vi, NS Vt Ndo, NS LV Nsc, or NS LV Adj-c.

1. The cart is standing in the hall.

2. The paintings look restful.

3. The kitten tasted the milk.

4. Mr. Danton became a counselor.

5. The runner appeared exhausted after the race.

6. The watchman appeared suddenly.

7. The firefighters sounded the alarm.

8. The crowd became silent.

9. The delivery boy proved unreliable.

10. Don's parents will be camp supervisors next month.

COMBINING SENTENCES

After writing two or three sentences which describe a person or a thing, you may want to combine the sentences in order to leave out some of the repeated words. Study the following example:

NS Vt Adj Ndo NS LV Adj-c NS
The typist completed three letters. The typist is efficient. The typist

LV Adj-c
is accurate.

You can see that the first sentence contains the information to be emphasized. Place X before the first sentence to show that it is the base sentence. Then use the second and third sentences to add information about the typist. Draw a line to delete (omit) unnecessary words. The words that remain are *efficient* and *accurate,* adjective complements that describe the subject *typist.* Therefore, they can be placed before *typist* in the first sentence:

SINGLE SENTENCES

X   The typist completed three
    letters.
    ~~The typist is~~ efficient.
    ~~The typist is~~ accurate.

COMBINED SENTENCES

The **efficient, accurate** typist completed three letters.

Place a comma between *efficient* and *accurate* because the word *and* has been omitted. (See Lesson 18.)

If you have also described the letters, you can put this information into the first sentence:

SINGLE SENTENCES

X   The efficient, accurate typist completed three letters.
~~The letters were~~ long.
~~The letters were~~ detailed.

COMBINED SENTENCE

The efficient, accurate typist completed the three **long, detailed** letters.

EXERCISE 21C

Read each group of sentences. The first sentence contains the idea to be emphasized. The sentences listed below it contain additional information. Draw a line through the words in the sentences below, and place the words that remain in the first sentence. Write the combined sentence, using appropriate punctuation.

1. Two men sailed to the island.

   The men were thirsty.

   The men were hungry.

   The island was small.

   The island was deserted.

2. A storm had damaged their boat.

   The storm was sudden.

   The storm was violent.

   Their boat was small.

   Their boat was unsafe.

3. They gathered pieces of wood for a fire.

   The pieces were large.

   The pieces were small.

   The fire was huge.

4. They waited through the night for help.

   The night was long.

   The night was dark.

   The night was stormy.

5. A freighter sent a boat for them the next morning.

   The boat was small.

EXERCISE 21D

Write sentences to match the following sentence patterns.

1. NS LV Adj-c

2. NS Vt Ndo

3. NS LV Nsc

4. NS and NS LV Nsc

5. NS VI

Show these sentences to your instructor or tutor.

Lesson 22

Sentences with Indirect Objects

When you write a sentence with a transitive verb and a direct object, you are telling how the subject and the action of the verb are affecting something else:

NS   Vt   Ndo
Jerry bought candy.   Jerry bought what? . . . candy.

Sometimes in a similar kind of sentence you may want to tell to whom or for whom something was done. You can do this by adding the information to the end of the sentence in a prepositional phrase:

NS Vt   Adj   Ndo   Adv————
He gave some candy to Nell.

Another way to tell your readers the same thing is to place the noun or pronoun telling to whom or for whom something is done **before** the direct object:

He gave   some candy to Nell   He gave Nell some candy.

The word *Nell* or any other word telling to whom or for whom something is done is called the **indirect object** (Nio). It always comes before the direct object. The verb in the sentence must be a verb like *give, find, send, bring, buy, sell, make, write, ask, play, build, teach, assign, feed, offer, throw, pass, pay, hand, read, save,* and a few others. The sentence pattern is NS Vt Nio Ndo. Compare the following sentences:

NS   Vt————   Ndo
Susan is making a sweater
Adv————
for Victor.

NS   Vt———— Nio   Ndo
Susan is making **Victor** a sweater.

NS   Vt   Ndo
My mother wrote a letter
Adv——————
to the company.

NS   Vt   Nio
My mother wrote the **company** a
Ndo
letter.

Vt   Ndo Adv————
Throw the ball **to me.**

Vt   Nio   Ndo
Throw **me** the ball.

To find indirect objects in sentences, use the Sentence Keys that you learned in Unit One. Then complete the fourth step.

Sentence Keys

1, 2, 3. Follow the steps on pages 17–18 in the order they are given:

NS————— Vt   Ndo NS Vt Ndo   NS Vt
Mr. Stevens offered Pat the job. He made Pat personnel manager. He believed

Ndo
Pat capable.

4. Read the subject, verb, and direct object together. If the word that tells *to whom* or *for whom* comes before the direct object, it is the **indirect object.** Write Nio above it.

NS————— Vt Nio Ndo
Mr. Stevens offered Pat the job. (Mr. Stevens offered the job to whom?
               ... Pat)

EXERCISE 22A

In the following sentences, the prepositional phrase in bold type tells to whom or for whom something was done. Rewrite the sentences to make the nouns in the phrases indirect objects by placing them in front of the direct object. Label all the parts of the sentence.

EXAMPLE: Jim gave pieces of liver **to his cat.**

NS Vt Adj Nio Ndo Adj———
Jim gave **his cat** pieces of liver.

1. Sid wrote a letter **to Tony.**

2. Mr. Richards sold an old farmhouse **to June and her mother.**

3. Steve built a house **for his dog.**

4. The twins gave a bright-colored tie **to their father** for his birthday.

5. The director found a position **for Terry.**

EXERCISE 22B

Using the Sentence Keys, identify the sentence patterns in the following sentences. Write NS Vt Ndo, NS Vi, NS LV Nsc, or NS Vt Nio Ndo above each sentence.

1. Trudy is Tom's boss.

2. Trudy and Tom sold Mr. Hirsch a computer.

3. Tom gave Mr. Hirsch instructions.

4. Trudy gave Tom a bonus.

5. After the trip they returned to Chicago and reported their success.

EXERCISE 22C

Study the example given, and then write your own sentences according to the directions.

1. First, write two nouns that name a person and a thing.

               N   N

EXAMPLE: mother   necklace   YOUR NOUNS: _____ _____

Next, choose one of the verbs you may use to write a sentence with an indirect object (see page 130).

             V

EXAMPLE: buy   YOUR VERB: _____

Finally, give the verb a subject, and combine all the words into a sentence with an indirect object. Label all the parts of the sentence.

            NS   Vt   Nio   Ndo

EXAMPLE: Jane bought her mother a necklace.

YOUR SENTENCE:

2. Write two more sentences with indirect objects.

Show these sentences to your instructor or tutor.

EXERCISE 22D

Write sentences to match these patterns. Label all the parts of the sentence.

1. NS Vt Nio Ndo

2. NS Vt Ndo and Ndo

3. NS Vi Adv

Show these sentences to your instructor or tutor.

Lesson 23

Sentence Keys for Five Sentence Patterns

You have now studied five basic sentence patterns for sentences written in English. A brief review now will help you summarize the main points you have been studying:

SUBJECTS AND PREDICATES

Sentences have a **subject** and a **predicate.** The subject tells what the sentence is about, and the predicate tells something about the subject.

In analyzing a sentence you may identify either the **simple subject** and **simple predicate,** or your may identify the **complete subject** and **complete predicate.**

The **simple subject** is the noun or pronoun that functions as the subject of the sentence. The **simple predicate** is the verb or verb phrase in the sentence.

The **complete subject** is the noun and its modifiers. The **complete predicate** is the verb, its objects or complements, and its modifiers.

In the following sentences S appears above the simple subject and V above the simple predicate:

(PREDICATE)	COMPLETE SUBJECT	COMPLETE PREDICATE
	S	V
For many years*	the highly skilled artists	designed very comfortable, practical furniture.
	S	V
	Their unusual designs	sold extremely well throughout the country.

* *For many years* is not part of the subject. It is an an adverb. See Lesson 6.

EXERCISE 23A

Identify the complete subject and complete predicate in the following sentences. Write S and draw a line above the subject. Write P and draw a line above the predicate. Use the Sentence Keys if you need help.

EXAMPLE:

$\overset{\text{S}\rule{2cm}{0.4pt}}{}$ $\overset{\text{P}\rule{5cm}{0.4pt}}{}$

An old shepherd lived alone in the Swiss Alps.

$\overset{\text{S} \quad \text{P}\rule{7cm}{0.4pt}}{}$

During the day he tended his flock of sheep with his two collies.

1. The one dog worked all day.

2. He kept the sheep in one part of the grassy meadow.

3. The other dog chased rabbits and gophers.

4. At night the shepherd cooked his meal and fed the dogs.

5. Sometimes he sat outside and watched the stars in the black sky.

BASIC SENTENCE PATTERNS

Next, you studied three main sentence patterns in Unit One:

SUBJECT	PREDICATE	
NS	Vi	(Lesson 4)
NS	Vt Ndo	(Lesson 4)
NS	LV Nsc	(Lesson 5)

In this unit you have studied one more pattern with transitive verbs (Vt) and one more pattern with linking verbs (LV):

SUBJECT	PREDICATE	
NS	LV Adj-c	(Lesson 21)
NS	Vt Nio Ndo	(Lesson 22)

If you have questions about either of these patterns, review the lessons in which they are discussed.

Three other sentence patterns have not been included in this unit because they seldom cause writing problems. They are listed below with examples for reference:

1. The adverb complement (Adv-c) in the following sentences follows a form of *be* and tells where:

NS LV Adv-c

NS   LV Adv-c   NS   LV Adv-c————
Janell is home. She is in the living room.

2. The object complement (Noc) follows the direct object and renames the direct object. It usually appears after verbs such as *call, appoint, choose, name, select, elect, make, consider,* and others.

NS Vt Ndo Noc

NS   Vt   Ndo————
The Corvette Club members elected Tony Davis

Noc
president.

3. The adjective complement (Adj-c) may follow the direct object and describe the direct object. It usually appears after verbs such as *paint, believe, like, prefer, report, want, get, have, set,* and a few others.

NS Vt Ndo Adj-c

$$\overset{\text{NS}}{\text{The rescuers}} \overset{\text{Vt}}{\text{found}} \overset{\text{Ndo}}{\text{the child}} \overset{\text{Adj-c}}{\text{safe}} \text{and} \overset{\text{Adj-c}}{\text{unharmed.}}$$

Below is a summary of all the Sentence Keys you learned in preceding lessons.

Sentence Keys

1. Find the verb by using the Verb Test (Lesson 2). The verb may be more than one word. Write V and draw a line above the entire verb:

    V————————
    Sharks have frightened swimmers.   **(They** have frightened)

    V
    Sometimes sharks attack.   **(They** attack)

    V
    A shark is a dangerous fish.   **(It** is)

2. Ask *who* or *what,* and then say the verb. The word that answers the question is the **subject.** Write NS above it.

    NS   V————————
    Sharks have frightened swimmers.   (What have frightened swimmers?
                                               Sharks . . .)

3. Read the subject and verb together and ask *who(m)* or *what.*
    a. If the word that answers the question completes the verb and is different from the subject, it is the **direct object.** Write Ndo above it. The verb is **transitive.** Write Vt above the verb:

        NS   Vt——————— Ndo
        Sharks have frightened swimmers.   (Sharks have frightened whom? . . .
                                                   swimmers)

    b. If there is no answer to *whom* or *what,* the verb is **intransitive.** Write Vi above the verb:

        NS   Vi
        Sometimes sharks attack.   (Sharks attack *what?* No answer.)

    c. If the word that answers the question renames the subject, the word is a **subject complement.** Write Nsc above it. The verb is a **linking verb.** Write LV above the verb:

        NS LV   Nsc
        A shark is a dangerous fish.   (Shark = fish)

    d. If the word describes the subject, the word is an **adjective complement.** Write Adj-c above it and LV above the verb:

NS   LV   Adj-c

Sharks look evil.   (evil sharks)

4. If the sentence has a transitive verb, read the subject, verb, and direct object together. If the word that tells *to whom* or *for whom* comes before the direct object, it is the **indirect object.** Write Nio above it:

NS   Vt   Nio   Ndo

Lifeguards give swimmers warnings.   (Lifeguards give warnings *to whom?*
                                          . . . swimmers)

EXERCISE 23B

Use the Sentence Keys to analyze the following sentences. Write the basic sentence pattern in the blank at the right. Omit modifiers and connectors.

NS   Vt   Ndo

EXAMPLE: The goat chewed the tin can vigorously.   _____NS Vt Ndo_____

1. The weary pioneers made frequent stops along the route.   _____

2. Many people prefer steak and potatoes for dinner.   _____

3. Autumn is a relaxing season.   _____

4. The modern camera takes remarkable pictures.   _____

5. Bruce Bennett is an amateur photographer.   _____

6. He is extremely talented.   _____

7. The skydivers awarded Elaine the trophy.   _____

8. Last year Tom traveled extensively in Africa.   _____

9. Dan Baker appointed a new chairperson of the board.   _____

10. Karen has been resting since her car accident.   _____

11. The college president gave the graduates their diplomas.   _____

12. The pilot flew the plane for the first time yesterday.   _____

MODIFIERS: ADJECTIVES AND ADVERBS

As you review the basic sentence patterns, you can see that they are made up mainly of nouns and verbs. One pattern contains an adjective complement. You have also learned that adjectives, which modify nouns or pronouns, can be placed before or after

all the nouns in the basic sentence patterns. They tell *which one* or *how many.* Adverbs, which modify verbs, adjectives, and other adverbs, can appear at the beginning, in the middle, or at the end of sentences. They answer the questions *when, where, why,* or *how.*

Both adjectives and adverbs are ADDITIONS to the basic sentence patterns. If you leave them out, you still have a grammatical sentence:

<pre>
                                    Adv-when——— Adj Adj   NS   Adj
SENTENCE WITH MODIFIERS: Late at night the giant monster, frightening
C   Adj   Vi   Adv-how Adv-where————————— Adv-why———————
and powerful, traveled quickly through the small town in search of the
————
scientist.
</pre>

<pre>
                         NS   Vi
BASIC SENTENCE: The monster traveled.
</pre>

EXERCISE 23C

Using the Sentence Keys, identify the patterns in the following sentences. Modifiers (adjectives and adverbs) have been added to them. Write the basic sentence—ONLY THE NOUNS AND VERB—in the blank at the right. You may include *the* in your basic sentence.

<pre>
         Adv   Adj Adj
EXAMPLE: Unfortunately the frightened,
         Adj   NS Vt   Adv
         trembling man could not
         Vt   Adj Adj   Ndo
         remember his home address.
</pre>

The man could remember the

address. _____

1. Careful research revealed the reason for the

   widespread illness. _____

2. Thoroughly cleaned kettles and pans should

   prevent the spread of disease. _____

3. Very few people know Mark's last name. _____

4. The hungry and thirsty two-year-old boy eagerly

   ran home. _____

5. The captain's privately owned plane, damaged

   and scorched, landed safely. _____

EXERCISE 23D

Use the Sentence Keys to analyze the following sentences. Then identify the word group in bold type by writing its label in the blank.

Subject: noun and its modifiers
Predicate: verb and its complements and modifiers
Modifiers: adjectives and adverbs

EXAMPLE:
```
           Adv──────── NS   C   NS    Vt      Adj
```
Last summer Kent and Andrea **planned their**
```
Ndo
```
wedding.   _____Predicate_____

1. **Their wedding day** finally arrived.   _____

2. Andrea, **happy and smiling,** wore a long white dress.   _____

3. The nervous bridgegroom paced **back and forth for an hour**

   before the ceremony.   _____

4. After the ceremony **friends and relatives of the happy couple**

   drank toasts and ate wedding cake.   _____

5. That evening the newlyweds **began the long drive to Miami**

   Beach.   _____

EXERCISE 23E

Write a sentence to match each of the following patterns. Add modifiers to your basic sentences. Label all the parts of the sentences.

1. NS Vt Ndo

2. NS LV Nsc

3. NS Vi

4. NS Vt Nio Ndo

5. NS LV Adj-c

Show these sentences to your instructor or tutor.

EXERCISE 23F

Use the sentences you wrote for Exercise 23E, and write the COMPLETE SUBJECT under the first heading and the COMPLETE PREDICATE under the second heading below.

COMPLETE SUBJECT   COMPLETE PREDICATE

1.

2.

3.

4.

5.

Show these sentences to your instructor or tutor.

Unit Five Review

Practice Test

PART I

A. Identify the simple subjects and the simple predicates (verbs) in the following sentences by writing the subject in the first blank and the verb or verbs in the second blank. Remember to list auxiliary verbs and main verbs.
(20 points—2 points each)   (Lesson 23)   Score _____

	SIMPLE SUBJECT (NOUNS)	SIMPLE PREDICATE (VERBS)
1. Linda Thompson had been developing new selling techniques for sportswear.	_____	_____
2. At a sales conference in New York she demonstrated these techniques before a small group.	_____	_____
3. John Holt had listened to Linda.	_____	_____
4. He had not spoken to her at the meeting and praised her speech.	_____	_____
5. Soon John was asking Linda for help in long, friendly letters.	_____	_____
6. Happily she arranged a meeting with him at his office in Chicago and flew to Chicago.	_____	_____
7. She smiled broadly at the tall, slender man and extended her hand.	_____	_____

8. She pulled her hand quickly from his cold, wet, limp hand.

_____ _____

9. She talked for hours and could not make her ideas clear to him.

_____ _____

10. She quickly hurried home after a boring, disappointing meeting.

_____ _____

B. The sentences in Exercise A tell a story. Reread the sentences. Then write sentences to answer the questions below.
(9 points—3 points each)   Score _____

1. What did Linda Thompson do at the conference in New York?

2. Where did Linda arrange to meet John Holt?

3. What kind of meeting did Linda have with John Holt?

C. Identify the word groups in bold type by writing *Subject, Predicate,* or *Modifiers* in the blanks at the right.
(12 points—2 points each)   (Lesson 23)   Score _____

    Subject: noun and its modifiers (adjectives)
    Predicate: verb and its modifiers (adverbs) and complements (Ndo, Nio, Nsc, Adj-c)
    Modifiers: adjectives and adverbs

1. **Several shiny red** apples hung on the tree.

_____

2. **Five thousand people** attended the jazz concert.

_____

3. **Ten bottles of grape juice** stand on the shelf.

_____

4. Five students **walked noisily into the classroom.**

_____

5. The young violinist **stood nervously on the stage.**

_____

6. The express bus stops **near the bank on Broadway.**

_____

D. Write the basic sentence pattern for each of the following sentences in the blanks at the right. The patterns may be one of the following:

    NS Vt Ndo   NS Vt Nio Ndo   NS LV Adj-c
    NS Vi   NS LV Nsc

(15 points—3 points each)   (Lessons 21, 22, 23)   Score _____

1. Thousands of cars travel on freeways every day. _____

2. The sheriff showed the audience burglar-proof locks for doors and windows. _____

3. Lisa Farraday has been an employee of the company for two years. _____

4. Visitors enjoyed the dinners at the new hotel. _____

5. The actors felt depressed at the end of the play. _____

E. Read each group of sentences. The first sentence contains the idea to be emphasized. The sentences listed below it contain additional information. Cross out repeated words in the sentences below, and place the words that remain in the first sentence. Write the combined sentence, using appropriate punctuation.
(9 points—3 points each)   (Lesson 21)   Score _____

1. The lamp hung from the ceiling.

   The lamp was huge.

   The lamp was circular.

   The ceiling was carved.

   The ceiling was wooden.

2. The swimmer rapidly crossed the Olympic-sized pool.

   The swimmer was tanned.

   The swimmer was muscular.

3. The bricklayer placed his hand on the table.

   The bricklayer was injured.

   His hand was bleeding.

   The table was white.

   It was an examining table.

F. Write sentences according to the directions given below. **Label all the parts of the sentences.**
(35 points—7 points each)   (Lessons 21, 22, 23)   Score _____

1. Write a sentence with a transitive verb and a direct object. (NS Vt Ndo)

2. Write a sentence with a linking verb and a subject complement. (NS LV Nsc)

3. Write a sentence with a transitive verb and a noun that tells to whom or for whom something is done. (NS Vt Nio Ndo)

4. Write a sentence with an intransitive verb. (NS Vi)

5. Write a sentence with a linking verb and an adjective complement. (NS LV Adj-c)

PART II

A. Write ten sentences about ONE topic.
   (80 points—8 points each)   Score _____

   1.

   2.

   3.

   4.

   5.

   6.

   7.

   8.

   9.

   10.

B. Using the first FIVE sentences you wrote above, write the complete subject under the first heading and the complete predicate under the second heading. The complete subject includes nouns and their modifiers. The complete predicate includes the verb and its complements (Nio, Ndo, Nsc) and modifiers (Adj and Adv).
   (20 points—4 points each)   Score _____

   COMPLETE SUBJECT   COMPLETE PREDICATE

   1.

   2.

3.

4.

5.

Unit Six

Pronouns and Agreement

Pronouns are a small group of words that take the place of nouns in sentences. They allow us to refer to the same person or thing again and again without repeating the noun that names the person or thing. In the sentence below the pronoun *he* replaces *the lonely man* and *it* replaces *basket:*

     NS   NS   Ndo   NS
The lonely man opened the door. **He** found a **basket** on the step. **He** took

Ndo
It   inside.

Pronouns also allow us to refer to people or things we cannot name. In the following example we use the pronoun *someone* because we cannot identify who left the basket:

NS
Someone had left the basket there.

Although pronouns are always used in noun positions, they are different from nouns:

1. Pronouns cannot be identified by using the Noun Test:

     the people   *the* question   NOT: *the* you   *the* everyone

2. Unlike nouns, some pronouns may have different forms depending on their function in a sentence:

     NS   Ndo
     She worked hard. The instructor praised **her.**

In this unit you will learn about the various kinds of pronouns and their forms. You will also cover the agreement of subject and verb, which you studied briefly in Lesson 7, and pronouns that sometimes cause writers problems in making subjects and verbs agree.

Lesson 24

Personal Pronouns

When you speak to another person about your experiences or ideas, you use the pronoun *I* to identify yourself as the speaker:

I made my decision.   I will not change my mind.

When you talk to someone else, you use the pronoun *you* to address that person:

You understand my reasons.

If you speak to a friend about another person, you usually mention the person's name first; then you use *he* or *she* to refer to the person again:

Doug will argue with me.   **He** wants his way.

And if you refer to objects or ideas, you use *it* or *they* to talk about them:

The car stopped.   **It** needed gasoline.
The tires were flat.   **They** needed air.

In each case you use a particular personal pronoun to refer to each of the persons or things. The personal pronouns, then, represent three persons:

First person *(I, we)*—the person or persons speaking
Second person *(you)*—the person or persons spoken to
Third person *(he, she, it, they)*—the person, persons, thing, or things spoken about

NOTE: All nouns except words of direct address, as in "John, come in," are third person.

PERSONAL PRONOUN FORMS

Personal pronouns may have different forms depending on their function in a sentence. The **subjective** forms are used for subject and subject complement. The **objective** forms are used for direct object, indirect object, and object of the preposition. The **possessive** forms may be used alone to show possession in all noun positions, or they may function as determiners before another noun (see Lesson 16). The following chart shows the forms of all the personal pronouns:

	Subjective (NS, Nsc)	Objective (Ndo, Nio, Nop)	Possessive (NS, Nsc, Ndo, Nio, Nop)	Possessive (Adj)
SINGULAR				
First person	I	me	mine	my
Second person	you	you	yours	your
Third person				
(M)*	he	him	his	his
(F)*	she	her	hers	her
(N)*	it	it	its	its
PLURAL				
First person	we	us	ours	our
Second person	you	you	yours	your
Third person	they	them	theirs	their

*Masculine, feminine, neuter.

Personal Pronouns in Subject and Object Positions

The examples below show how the first and second person pronouns function in sentences. Compare the following pairs of sentences:

SUBJECTIVE	OBJECTIVE
Nsc This is **I**.	Nio Terry gave **me** theater tickets.
NS Do **you** want to go Thursday night?	Ndo Terry will call **you** later.
NS Afterwards **we** can go out for dinner.	Nop Terry will meet both of **us** there.

The next examples show how the third person pronouns function in place of nouns, which are also third person. Study the following sentences:

	SUBJECTIVE	OBJECTIVE
NS The **traveler** went to Japan.	NS **He** stayed a month.	Ndo The trip pleased **him**.
NS **Dave** went on a tour.	NS **He** visited several shrines.	Nio A guide told **him** many interesting stories.
The guide took the Ndo **travelers** to five cities.	NS **They** rode a bus.	Nop All of **them** enjoyed the trip very much.

Possessives

The possessive forms listed in the third column of the chart on page 147 take the place of nouns, and those listed in the fourth column function as determiners. Compare the following pairs of sentences:

PRONOUNS   ADJECTIVES

                          Nsc   Adj   Nsc

The oil paints on the table are **mine.**   They are **my** oil paints.

  NS   Adj   NS

Are **yours** in the cabinet?   **Your** brushes need cleaning.

                     Ndo   Adj   Ndo

Margie will lend me **hers.**   She is not using **her** brushes now.

EXERCISE 24A

Underline the personal pronouns or possessives in the following sentences and label them NS, Nsc or Ndo, Nio, Nop, Adj, according to their function in the sentence. Use the Sentence Keys.

                         NS   Adj

EXAMPLE: Ken and <u>I</u> are engaged. Here is <u>my</u> ring.

1. Jane bought me a ticket for the play.

2. Carol gave them their keys.

3. He attended your meeting.

4. They told us the details of the accident.

5. Are you Man of the Year?

6. We received our awards.

7. She sent him a part of mine.

8. A part of his belongs to you.

9. Mary likes his cooking.

10. I am I.

USING PERSONAL PRONOUNS

An easy way to decide which pronoun form to use is to label words in your sentence with the basic sentence pattern. For example, would you use *I* or *me* in the following sentence? Label all the sentence parts first:

    NS   Vt   Nio   Ndo   Adv————————
    Mike gave _____ a parrot for my birthday.

Then look at the chart. Even better, remember that *me* is an objective form, and you will know that you should use *me* as the indirect object in your sentence. The letter *o* in *Nio* tells you to use the objective form:

    NS   Vt   Nio   Ndo   Adv————————
    Mike gave **me** a parrot for my birthday.

Try another sentence. Would you use *I* or *me?*

> Sally invited everyone except _____.

If you label the sentence parts, you will see that *except* is a preposition which is followed by an object. As a result, you would use the objective form *me* in the blank:

> NS   Vt   Ndo   Pr   Nop
> Sally invited everyone except **me.**

If you knock on a door and a person you know asks, "Who's there," do you say, "It's me" or "It is I"? It may seem more natural to say, "It's me," but the pronoun *I* is preferable because it is the form used for a subject complement:

> NS LV Nsc
> It is **I.**

On the other hand, some people try to use the pronoun *I* in every part of the sentence—as NS, Nsc, Ndo, Nio, and Nop—because they learned early that they should use *I*, not *me*, in sentences like these:

> NOT: **Me** and Bob won the race.
> BUT: **I** and Bob (Bob and **I**) won the race.
>
> NOT: **Me** want a drink.
> BUT: **I** want a drink.

Because they had been told frequently to use *I*, they use it even in sentences where they should use objective forms. Examine the following sentences. When you label the sentence parts, you can see immediately whether you should use the subjective or objective form:

> NOT: Mr. Walker bought Alan and **I** ice skates.
>
> NS————   Vt   Nio   C   Nio Adj Ndo
> BUT: Mr. Walker bought Alan and **me** ice skates.
>
> NOT: All the class members except Dale and **I** attended the prom.
>
> Adj Adj Adj   NS   Pr   Nop C   Nop Vt   Adj Ndo
> BUT: All the class members except Dale and **me** attended the prom.

The next example shows the object form *him* incorrectly used as a subject in the sentence:

> NOT: Dick and **him** hitched a ride to town.
>
> NS   C   NS Vt   Ndo Adv————
> BUT: Dick and **he** hitched a ride to town.

If a noun and a pronoun are joined by *and*, as in the sentences above, you can check the form to be used by reading the sentence with only the pronoun:

> NOT: Dick and **him** hitched a ride to town.
> BUT: . . . **he** hitched a ride to town.
>
> NOT: Mr. Walker bought Alan and **I** ice skates.
> BUT: Mr. Walker bought . . . **me** ice skates.

If you use a noun as a subject, you should not use a pronoun immediately after it. Use either the noun or the pronoun:

NOT: **Glenn he** drove to New York.
BUT: **Glenn** drove to New York.
OR: **He** drove to New York.

However, you may use the pronoun *we* before a plural noun to indiciate that you include yourself in the group:

NOT: **Us** workers have certain rights.
BUT: **We** workers have certain rights.

REFLEXIVE AND INTENSIVE PRONOUNS

Pronouns ending in *-self* or *-selves* may function as **reflexive pronouns** when they "reflect" action back to a noun or pronoun in the sentence:

NS Vt————— Ndo   NS Pr Nop Vt   Ndo   Adv—————
The girl had hurt **herself.** All of us blamed **ourselves** for the accident.

The same forms function as **intensive pronouns** when they come immediately after a noun or a pronoun to emphasize it:

NS   NS   Vt   Adj Ndo NS NS   Vi   Adv—————
Gordon himself rescued the girl. I myself dived into the water.

Reflexive and intensive pronouns may function in all noun positions. The following chart shows the forms of reflexive and intensive pronouns:

	SINGULAR	PLURAL
First person	**myself**	**ourselves**
Second person	**yourself**	**yourselves**
Third person	**himself** NOT: hisself	**themselves** NOT: theirselves
	herself	
	itself	

Though some people use *myself* as a part of the subject with another noun, this usage is considered unacceptable:

NS   C   NS   Vt   Adj Ndo
NOT: Ruth and **myself** enjoyed the play.

NS   C   NS Vt   Adj Ndo
BUT: Ruth and I enjoyed the party.

If you have trouble deciding whether to use *I* or *myself*, simply leave out the first noun in the subject:

NOT: Ruth and **myself** enjoyed the play.
BUT: . . . I enjoyed the play.

EXERCISE 24B

In the following sentences the forms of the pronouns are **not** the forms preferred in Standard English. First, underline the pronoun in each sentence. Then write the preferred form in the blank at the right.

EXAMPLE: Wynn and <u>me</u> applied for the job.   ___I___

1. Christine and him found a small snake on the sidewalk.   _____

2. The store manager gave John and I new assignments.   _____

3. Us players found new team members.   _____

4. Dale told that lie to Tim and I several times.   _____

5. Carrie sent an announcement to everyone except Karen and I.   _____

6. Mr. Walker and myself presented our report this morning.   _____

7. Tony and Sandra bought theirselves furniture.   _____

8. Linda and them offered help.   _____

9. Me and Diane liked the music.   _____

10. The advertiser sent Jim and I the photograph for the magazine.   _____

Lesson 25

Other Pronouns

When you write sentences using personal pronouns, the pronouns usually refer to specific persons or things. In the following example the pronoun *he* refers to *Brian*, a specific person, and the pronoun *it* refers to *his car*, a specific thing:

Brian took his car in for repair. He knew it was not running properly.

However, it is not always possible to name specific persons or things. When you want to refer to people or things in a general way, you can use indefinite pronouns like *someone, each, many,* and *few* to take the place of nouns you cannot or do not name.

You will learn about this group of indefinite pronouns in this lesson. In addition, you will study two other kinds of pronouns, demonstrative and interrogative pronouns.

INDEFINITE PRONOUNS

Indefinite pronouns, as their name suggests, refer to general groups of people or things rather than to specific persons or things. They are all third person. They function in all noun positions, and a few of them can be made possessive by adding -'s. The following words may function as indefinite pronouns.

1. The following indefinite pronouns are always singular:

another	everybody	no one
anybody	everyone	nothing
anyone	everything	one
anything	much	somebody
each	neither	someone
either	nobody	something

NS Adj————— Vt   Ndo   Adv—————
One of my friends reads a newsmagazine every week.

NS Vi   Adv Vi   Pr   Nop   Adj—————
She does not agree with **everything** in the magazine.

Adj   NS   LV Adj-c
Everyone's opinion is different.

2. The following indefinite pronouns are always plural:

both	few	many	several

NS   Vt Adj Ndo   C Adj   Ndo   NS   Adv Vt Ndo
Many want easy answers and objective reporting. Newsmagazines rarely give **both.**

3. The remaining indefinite pronouns may be either singular or plural:

all   any   enough   none   some

For example, *enough* in the first example on the left is singular because *of the reporting* which follows it contains the singular noun *reporting*. *Enough* is considered plural in the example on the right because *reporters* is plural:

SINGULAR
Enough of the reporting *makes* sense.

Any of the information *is* well written.

PLURAL
Enough of the reporters carefully *research* their articles.

Any of the magazines *are* available.

Some of these words may function as indefinite pronouns in some sentences, and they may function as determiners in others. Compare the following pairs of sentences:

DETERMINER

Adj NS   LV   Adj-c
All sugar tastes sweet.

PRONOUN

NS Vt   Ndo Adj————— ‚Adv—————
He used all of the sugar for the cake.

Adj NS   Vt   Adj Ndo
Both women tasted the candy.

NS Vt   Ndo
Both liked it.

NS Vt   Adj Ndo Adj_____
Max chose **one** kind of car.

NS Vt   Adj Adv Adj   Ndo
He chose the most expensive **one**.

EXERCISE 25A

Underline the indefinite pronouns in the following sentences. Determine whether they are singular or plural. Sometimes examining the verb and the possessive (if there is one) in the sentence or substituting *he* or *they* gives a clue. Then write S (singular) or P (plural) in the blank at the right.

1. Each one has chosen a partner.   _____

2. Few take the time to write letters.   _____

3. Several have given their help eagerly.   _____

4. Anything satisfies the elderly man.   _____

5. Lynn will tell both of them the good news.   _____

6. Joe talks to anybody on the street.   _____

7. Neither is really capable.   _____

8. Sarah selected some of the books.   _____

9. All of Jonathan's money is gone.   _____

Write sentences using the following words as pronouns. Label the parts of the sentence.

1. anyone

2. something

3. both

4. all

5. one

Show these sentences to your instructor or tutor.

DEMONSTRATIVE PRONOUNS

The demonstrative pronouns are four words, two singular and two plural, which refer to specific persons or things:

SINGULAR	PLURAL
this	these
that	those

The demonstrative pronouns may replace nouns in some sentences, and they may function as determiners in other sentences. If they are pointing to a noun, they are functioning as determiners. If they are replacing nouns, they are functioning as nouns. Compare the following sentences:

DETERMINER

Adj   NS   Vi————— Adv——
Those draperies will hang in the
————
house.

Adj   NS   Adj————— LV Adv Adj-c
That kind of candy is too sweet.

NS   Vt   Adj   Nio
Cathy gives **these** children

Ndo————
ice cream.

PRONOUN

NS   Vi——————— Adv—————
These will hang in the office.
(*these* draperies)

NS   Vt   Ndo
I   prefer **this**.   (*this* kind)

NS   Vt   Ndo   Pr   Nop
She plays games with **those**.
(*those* children)

To refer to singular nouns use *this* or *that*. Use *these* or *those* to refer to plural nouns.

INTERROGATIVE PRONOUNS

The interrogative pronouns *who, which,* and *what* allow us to ask questions about persons or things we cannot name. *Which* and *what* are easy to use because their forms remain the same for subject or object:

Ndo   Vt NS   Vt
What can they do?

Ndo   Vt NS   Vt
Which will they choose?

NS   LV Adj   Nsc
What is their decision?

NS   LV Nsc
Which is it?

Only *who* has different forms for subjective, objective, and possessive functions:

NS   LV Adj Nsc
SUBJECT: **Who** is the winner?

Ndo   Vt Adj NS   Vt
OBJECT: **Whom** did the people elect?

NS   LV Adj Adj   Nsc
POSSESSIVE: **Whose** is the successful party?

If you are not sure whether to use *who* or *whom,* substitute *he, she,* or *they* for *who* and *him, her,* or *them* for *whom:*

NS   NS
Who won the election? (Did **he** win the election?)

    Nop
To **whom** did the people give their support? (Did the people give their support

    Nop
to **her?**)

The words *which, what,* and *whose* may also be used as determiners to ask questions:

Adj   Ndo   Vt NS————— Vt
Which election did Tina Harms win?

Adj   NS   Vt   Nio Adj Adj
What group gave her the most
Ndo
support?

Ndo   Vt NS————— Vt
Which did Tina Harms win?

NS   Vt   Nio Adj Adj   Ndo
What gave her the most support?

EXERCISE 25C

Write questions using the following words as interrogative pronouns or adjectives. Label all parts of the sentence.

1. who

2. what

3. whom

Show these sentences to your instructor or tutor.

Lesson 26

Pronoun Reference and Agreement

When you speak or write about someone or something, you usually name the person or thing first by using nouns. Then if you want to speak or write about the person or thing again, you usually use third-person personal pronouns to refer to the nouns plus their determiners and modifiers. In the following example, *he* refers to *Tom,* and *it* refers to *a new rifle:*

> NS   Ndo   NS   Ndo
> **Tom** owns **a new rifle. He** shoots **it.**

In this way you avoid repeating the same nouns over and over again:

> NOT: **Tom** owns **a new rifle. Tom** shoots **the new rifle. Tom** cleans **the new rifle.**
>
> BUT: **Tom** owns **a new rifle. He** shoots **it. He** cleans **it.**

You may show that Tom owns the rifle by using the possessive *his* before the noun *rifle:*

> **Tom** shoots **his** new rifle.

Because one pronoun, like the words *he* and *it,* can refer to other nouns besides *Tom* and *rifle,* you have to be sure that the pronouns you use refer to particular nouns. When you write about one person, as in the example below, your readers can easily see that *she* refers to *Beth:*

> **Beth** enjoys working in the Book Nook.
> ↑
> **She** is the assistant manager.

Beth is the antecedent of the pronoun *she.* The word *antecedent* means *going before.*
The antecedent is the word or words the pronoun refers to and replaces.

PRONOUN-ANTECEDENT AGREEMENT

When you choose a pronoun or possessive to refer to a noun or pronoun antecedent, the pronoun or possessive must agree with its antecedent in

> number—singular or plural
> person—first, second, or third person
> gender—masculine (he), feminine (she), or neuter (it)

The following list of personal pronouns and their antecedents may look complicated, but it really is not. Only the first two pronouns, *I* and *we,* can be first person, and only the third one, *you,* can be second person. All the remaining nouns, nouns with determiners and modifiers, and pronouns are third person.

ANTECEDENT	PRONOUN	POSSESSIVE	PERSON	NUMBER	GENDER
I	me	my/mine	first	singular	masc. or fem.
we	us	our/ours	first	plural	masc. or fem.
you	you	your/yours	second	sing., pl.	masc. or fem.
Mary	she/her	her/hers	third	singular	feminine
Dan	he/him	his	third	singular	masculine
a child	he/him or she/her	his or her	third	singular	masc. or fem.
the man	he/him	his	third	singular	masculine
his mother	she/her	her/hers	third	singular	feminine
a large dish	it	its	third	singular	neuter
the gray cat	he/him or she/her or it	his/her(s)/its	third	singular	neuter, masc., fem.
idea	it	its	third	singular	neuter
everyone	he/him or she/her	his or her	third	singular	masc. or fem.
contracts	they/them	their/theirs	third	plural	neuter
employees	they/them	their/theirs	third	plural	masc., fem.
many	they/them	their/theirs	third	plural	masc., fem., neuter

Pronouns which replace nouns should always be third person because all nouns, except nouns of direct address (like "**John,** please help Sandy"), are third person. In the first example below, *Sarah* is third person singular feminine. As a result, you cannot use *you* in the second sentence to refer to her. *You* refers to the person spoken to:

NOT: **Sarah** makes **her** clothes. **You** design them **yourself.**

BUT: **Sarah** makes **her** clothes. **She** designs them **herself.**

In the next example *Americans* is third person plural; as a result, you cannot use *we* to refer to Americans unless you use *we* in the first sentence also:

NOT: **Americans** are world travelers. **We** have visited most of the globe.

BUT: **Americans** are world travelers. **They** have visited most of the globe.

OR: **We Americans** are world travelers. **We** have visited most of the globe.

EXERCISE 26A

Given on page 158 is a list of nouns and pronouns that can be antecedents in sentences. In the blanks at the right, write the pronoun or possessive that can refer to the antecedent. Also write the person, number and gender of the antecedent and pronoun.

ANTECEDENT	PERSONAL PRONOUN AND POSSESSIVE	PERSON	NUMBER	GENDER
somebody	he/him/his she/her/hers	third	singular	masc. or fem.
1. collar	_____	_____	_____	_____
2. anyone	_____	_____	_____	_____
3. friends	_____	_____	_____	_____
4. mother	_____	_____	_____	_____
5. both	_____	_____	_____	_____
6. houses	_____	_____	_____	_____
7. Mr. Hunt	_____	_____	_____	_____
8. you	_____	_____	_____	_____
9. I	_____	_____	_____	_____
10. we	_____	_____	_____	_____

Singular Antecedents

The singular pronouns or possessives *he/him/his*, *she/her/hers*, *it/its*, and *this/that* refer to and replace singular noun and pronoun antecedents.

1. Singular noun antecedents:

> **Mike** damaged **his car** yesterday.

> **He** drove **it** into a ditch.

2. Singular indefinite pronoun antecedents—words like *anybody*, *each*, *everyone*, *neither*, *something*:

> **Everyone** wants **his** own paints and brushes.   **Each** of the painters brought **his** ladder.

Notice that when a singular indefinite pronoun is followed by a prepositional phrase containing a plural noun, the pronoun used to refer to the indefinite pronoun is singular.

NOTE: Since *everyone* and *each* are indefinite pronouns, they may refer to either men or women. In recent years some people have suggested using both pronouns—*his or her*—in sentences like the preceding examples to show that women are included in the group:

Everyone wants **his or her** own paints and brushes.

Others believe that repeating the two pronouns in several sentences is unnecessary. One way to avoid the repetition is to use plural nouns and pronouns:

The **painters** want **their** own paints and brushes.

3. Collective nouns as antecedents—words like *committee, group, band, jury, team:*

The **team** won **its** fifth game. The **jury** announced **its** verdict.

A collective noun represents a group. When the group is working as a unit, the noun is considered to be singular. Therefore, a singular pronoun must be used to refer to it. *Team* and *jury* in the examples above are singular because the members of the team and jury are working together.

Plural Antecedents

The plural pronouns or possessives *they/them/their/theirs* and *these/those* refer to and replace plural noun and pronoun antecedents.

1. Plural noun antecedents:

The **students** packed **their backpacks** for the trip.

They hoisted **them** onto their backs.

2. Two or more nouns or pronouns joined by *and:*

Michael and his sister watch **their** weights constantly. **They** eat very little.

3. Plural indefinite pronoun antecedents—words like *both, many, several:*

Many of the employees like **their** jobs. **Several** are unhappy with **their** pay.

4. Collective nouns as antecedents:

The **team** ordered **their** meals before the game.

When members of a group act individually, the collective noun is considered plural, and the pronouns referring to it must be plural. In the example above, each member of the team orders a separate meal.

EXERCISE 26B

In the following sentences, change the nouns to pronouns. Write the pronouns above the nouns.

EXAMPLE:
They   them   it

Virginia and Sam planted seeds in their garden.

1. Virginia and Sam grew many vegetables.

2. Sam liked beets and carrots.

3. Virginia preferred tomatoes.

4. Virginia and Sam prepared a salad for Barry and Jean.

5. Sam brought lettuce, cucumbers, and peppers from the garden.

6. Virginia, Sam, Jean, and Barry ate the salad.

EXERCISE 26C

In the following sentences, underline each pronoun or possessive and its antecedent. Write the antecedent in the first blank and the pronoun or possessive in the second blank. If the pronoun does not agree with the antecedent, write the preferred form of the pronoun in the second blank.

	ANTECEDENT	PRONOUN
EXAMPLE: Jack bought a <u>motorcycle</u>. <u>It</u> cost a thousand dollars.	motorcycle	It
<u>Everyone</u> has <u>their</u> luggage.	Everyone	his/her
1. Each bird has a spot of orange on its throat.	_____	_____
2. Each piece of equipment has their own place in the tool room.	_____	_____
3. Someone stole the yellow sports car. The police found it the next day.	_____	_____
4. Occasionally someone whistles, but I do not look at them.	_____	_____
5. Renee and Bob bought themselves clothes.	_____	_____

6. The team played last Saturday. They won another trophy.

_____   _____

7. Every one of the candidates should send their name to Joe King.

_____   _____

8. Frank had dinner with Sue and Tim Evans. Sue had invited him last week.

_____   _____

9. The children want radios. They will have to earn money first.

_____   _____

10. The mothers of the boys offered her help at the fund raising event.

_____   _____

FAULTY PRONOUN REFERENCE

As long as the personal pronouns you use refer to particular nouns or pronouns, your readers should have no problem understanding what you have written. However, if pronoun reference is unclear, the readers will feel confused. For example, it is difficult to decide when reading the following sentences whether Beth or Florence is lonely at night. The pronoun *she* could refer to either woman:

> After work **Beth** frequently calls **Florence.**
> ?
> **She** feels lonely at night.

To eliminate the confusion, use the name of either woman in place of *she:*

> **Beth** feels lonely at night.   OR: **Florence** feels lonely at night.

If you use pronouns, like *they* or *it* in the following examples, without an antecedent, the meaning will not be clear:

> ?
> ↑
> NOT: **They** wear uniforms in the hospital.
> BUT: **Doctors** and **nurses** wear uniforms in the hospital.

> ?
> ↑
> NOT: **It** was a disaster.
> BUT: **The game** was a disaster.

Using a noun in one sentence and then writing a second sentence with a pronoun that seems to refer to the noun in the preceding sentence is another source of confusion:

> Three **cars** were in the parking lot outside the building.
> NOT: **They** were signing a contract in Mr. Brent's office.
> BUT: The **drivers** were signing a contract in Mr. Brent's office.

The girl had **appendicitis.**
NOT: The doctor removed **it.**
BUT: The doctor removed the **appendix.**

John wants to buy a used sofa.
NOT: He saw **one** in the paper yesterday.
BUT: He saw an **ad** for one in the paper yesterday.

IT, THIS, THAT, WHICH

When you read sentences such as the following, you probably understand generally what the writer is saying:

Susan collected clothing for the refugees. **This** pleased them.
They told other refugees about the collection center. **It** brought many needy people there.

If you think about the first two sentences and ask yourself **what pleased them,** the answer you get is *this,* which refers to the whole idea in the preceding sentence instead of a single noun or pronoun. If you ask what brought needy people there, the answer is *it,* another pronoun that refers to a whole idea. This kind of general reference is acceptable if you use it occasionally in a paper, but if you write several sentences beginning with *this, it, which,* or *that,* your readers will not be able to follow your reasoning because the relationship of ideas will be vague rather than precise.

A satisfactory way to revise the second and fourth sentences in the preceding example is to replace *this* or *it* with a noun that summarizes the meaning of the preceding sentence. For example, you can change the verb *collected* in the first sentence to the noun *collection.* Then use *The collection* or *Susan's collection* in place of *this* in the second sentence:

What pleased them?   **The collection**
                                          Susan's collection
Susan collected clothing for the refugees. **This**   pleased them.

Or you may prefer to use nouns other than *collection* in place of *this.* Here are three more examples:

Susan collected clothing for the refugees. **The donations** pleased them.
                                           Her concern for them pleased them.
                                           Susan's concern for them pleased them.

In the next pair of sentences you cannot change the verb *told* to a noun form that would be entirely satisfactory in the second sentence. The noun form would be *telling.* But keep the idea of telling in mind as you think of other possibilities. You might use *news* or *information.*

They told other refugees about the collection center. **The news (the information)** brought many people there.

Or you might prefer *their extreme need* in place of *it:*

Their extreme need brought many people there.

Sometimes you can change an adjective in the first sentence to a noun for the second sentence, as in the following example:

Her cheerfulness
The nurse always seems cheerful. **This** keeps the patients relaxed.

EXERCISE 26D

Given below are verbs and adjectives you might use in sentences. In the blanks at the right write the noun form of each word. Use your dictionary if you need help.

	VERB OR ADJECTIVE	NOUN
EXAMPLE:	express (V)	expression
	leak (V)	leakage
1.	notify (V)	_____
2.	operate (V)	_____
3.	clerical (Adj)	_____
4.	break (V)	_____
5.	gratify (V)	_____
6.	removable (Adj)	_____
7.	thick (Adj)	_____
8.	valuable (Adj)	_____

EXERCISE 26E

In each of the following sentences pronoun reference is faulty because the pronoun does not have an antecedent. First, underline the pronoun that has no antecedent. Then, rewrite the sentence using a noun in place of the pronoun.

EXAMPLE: Jim drove down the street in his new car. They waved and cheered.
REVISED: **His friends (neighbors, family)** waved and cheered.

EXAMPLE: The restaurant serves excellent food. This pleases the customers.
REVISED: **The wide variety** pleases the customers.

1. The supervisor ended his inspection. They drove him to the airport.

2. Dick had a hard life. That made him unhappy.

3. The potluck supper was finally organized. She bought all the supplies.

4. Harvey was very angry. This bothered Jane.

5. Judy took a shower in the locker room after the game. They stole Judy's watch.

6. Bob studies engineering in order to become one.

7. The old brick house has been empty for a year. They say the house is haunted.

8. Meg is learning to speak French in order to visit it.

9. Barbara and Phil still date. It goes on and on.

10. Tami hates school. This upsets her parents.

EXERCISE 26F

First, write five sentences about one topic. Use personal pronouns to refer to the preceding nouns or pronouns. Next, underline each pronoun. Then, if the pronoun has an antecedent, draw a line from the pronoun to its antecedent.

EXAMPLE: The neighbors brought food to the party.
            They had prepared it for the occasion.
            They also had soft drinks and beer.
            All of the neighbors enjoyed themselves.

1.

2.

3.

4.

5.

Show these sentences to your instructor or tutor.

Lesson 27

Subject-Verb Agreement

When you studied verb tenses in Units Two and Three, you learned that Part 1 (Base) and Part 2 (Verb + *s*) are both used for present tense verbs. Part 1 is used with plural subjects and the pronouns *I* and *you.* Part 2 is used with singular subjects:

	SUBJECT	PREDICATE
Part 1:	I	cheer.
Part 1:	You	cheer.
Part 2:	She	cheers.
Part 2:	The crowd	cheers.
Part 2:	Everyone	cheers.
Part 1:	They	cheer.
Part 1:	The crowds	cheer.
Part 1:	Many	cheer.

In the present perfect tense (Lesson 10), the auxiliary verb *have* (Part 1) or *has* (Part 2) is used with Part 4 (V-ed) of the verb. In the progressive tenses (Lesson 11), the auxiliary verb *is* (Part 2) or *am/are* (Part 1) is used with Part 5 (V-ing) of the verb:

has + Part 4:	The crowd	has left.
have + Part 4:	The crowds	have left.
is + Part 5:	The crowd	is leaving.
are + Part 5:	The crowds	are leaving.

With the other verb tenses you do not have to make such a decision because the verb form is the same for both singular and plural nouns and pronouns:

SUBJECT	PREDICATE
The crowd	had left.
The crowds	had left.

For most writers, the problem is usually not deciding which form of the verb to use but recognizing singular or plural subjects. If you are not sure whether a noun is singular or plural, use *he, she, it,* or *they* in place of the noun:

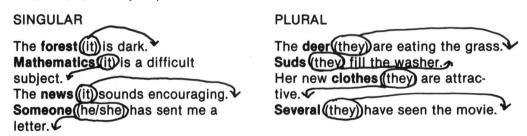

SINGULAR

The **forest** (it) is dark.
Mathematics (it) is a difficult subject.
The **news** (it) sounds encouraging.
Someone (he/she) has sent me a letter.

PLURAL

The **deer** (they) are eating the grass.
Suds (they) fill the washer.
Her new **clothes** (they) are attractive.
Several (they) have seen the movie.

USING SINGULAR AND PLURAL VERBS

When Part 2 of the verb is used with singular subjects and Part 1 of the verb is used with plural subjects, we say that the subject and the verb agree. To help you decide which form of the verb to use, study the following list of singular and plural subjects.

Singular Subjects

1. When the subject is a singular noun or pronoun, the verb is Part 2:

> Mike's **car** *needs* repairs. **It** *is* an old car.

2. When the subject is a singular indefinite pronoun, the verb is Part 2:

> **Neither** of the dancers *is* ready for the contest.
>
> **Each** *is practicing* day and night.

(*Dancers* is not the subject because it is the object of the preposition *of*.)

3. When a singular subject is followed by a phrase beginning with *together with, along with, as well as, besides,* and *in addition to,* the verb is singular:

> The **cat** together with its kittens *is looking* for food.
> The **actor** as well as the director and his assistant *lives* in the trailer.

4. When two or more singular subjects are joined by *or* or *nor,* the subject is singular because each noun is considered separately, and the verb is singular:

> Neither the **sound** nor the **color** *is* good.
> Either the **pump** or the **motor** *is* not *functioning.*

Plural Subjects

1. When the subject is a plural noun or pronoun, the verb is plural Part 1:

> **Horses** *feed* on the range. **They** *are* beautiful animals.

2. When the subject is a plural indefinite pronoun, the verb is Part 1:

> **Many** *ask* favors. **Few** *give* them.

3. When two or more singular nouns are joined by *and,* the verb is Part 1:

> **Soil, water, air,** and **sunshine** *help* plants grow.

Singular or Plural Subjects

1. When a sentence begins with the words *there* or *here,* the verb agrees with the subject which follows:

> There *are* several **snapshots** of Miranda.   (snapshots are . . .)
> Here *is* my favorite **one.**   (one is . . .)

2. The indefinite pronouns *any, all, none,* and *some* may take Part 1 or Part 2 verbs:

    Any of the contestants *are* eligible. **None** *are* winners yet.
    Any of the information *is* correct.   **None** *is* badly written.

3. When two subjects, one singular and one plural, are joined by *either . . . or* or *neither . . . nor,* the verb agrees with the noun nearer to it:

    Neither Mrs. Anderson nor her **sisters** *believe* the strange story.
    Either the sisters or **Mrs. Anderson** *intends* to talk with the neighborhood gossip.

4. When a collective noun representing a group is considered to be acting as a unit, the verb is Part 2. When members of the group are considered to be acting individually, the verb is Part 1:

    The **band** *is practicing* today. The **faculty** *is attending* the rehearsal.
    The **band** *have forgotten* their instruments. The **faculty** *are attending* committee meetings.

5. When the subject appears to be plural but represents a unit, the verb is Part 2. When the subject is plural and does not represent a unit, the verb is Part 1:

    Ham and eggs *is* my favorite breakfast.
    Ham and **eggs** *have* both *gone* up in price.

EXERCISE 27

In the following sentences, underline each simple subject and verb. Write the subject in the first blank and the verb in the second blank. If the verb does not agree with the subject, write the preferred form in the second blank.

	SUBJECT	VERB
1. Each of the boys have his own bicycle.	_____	_____
2. You and Meg are my friends.	_____	_____
3. Bill or John is coming to sell tickets.	_____	_____
4. The group of students intend to travel by bus.	_____	_____
5. None of my friends have read the book.	_____	_____
6. Peggy and Anne conduct craft classes.	_____	_____
7. Neither the man nor his son has a job.	_____	_____
8. The surgeon as well as the interns attend staff meetings.	_____	_____

9. *The Skyfighters* is a thrilling novel.   _____ _____

10. The team go to their homes after practice.   _____ _____

11. One of the representatives have not registered
    today.   _____ _____

12. Either Janice or her parents drives the car.   _____ _____

13. Ten dollars seem like a high price to pay.   _____ _____

14. Mathematics is a difficult subject for Steve.   _____ _____

15. Where is the treasures from the ocean?   _____ _____

16. The dog in addition to the cats make noise all
    night.   _____ _____

17. Here is Dick, Bob, and Barb.   _____ _____

18. Nobody likes to be the last one in line.   _____ _____

19. The rooms of the house needs painting.   _____ _____

20. Any of these students are ready for work.   _____ _____

Unit Six Review

Practice Test

SCORE PART I (Total—100 points) _____
SCORE PART II* (Total—100 points) _____
TOTAL _____
AVERAGE _____

*Average scores for Part I and Part II only if the Part I score is 85 percent or more.

PART I

A. Given below is a list of nouns and pronouns that can be antecedents (words to which pronouns refer). In the blanks at the right, write the pronouns and possessives that can refer to the antecedent. Also write the person, number, and gender of the antecedents and pronouns.
(20 points—4 points each)   (Lessons 24, 25, 26)   Score _____

	PRONOUNS OR POSSESSIVES	PERSON	NUMBER	GENDER
1. books	_____	_____	_____	_____
2. everyone	_____	_____	_____	_____
3. Nancy and I	_____	_____	_____	_____
4. several	_____	_____	_____	_____
5. employee	_____	_____	_____	_____

B. In the following sentences the forms of the pronouns are not the forms used in Standard English. First, underline the pronoun in each sentence. Then write the preferred form in the blank at the right.
(10 points—2 points each)   (Lesson 24)   Score _____

1. Me and Dana bought a big bag of candy.   _____

2. Mrs. Jenkins gave Bert and I a toaster.   _____

3. No one except Jim and I will help Joyce.   _____

4. Cary hurt hisself opening the tin can. _____

5. Us friends get together every Saturday. _____

C. Underline the indefinite pronouns in each of the following sentences. Determine whether they are singular or plural. Sometimes examining the verb and possessive in the sentence or substituting *he* or *they* gives a clue. Then write S (singular) or P (plural) in the blanks at the right.
(10 points—2 points each)   (Lesson 25)   Score _____

1. Many enjoy swimming in the ocean. _____

2. Everyone knows Stan's address. _____

3. One becomes nervous before a dental appointment. _____

4. Sally spoke to several at the meeting. _____

5. Jim wants all of the money. _____

D. In the following sentences, underline each pronoun or possessive and its antecedent. Write the antecedent in the first blank and one form of the pronoun or possessive in the second blank. If the pronoun or possessive does not agree with the antecedent, write the preferred form in the second blank.
(20 points—4 points each)   (Lesson 26)   Score _____

	ANTECEDENT	PRONOUN OR POSSESSIVE
1. Each guest entered the room, and their name was announced.	_____	_____
2. Neither miner would admit their part in the accident.	_____	_____
3. A carpenter may want to earn more money; they must work longer hours.	_____	_____
4. The child fell and broke his arm.	_____	_____
5. Both Carla and Jane completed their assignments.	_____	_____

E. In each of the following sentences, pronoun reference is faulty because the pronoun does not have an antecedent. Rewrite the sentence, using a noun in place of the pronoun.
(20 points—4 points each)   (Lesson 26)   Score _____

1. Aileen was unhappy all week. This concerned her husband.

2. The new book sold very well the first week, which pleased them.

3. Sandra likes working in the dentist's office. She plans to become one herself.

4. John has been going to college for ten years. It does not end.

5. One artist is outstanding. They all praised her paintings.

F. Underline each subject and verb in the following sentences. Write the subject in the first blank and the verb in the second blank. If the verb does not agree with the subject, write the preferred form in the second blank.
(20 points—4 points each)   (Lesson 27)   Score _____

	SUBJECT	VERB
1. The results is described in the report.	_____	_____
2. The collection of shells need a display case.	_____	_____
3. Here is Warren and Peggy.	_____	_____
4. The family eats dinner at five o'clock.	_____	_____
5. Each of the children want a bike.	_____	_____

PART II

First, write five sentences about one topic. Use personal pronouns to refer to the preceding nouns (antecedents). Next, underline each pronoun. Then, if the pronoun has an antecedent, draw a line from the pronoun to its antecedent. Be sure that subjects and verbs agree.
(100 points—20 points each)   (Lesson 26)   Score _____

1.

2.

3.

4.

5.

Unit Seven

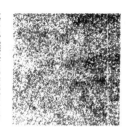

Coordination

As you read a well-written passage, you probably move through it smoothly and easily, aware only of what it is telling you. However, if you examine the way it is written, you can see that some sentences are long, and others are short. The short sentences, you discover, usually contain a single idea. The longer sentences, which frequently contain two or three ideas, are carefully constructed to show how the ideas are related to one another. The result is that readers experience little or no difficulty in understanding what the writer has said.

Experienced writers usually can produce long sentences with several related ideas because they have thought about their topic in detail, and they get daily practice writing. They know that they probably will not be satisfied with what they have written the first time. An important part of their writing is rewriting sentences of paragraphs two, three, or more times until they feel that what they have written is clear and understandable.

To develop the ability to produce mature sentences with ideas carefully related to one another, you will study coordination, the joining of two or three ideas of equal importance, in this unit. In the two units that follow, you will study subordination, emphasizing one idea and relating others to it.

Lesson 28

Compound Sentences

The sentences you have studied in the first six units of this book have all been **simple sentences,** consisting of a subject and a predicate:

Subject——————— Predicate————————————————
Natural disasters sometimes strike with little warning.

Subject——————————— Predicate——————————
Flash floods and earthquakes take people by surprise.

In this lesson you will discover that you can combine two or more sentences about closely related ideas into a single sentence called a **compound sentence.** *Compound* means *made up of two or more equal parts.* By combining sentences you can make your writing cohesive (hang together) and help your readers understand your ideas because you have shown how ideas are related to one another. To show the relationships you use suitable connectors, called coordinating conjunctions, with punctuation, or with punctuation alone.

COMBINING SIMPLE SENTENCES

Compound sentences are made up of two or more simple sentences. The ideas in both sentences are emphasized equally. In the following example the two simple sentences on the left give readers two pieces of information that the readers must put together for themselves. The compound sentence on the right, however, contrasts the two ideas for readers with the coordinating conjunction *but:*

SIMPLE SENTENCES	COMPOUND SENTENCES
NS V Earthquakes happen throughout the	NS V Earthquakes happen throughout the
NS V world. People are seldom prepared.	, C NS V world, **but** people are seldom prepared.

Although a compound sentence is made up of two or more simple sentences, the parts of the compound sentence are no longer called simple sentences. Instead they are called **independent clauses.** *An independent clause has a subject and predicate and can stand alone as a sentence:*

Independent clause——————————————————— C   Independent clause——————
Earthquakes happen throughout the world, **but** people are seldom prepared.

COORDINATING CONJUNCTIONS

You have already used *and* as a connector between two or more nouns and verbs, and you know that *and* is called a **coordinating conjunction.** *Coordinating* means *placing at equal levels*, and *conjunction* means *connector.* Coordinating conjunctions may also connect two or more sentences of equal rank.

Other words that may also function as coordinating conjunctions are listed below. After each one you find words such as *addition, contrast, cause,* and *alternation.* These words indicate the relationship that the coordinating conjunctions express when they are used to combine sentences:

CONNECTOR	RELATIONSHIP	EXAMPLE
and	addition	A severe earthquake shook the city, **and** the people fled into the streets.
but, yet	contrast	Many buildings collapsed, **but** not more than one hundred people were injured.
for	cause	Rescuers worked feverishly into the night, **for** they wanted to locate the victims quickly.
or, nor	alternation	In some cases they could not get into the destroyed apartments, **nor** could they lift the huge pieces of walls and floors.

SEMICOLON

In some cases you may choose to use only a semicolon (;) between two independent clauses. The semicolon acts as a stop sign; it tells your readers that they have reached the end of one idea and that they will go on to a related idea in the second part of the sentence:

> Scientists sometimes predict earthquakes; they are working to improve their accuracy.

PUNCTUATING COMPOUND SENTENCES

A compound sentence, then, consists of at least two independent clauses joined by a comma and conjunction or by a semicolon. In other words, a compound sentence must have a subject and a verb before the connector and another subject and verb after the connector. The following examples show simple sentences on the left and compound sentences on the right. You will find one of these patterns in the compound sentences: NS V, C NS V or NS V; NS V.

SIMPLE SENTENCES	COMPOUND SENTENCES
NS V Jerry completed his experiment.	NS V , C Jerry completed his experiment, **but**
NS V V He did not write his final report.	NS V V he did not write his final report.
NS V———— Jerry was studying the texture and quality of bread.	NS V———— Jerry was studying the texture and ; NS quality of bread; each recipe
NS V Each recipe contained different amounts of the same ingredients.	V contained different amounts of the same ingredients.
NS V He baked the breads.	NS V , C NS He baked the breads, **and** then he
NS V Then he examined slices from each loaf.	V examined slices from each loaf.

If a compound sentence contains three or more independent clauses, you may separate them with commas and use **and** before the last clause. The pattern is NS V, NS V, C NS V:

     NS   V   , NS   V
Jerry's friends tasted the different kinds of bread, they answered questions

               , C   NS   V
about each sample, **and** they indicated the best loaf.

However, you may separate the independent clauses with semicolons if *and* does not appear before the last clause:

> Jerry's friends tasted the different kinds of bread; they answered questions about each sample; they indicated the best loaf.

EXERCISE 28A

Combine each of the following pairs of sentences into one compound sentence. Write NS above each subject and V above each verb. Use either a comma and a coordinating conjunction or a semicolon between the two independent clauses. In the first three sets of sentences below, the punctuation and connector to be used are given. Choose your own punctuation and connector, or use punctuation alone, for the remaining sentences.

1.   Many Eskimos in the Arctic are changing their ways of living. /,/
    /but/ Some still like the old ways.

2. In some places Eskimos now live in houses along paved roads. /,/
    /**and**/ They wear cotton and woolen clothes.

3. Eskimo children probably will not build igloos in the future.
    They will not use dog sleds for transportation.

4. Eskimos may no longer carve animals and other figures from walrus tusks.
    The art of woodcarving may also disappear.

5. Eskimos have used the meat and furs of the seal, walrus, and other animals.
    Now they are gradually acquiring the ways of the Western world.

Run-on or Fused Sentences

If you write a compound sentence and use no punctuation or conjunction between the
independent clauses, the result is a **run-on** or **fused sentence.** The correction symbol
used to indicate this problem may be **R** or **Run-on.** As your readers move rapidly
through the sentence, they probably will read the second independent clause as part of
the first one and feel confused. They have to stop, read again, and break the compound
sentence into meaningful parts. To correct the problem, either add a comma and conjunction or a semicolon alone between the two independent clauses:

> NOT: The speakers at the conference gave summaries of their speeches to
>   the chairperson after the meeting he made the summaries available to
>   the public.
>
>   NS   V
> BUT: The speakers at the conference gave summaries of their speeches to
>
>   NS V
>   the chairperson; after the meeting he made the summaries available
>   to the public.

Comma Splice or Comma Fault

If you use only a comma between two independent clauses in a compound sentence,
the result is a **comma fault** or **comma splice.** The correction symbol may be CS or CF.
To eliminate the problem, either add a conjunction after the comma, or use a
semicolon instead of the comma:

> NOT: The chairperson had planned the conference carefully, he had one
>   problem after another.
>
>   NS   V———————   C NS V
> BUT: The chairperson had planned the conference carefully, **but** he had one
>   problem after another.

EXERCISE 28B

The following compound sentences need the punctuation corrected, and they may also need connectors between the independent clauses. Read each sentence. Then in the blank at the right write the correction symbol to indicate the kind of problem. Use *CS* for comma splice and *Run-on* for a run-on sentence. Finally, correct the sentence with a conjunction, with punctuation, or with punctuation and a conjunction.

1. People are collecting heat from the sun they are using the energy in several ways. _____

2. Some people have designed solar ovens, they cook all their meals outdoors. _____

3. Others install solar panels on the roofs of their houses they collect energy for heating their houses and the water in hot water tanks. _____

4. People find the system reliable on sunny days, on cloudy days they may use gas or electricity for heating. _____

EXERCISE 28C

Write sentences according to the directions given after each number. Write NS above each subject and V above each verb.

1. Write a compound sentence with *and* as the connector.

2. Write a compound sentence with *but* as the connector.

3. Write a compound sentence with *or* as the connector.

4. Write a compound sentence with three independent clauses connected by semicolons.

5. Write a compound sentence with three independent clauses connected by commas and a conjunction.

Show these sentences to your instructor or tutor.

Lesson 29

Transitional Expressions

In Lesson 28 you learned to combine two or more sentences with related ideas into a single sentence, called a compound sentence. To show how the ideas are related, you used coordinating conjunctions such as *and* to show addition and *but* to show contrast. You also used a semicolon between the independent clauses in a compound sentence in place of the comma and conjunction:

NS   V   C   NS   V

The television actor met the writer on a flight to Hawaii, and they discussed a

NS   V

script for a new episode in the television series. The writer began working

; NS V

immediately; she produced a completed script a month later.

In this lesson you will learn to show the relationship of ideas between independent clauses by using **transitional expressions** such as *however, moreover,* or *as a result.* You may place a transitional expression, also called a **conjunctive adverb,** at the beginning of the second independent clause or within it. In the following example *however* functions as a transitional expression that contrasts the idea expressed in the second sentence with the idea in the first sentence. The transitional expression is labeled TE:

NS   V

In the past libraries were mainly large collections of books; in more recent

TE   NS   V   V

years, **however,** libraries have also made magazines and pamphlets available.

You may also place the transitional expression within a simple sentence. In the following example *moreover* indicates that a third idea has been connected to the discussion of libraries begun in the sentence above:

NS   TE   V

Many libraries, **moreover,** now make films, slides, audio tapes, and videotapes available to borrowers.

COMPARISON OF COORDINATING CONJUNCTIONS AND TRANSITIONAL EXPRESSIONS

Transitional expressions are similar to coordinating conjunctions because both connect two related ideas. However, they are different in this way: A coordinating conjunction such as *and* or *but* preceded by a comma serves as a connector between two

independent clauses. The connector must always appear at the beginning of the second independent clause. In the following sentence *but* connects the two sentences and shows contrast between the two. *But* cannot appear within the second independent clause:

NOT: Steve rides a motorcycle in races, he does not **but** ride a motorcycle in traffic.

BUT: Steve rides a motorcycle in races, **but** he does not ride a motorcycle in traffic.

In contrast, a transitional expression such as *however* cannot connect two independent clauses in the same way that a coordinating conjunction can. As the word *transitional* indicates, the transitional expression carries one idea across to another. In the following example, *however* can follow the semicolon at the end of the first independent clause, or it can appear within the second independent clause:

Steve rides a motorcycle in races; **however,** he does not ride a motorcycle in traffic.

Steve rides a motorcycle in races; he does not, **however,** ride a motorcycle in traffic.

Or you may prefer to write the two independent clauses as separate sentences with *however* in the second sentence:

Steve rides a motorcycle in races. He does not, **however,** ride a motorcycle in traffic.

Knowing how to use the transitional expressions is especially important to connect ideas in a set of related sentences or to combine a set of sentences. For example, if you want to show result or effect, you state the cause in the first part of your sentence, then connect the explanation of the result by using *as a result* in the second independent clause:

CAUSE: Last January Friedrich did not carry tire chains in his car on his trip from San Francisco to Reno;

RESULT: **as a result,** he could not cross the Sierra Nevada mountains during a snow storm.

You can also use transitional words such as *first, next,* and *finally* or *first, second,* and *third* to show a time order or to show the steps taken. The set of sentences below tell about the changes in a woman's feelings and actions. When these sentences are introduced with *first, next,* and *finally,* they clearly show the order in which the changes took place:

SEPARATE SENTENCES

The woman talked at great length about her family's problems.
She smiled and praised her husband and four children.
She gradually gave details about her husband's and children's faults.
She cried and blamed all of them for her unhappiness.

COMBINED SENTENCES

The woman talked at great length about her family's problems. **First,** she smiled and praised her husband and four children; **next,** she gradually gave details about her husband's and children's faults; **finally,** she cried and blamed all of them for her unhappiness.

To help you understand the relationships that coordinating conjunctions and transitional expressions show, study the following chart carefully and use it to select a transitional expression when you want to relate two or more ideas to one another. In the column on the right you will find subordinating conjunctions, which you will study in Lesson 33.

RELATIONSHIP EXPRESSED	COORDINATING CONJUNCTIONS (C)	TRANSITIONAL EXPRESSIONS (TE)	SUBORDINATING CONJUNCTIONS (SC)
Addition	and	furthermore in addition moreover also again besides too	
Time	and (then)	then first, second, third first, next, finally next later still later finally	when whenever while as before since after as long as until now (that) once as soon as
Cause	for		because since
Result (effect)		consequently as a result thus therefore then hence	
Purpose			so that in order that
Similarity		similarly likewise in the same way also too	as as . . . as
Contrast	but and	on the one hand on the other hand nevertheless however on the contrary instead in comparison	than

Concession	yet but	nevertheless however admittedly to be sure	although though even though while whereas
Manner			as as if as though
Condition			if provided that unless
Alternation	or nor		
Emphasis		indeed in fact certainly to be sure	
Enumeration		first, second, third first, next, finally furthermore	
Summation		finally in summary in conclusion therefore	

PUNCTUATION WITH TRANSITIONAL EXPRESSIONS (TE)

Words identified as transitional expressions (TE) may function in two ways in a sentence—as transitions or as adverbs. The following set of sentences shows both functions and the punctuation used:

> Tony planned to hunt and fish the whole weekend; **however,** he had forgotten shells for the gun and hooks for the fishing line. Tony locked the car; then he walked to the dock. Tony had, **in addition,** no gasoline for the boat. **Finally,** he went home and read a book.

When the transitional expression such as *however* is inserted in a sentence or an independent clause, it is enclosed in commas because it is not a part of the sentence or independent clause. In the following sentence *however* serves as a transition between the two independent clauses. Because *however* follows the semicolon at the end of the first independent clause, no comma is needed before *however*, but a comma should appear after *however*:

> NS   V   TE   NS V————
> Tony planned to hunt and fish the whole weekend; **however,** he had forgotten shells for the gun and hooks for the fishing line.

When *however* appears within the second independent clause, it is enclosed in commas:

> Tony planned to hunt and fish the whole weekend; he had, **however,** forgotten shells for the gun and hooks for the fishing line.

When the transitional expression functions as an adverbial modifier in the sentence, it is not enclosed in commas. Transitional expressions that may function as adverbial modifiers are *still, hence, then, too, certainly, besides, again, later,* and *finally.* In the following sentence *then* functions as an adverbial modifier telling *when* and links the sentence to the one on the preceding page about Tony:

<pre>
NS   V   Adv NS V.
</pre>
Tony locked the car; **then** he walked to the dock.   OR
Tony locked the car; he **then** walked to the dock.

In the single sentence that follows *in addition* is a transitional expression that is enclosed in commas:

<pre>
NS   V   TE
</pre>
Tony had, **in addition,** no gasoline for the boat.

In the first example below, *finally,* which appears at the beginning of the sentence, is followed by a comma because it is not a part of the sentence. In the second and third examples, *finally* functions as an adverbial modifier and is not enclosed in commas. Notice the slight change in meaning:

TE: **Finally,** Tony went home and read a book.
ADV: **Finally** Tony went home and read a book.
ADV: Tony **finally** went home and read a book.

Occasionally you may write a sentence with three independent clauses that needs both a conjunction and a transitional expression. Use the punctuation required with each kind of connector:

Peaches ripened early, but the pickers had not arrived in the area; as a result, fruit began falling to the ground.

STEPS TO FOLLOW IN PUNCTUATING COMPOUND SENTENCES WITH TRANSITIONAL EXPRESSIONS

To keep yourself from becoming confused about punctuating compound sentences, follow these steps:

1. Read the entire sentence, label all the verbs first, then label the subjects. In the following example the sentence contains two subject-verb combinations, indicating that the sentence is compound:

<pre>
NS———— V   NS V
</pre>
The Great Dane jumped over the fence and he ran away.

2. Find the coordinating conjunction, and place a comma before it. In the following sentence *and* is the coordinating conjunction:

<pre>
NS———— V   , and NS V
</pre>
The Great Dane jumped over the fence, **and** he ran away.

If there is no connector, place a semicolon between the two independent clauses:

<pre>
NS   V   V   ; NS   V
</pre>
The owner could not find him; she looked everywhere.

If you find no coordinating conjunction but you find a transitional expression, place a semicolon at the end of the first independent clause. Then place a comma after the transitional expression or enclose it in commas:

```
     NS   V                 TE          NS   V
```
She waited a week; **finally,** the dog returned.

EXERCISE 29A

Label the subjects and verbs in each sentence to decide whether the sentence has one or more independent clauses. Next, write TE above each transitional expression. Use the list on pages 181–82 to help you identify them. Then add appropriate punctuation if it is needed.

1. Tom was poorly prepared for the meeting with the typing pool supervisors as a result they were not impressed with his company's word processor.

2. The office manager nevertheless arranged a second meeting for Tom with the supervisors.

3. The supervisors still wanted no part of Tom's plan or equipment.

4. The supervisors had discussed every aspect however they could see no merit in the plan.

5. Finally the office manager called Tom in for a conference.

6. Tom refused consequently the supervisors cancelled further negotiations.

7. Tom as a result lost the contract.

EXERCISE 29B

Combine each of the following pairs of simple sentences into one compound sentence. Write the combined sentence, using the connector indicated and appropriate punctuation. CC means *coordinating conjunction,* and TE means *transitional expression.* If you need help, refer to the list of connectors on pages 181–82.

EXAMPLE: The science club members planned to spend the weekend at the ocean.   /TE: result/
They had to gather equipment and supplies.

The science club members planned to spend the weekend at the ocean; **consequently,** they had to gather equipment and supplies.

1. The orchestra played several concerts last season. /Punctuation only/
   For the first time in years they made money.

2. Gail plans to attend medical school next fall.   /TE: result/
   She has to work this summer to make money for tuition.

3. Molly and George will give a dinner party.   /Punctuation only/
   Only their best friends will come.

4. Ed traveled two thousand miles on a bus.   /CC: contrast/
   He found the trip too hard to try again.

5. Michael considered taking a postgraduate engineering course.   /TE: contrast/
   It seemed wise to take the position offered him first.

6. Tim likes to walk through the forest.   /CC: contrast/
   He always watches for rattlesnakes.

7. Carol acknowledged Jon as her brother.   /TE: contrast/
   She would not allow him to reveal the fact to anyone.

8. Warren likes to fish, hunt, and hike.   /TE: addition/
   He likes to read novels and science books.

Show these sentences to your instructor or tutor.

EXERCISE 29C

Using the chart of coordinating conjunctions and transitional expressions on pages 181–82, write either a simple or compound sentence as indicated in the parentheses, and choose a transitional expression to express the relationship indicated.

1. (Compound sentence: time)

2. (Compound sentence: result)

3. (Compound sentence: contrast)

4. (Simple sentence: summation)

Show these sentences to your instructor or tutor.

EXERCISE 29D

Write at least five or six sentences about ONE topic. Use transitional expressions between independent clauses and within sentences. See Exercise 29A as an example of the kinds of sentences to write.

1.

2.

3.

4.

5.

Show these sentences to your instructor or tutor.

Lesson 30

Compound Subjects and Compound Predicates

You have been combining two or more simple sentences in Lessons 28 and 29 to make a compound sentence. In this lesson you will learn to combine sentences by deleting (omitting) repeated words or word groups that are not needed. The remaining words will be combined, and you might then have a sentence with a compound subject or a compound predicate or both.

COMPOUND SUBJECTS

A subject made up of two or more nouns joined by *and* is called a **compound subject**. For example, *Mary and the professor* is the compound subject in the first example that follows; *Jeff, Jim, and Susan* is the compound subject in the second example. On the left are simple sentences that have been combined into a single sentence on the right. Lines have been drawn through repeated words that can be deleted. *And* in slash marks at the beginning of the second line is placed before *the professor* to connect it with *Mary* from the first line. The pattern of the combined sentences is NS C NS V:

SIMPLE SUBJECTS	COMPOUND SUBJECT
NS V **Mary** ate lunch on the lawn.	NS C NS V **Mary and the professor** ate lunch on the lawn.
NS /and/ **The professor** ate lunch on the lawn.	

The next sentence with three nouns as the subject is actually made up of the three sentences on the left. The pattern of the combined sentences is NS, NS, C NS V. To keep the subjects from running together, the writer has placed a comma between the first two nouns because *and* does not appear, and a comma and *and* between the second and third nouns in the series. The comma between the slash marks at the end of the first and second sentences indicates that the comma follows *Jeff* in the first sentence and *Jim* in the second sentence. *And* in slash marks at the beginning of the third sentence indicates that *and* precedes *Susan* in the third sentence:

SIMPLE SUBJECTS   COMPOUND SUBJECT

       NS V
       Jeff joined them. /,/

       NS V
       Jim ~~joined them.~~ /,/

       NS V   NS NS C NS   V
/and/ **Susan** ~~joined them.~~   **Jeff, Jim, and Susan** joined them.

COMPOUND PREDICATES

Two or more verbs joined by *and* or *or,* like those in the following sentences on the right, make up a **compound predicate.** A predicate is compound only if it contains two or more verbs joined by *and* or *or.* The pattern for the first example is NS V C V. No comma is used before *and* because you do not want to separate the second verb from its subject:

SIMPLE PREDICATES   COMPOUND PREDICATE

       NS   V
       They **talked** for a short time.

            V   NS   V   C   V
/and/ ~~They~~ **laughed** ~~for a short time.~~   They **talked and laughed** for a short time.

The pattern for the next example is NS V, V, C V. Commas separate the three verbs:

SIMPLE PREDICATES   COMPOUND PREDICATE

       NS   V
       They **planned** a field trip. /,/

                        NS   V   V
                        They **planned** a field trip, **made** a

             V   C   V
      ~~They~~ **made** a list of equip-   list of equipment, **and chose** a date
      ment. /,/   for the trip.

             V
/and/ ~~They~~ **chose** a date
      for the trip.

NOTE: If a sentence has two or more direct objects but only one verb, the predicate is NOT compound. Only the direct object is compound:

```
       NS    V        Ndo
/and/  They selected Thursday for
       for the trip.
```

```
                      Ndo                 NS   Vt       Ndo      C  Ndo
/or/   ~~They selected~~ Friday for the   They selected Thursday or Friday
       ~~trip.~~                          for the trip.
```

COMBINING SEVERAL SENTENCES

You may have more than one compound structure in each sentence. Sometimes both the subject and the verb are compound, or two direct objects, adjectives, or adverbs may be compound. When the sentences on the left below are combined, the resulting simple sentence on the right contains a compound subject, compound predicate, and a compound direct object after *took:*

SINGLE SENTENCES   COMBINED SENTENCE
```
       NS   V
       Jeff arranged the transporta-
       tion.
```

```
       NS
/and/  Susan ~~arranged the transpor-~~
       ~~tation.~~
```

```
/and/  ~~Jeff~~ took reservations.
```

```
                                        NS   C  NS    Vt          Ndo
                                        Jeff and Susan arranged the trans-
```

```
       ~~Susan took reservations.~~
```

```
                                                 C   Vt  Ndo          C
/and/  ~~Jeff took~~ money for the      portation and took reservations and
       tickets.
       ~~Susan took money for the~~     Ndo
       ~~tickets.~~                     money for the tickets.
```

PUNCTUATING COMPOUND STRUCTURES

No comma is used when two words or word groups are joined by *and:*

> Mary and the professor...
> ... talked loudly and laughed frequently...
> ... soft-spoken and considerate...
> ... in the house and under the chair...

Commas are used when three or more words or word groups in a series are joined by *and:*

> Jeff, Jim, and Susan...
> ... clear, clean, and sparkling water...
> ... opened the book, wrote the check, and mailed it.

Combine the following sentences. First, write NS above each subject and V above each verb. Next, draw a line through repeated words you intend to delete. Then write the combined sentence, adding conjunctions and punctuation if needed. Finally, tell what part or parts of the sentence are compound by writing *compound subject, compound predicate, compound direct object, compound adjectives,* or *compound adverbs* in the blank at the right.

EXAMPLE:

          NS   V
The hardware store opened early.

           NS   V
/and/ The repair shop ~~opened early.~~

The hardware store and the repair shop opened early.
          compound subject

NS   V
Customers looked at the garden equipment. /,/

NS   V
~~Customers~~ purchased seeds. /,/

      NS   V
/and/ ~~Customers~~ brought lawn mowers for repair.

Customers looked at garden equipment, purchased seeds, and brought lawn mowers for repair.
        compound predicate

1.   Margery visited the science museum.
/and/ Janet visited the science museum.   _____

2.   Tom visits his family on weekends.
/and/ Tom visits his neighbors on weekends.   _____

3.   Mr. Stevens fired the bookkeeper last week.
/and/ Mr. Stevens hired a new bookkeeper this week.
/and/ Mr. Stevens hired a typist this week.   _____

4. At the picnic the people barbecued hamburgers.
   At the picnic the people toasted marshmallows. _____

5. Dr. Stone flew to New York for a medical conference.
   His partner flew to New York for a medical conference.
   Another doctor flew to New York for a medical conference. _____

6. Neil attends movies.
   Neil attends rock concerts.
   Neil attends motorcycle races.   _____

7. Last Saturday the hardworking gardener pruned the fruit trees.
   Last Saturday the gardener raked the leaves.
   Last Saturday the gardener mowed the lawn.   _____

8. The kindly dentist filled Susan's tooth quickly.
   The careful dentist filled Susan's tooth painlessly.   _____

9. The young pilot flew a twin-engine plane from San
   Francisco to Reno.
   The well-trained pilot returned the same day.   _____

COMPOUND PREDICATE OR COMPOUND SENTENCE?

You should be aware of the difference between compound predicates and compound sentences to help you become confident about using commas. Stated very simply, you place a comma before a coordinating conjunction when the conjunction is followed by another subject and verb (NS V, C NS V). You do not place a comma before a coordinating conjunction when the conjunction is followed by a verb alone (NS V C V). (Remember that you do use a comma before *and* or *or* in a series of three or more items.) If you have any questions about using a comma, write NS above each subject and V above each verb. Then look at the patterns:

COMPOUND PREDICATE

```
    NS        V                    C    V
The technician repaired the television and installed the antenna.
```

COMPOUND SENTENCE

```
    NS        V                    , C   NS V
The technician repaired the television, and he installed the antenna.
```

At times you may wonder whether to write a compound sentence or a simple sentence with a compound predicate when the subject of both simple sentences is the same. If you want to give equal emphasis to the subject in each sentence, then you probably should write a compound sentence:

Thomas Weatherbee has been president of the company for ten years; now he is chairperson of the board.

But if you want to direct your readers' attention to what the subject was doing, then you should probably write a compound predicate:

```
NS C  NS———————  V                    C   V
Joe and Sylvia March bought a new house and moved into it the next week.
```

If the second part contains *not* or *never*, you probably should repeat the subject and write a compound sentence:

NS   C   NS————— V   , C   NS   V   V
Joe and Sylvia March bought a new house, **but** they did not move into it for at least a month.

EXERCISE 30B

Write sentences according to the directions given after each number. Write NS above each subject and V above each verb.

1. Write a simple sentence with two verbs in a compound predicate.

2. Write a simple sentence with two nouns in a compound subject.

3. Write a simple sentence with three verbs in a compound predicate.

4. Write a simple sentence with three nouns in a compound subject.

5. Write a simple sentence with a compound direct object.

Show these sentences to your instructor or tutor.

Lesson 31

Appositives

The **appositive** is a noun that renames another noun in the sentence: subject, direct object, indirect object, subject complement, and object of the preposition. *Appositive* means *placing side by side.* In the following sentence *barber* renames *Mike,* and *Liza* renames *daughter:*

NS   NS (Appos)   Nio   Nio (Appos)

Mike, the **barber,**   gave his daughter **Liza**   a haircut.

A sentence with an appositive actually consists of two sentences. In the following example, you can see that the noun *Don* appears in both sentences on the left. In the second sentence, *Don,* the subject, is renamed by *the carpenter's helper,* the subject complement. To combine the two sentences, follow these steps: Place X before the first sentence to indicate that it is the base sentence. Then draw a line through *Don is* in the second sentence. Finally, combine the sentences by inserting words from the second sentence at the slash mark in the first sentence:

SINGLE SENTENCES

NS   Vi   Adv
X Don / learns quickly. /,/
NS LV Adj Adj   Nsc
~~Don is~~ the carpenter's helper. /,/

NS Vt   Ndo
X Don likes Bud Taylor /. /,/
NS   LV   Nsc
~~Bud Taylor is~~ the carpenter.

NS Vi   Adv———
X They work in Plainfield / . /,/
NS   LV   Nsc
~~Plainfield is~~ a small town.

COMBINED SENTENCES

NS   NS (Appos) Vi
Don, the carpenter's helper, learns
Adv
quickly.

NS Vt   Ndo   Ndo (Appos)
Don likes Bud Taylor, the carpenter.

NS Vi Pr Nop
They work in Plainfield, a small
Nop (Appos)
town.

Sometimes you may have three or four sentences to combine. However, the process is essentially the same.

SINGLE SENTENCES

X New York / attracts visitors from all over the world. /,/
~~It~~ is a cultural center.
/and/ ~~It~~ is headquarters for many international corporations.

COMBINED SENTENCE

New York, a cultural center and headquarters for many international corporations, attracts visitors from all over the world.

PUNCTUATION WITH APPOSITIVES

An appositive that is not necessary to identify the noun it renames is enclosed in commas. The appositive in the example below adds extra information about Ben Caldwell, a particular person:

> COMMAS: Ben Caldwell, the artist, teaches at Gibson Art Institute.

When the appositive is needed to make a general term more specific, the appositive is NOT enclosed in commas. The appositive *Ben Caldwell* in the sentence below tells which artist the sentence is about. The noun *artist* is a general term that needs further identification:

> NO COMMAS: The artist Ben Caldwell teaches at Gibson Art Institute.

Here are two more examples. In the first sentence the title *A Farewell to Arms* is needed to identify which Hemingway novel the sentence is about:

> NO COMMAS: Hemingway's novel *A Farewell to Arms* was made into a motion picture.

In the next sentence the modifiers *first war* identify the novel the sentence is about; therefore, the title *A Farewell to Arms* provides extra information:

> COMMAS: Hemingway's first war novel, *A Farewell to Arms,* was made into a motion picture.

If the title appears first, enclose the additional information in commas:

> COMMAS: *A Farewell to Arms,* Hemingway's first war novel, was made into a motion picture.

If the appositive consists of three or more nouns, it often has commas within it. Instead of using commas before and after the appositive, use dashes (—) to help readers see the appositive more easily:

> DASHES: Spring flowers—daffodils, tulips, and primroses—filled the garden with color.

If the appositive appears at the end of the sentence, use only the comma or dash before it and the period at the end of the sentence.

> Mike enjoys his new car, a Corvette.
> In recent years he has owned several cars—a Dodge, an Austin-Healey, and a Firebird.

EXERCISE 31A

Combine each of the following sets of sentences into one sentence. First draw a line through the words to be deleted. Next, place the remaining words in the base sentence. Then, write the combined sentence, adding punctuation only if the appositive adds extra information.

EXAMPLE: X   Otto / does tricks. /,/   X   The dog / does tricks.
               ~~Otto is~~ a dog. /,/   ~~The dog is~~ Otto.
               Otto, a dog, does tricks.   The dog Otto does tricks.

1. Mrs. Martin gives piano and organ lessons.
   She is our next-door neighbor.

2. The athletes gathered for the national competitions.
   The athletes are tennis players, golfers, and swimmers.

3. The actor has appeared in one hundred motion pictures.
   The actor is Bruce Manning.

4. Deep in the mountain is a huge cave.
   It is a hiding place for rustlers.

5. The *Concorde* flew for an hour above a raging storm.
   It is a supersonic jet.

6. The Blakes' house burned down last night.
   It was a Victorian mansion.

7. The names of George Washington and Abraham Lincoln appear in most history
   books.
   George Washington was president of the United States.
   Abraham Lincoln was president of the United States.

8. The knight charged wildly through the castle.
   He was Sir Gawain.

9. The third speaker at the conference outlined ten ways to prevent water pollution.
   She is the State Water Resources representative.

10. The high fence concealed the old house.
    The house was first the residence of a wealthy manufacturer.
    Then it was the hideout for jewel thieves.

Write three sentences with appositives in them. Draw an arrow from the appositive to the noun it renames.

EXAMPLE: Sylvia bought three books, two novels, and a book of poetry.

1.

2.

3.

Show these sentences to your instructor or tutor.

Lesson 32

Sentence Combining Review

Up to this point you have learned to combine sentences in several ways. Here is a brief review. A line has been drawn through the words to be deleted. The remaining words are added to the first sentence in each case.

1. Prepositional phrases:

    X   Students / conduct experiments /.
            ~~The students are~~ in high school.
            ~~The students are~~ in college.
            ~~The experiments are~~ in science labs.

            Students in high school and college conduct experiments in science labs.

2. Adjectives placed before nouns:

    X   / Students sometimes use / chemicals.
            ~~The students are~~ inexperienced.
            ~~The chemicals are~~ harmful. /,/
            ~~The chemicals are~~ dangerous.

            Inexperienced students sometimes use harmful, dangerous chemicals.

3. Compound predicate:

    X   The students might taste / the dangerous chemicals. /,/
            ~~They might~~ touch ~~the dangerous chemicals.~~ /,/
  /or/   ~~They might~~ inhale ~~them.~~

            The students might taste, touch, or inhale the dangerous chemicals.

4. Compound subject:

    X   Arsenic is an example of a dangerous chemical. /,/
            Potassium ~~is an example of a dangerous chemical.~~ /,/
  /and/ Sodium cyanide ~~is another example.~~

            Arsenic, potassium, and sodium cyanide are examples of dangerous chemicals. (Note that the verb must be made plural because the subject is plural.)

5. Compound sentence

> Some science teachers have removed harmful chemicals. /,/
> /and/ Students have been informing other students about the dangers.
>
> Some science teachers have removed harmful chemicals, and students have been informing other students about the dangers.

6. Appositive

> X Schools are providing safety features / for the students. /—/
> One is emergency showers. /,/
> Another is proper ventilation. /,/
> /and/ A third is safety equipment such as eye goggles. /—/
>
> Schools are providing safety features—emergency showers, proper ventilation, and safety equipment such as eye goggles—for the students.

EXERCISE 32

Combine each of the following sets of sentences into one sentence. Write NS above each subject and V above each verb to help you see the patterns of the sentences. Place X before the base sentence. Draw a line through words you intend to delete. Then place the remaining words in the base sentence. Add connectors and punctuation wherever they are needed.

1. Workers can sometimes help companies reduce their payrolls.
   The workers are temporary.
   The companies are large.
   The companies are small.

2. The companies hire the temporary workers for special projects.
   The companies hire workers during peak seasons.
   The companies later dismiss the temporary workers.

3. Temporary workers experience certain disadvantages.
   They lack the security of full-time employment.
   They cannot receive fringe benefits.
   They cannot collect unemployment insurance.

4. Clerical workers make up the largest number of temporary workers.
   Secretaries make up the largest number of temporary workers.

5. Technically skilled personnel are finding increasing opportunities for temporary employment.
   Technically skilled personnel may be data and word processors.
   They may be engineers.
   They may be accountants.
   They may be health care workers.

Unit Seven Review

Practice Test

SCORE PART I (Total—100 points) _____
SCORE PART II* (Total—100 points) _____
TOTAL _____
AVERAGE _____

*Average scores for Part I and Part II only if the Part I score is 85 percent or more.

PART I

A. Match the letter definitions to the numbered terms on the following page. Write the letter of the matching definition in the blank at the right of each term.
(10 points—1 point each)   (Lessons 28–31)   Score _____

a. A meaningful word group without a subject and predicate.

b. A mark of punctuation (;) used alone between two independent clauses.

c. A word group that contains two or more NS-V combinations connected by commas and conjunctions to-gether or by semicolons.

d. A mark of punctuation (.) used at the end of a sentence.

e. A word group that contains NS and V and can stand alone as a sentence.

f. A connector like *and, but,* and *or* used between two words, two phrases, or two clauses.

g. Two or more nouns joined by *and* to form the subject in a sentence.

h. Two or more verbs and their com-plements and modifiers joined by coordinating conjunctions to form the predicate in a sentence.

i. A noun that follows another noun in the sentence and renames it.

j. A single independent clause punc-tuated as a sentence.

k. A connector like *however* preceded by a semicolon and followed by a comma when it joins two indepen-dent clauses.

l. Two independent clauses joined with only a comma.

1. Compound subject	_____	6. Semicolon	_____
2. Appositive	_____	7. Conjunctive adverb	_____
3. Compound sentence	_____	8. Phrase	_____
4. Coordinating conjunction	_____	9. Independent clause	_____
5. Simple sentence	_____	10. Compound predicate	_____

B. Identify the kinds of compound constructions (those made up of two or more parts and joined by a coordinating conjunction) in the following sentences. First, underline the compound construction. Then, write one of the following labels in the blank at the right: *compound subject, compound predicate, compound direct object, compound sentence.*
(20 points—4 points each)   (Lessons 28, 29, 30)   Score _____

1. Paula bought brightly colored napkins and tablecloths for the dinner party.   _____

2. The skiers rode the ski lift to the top of the mountain and enjoyed the spectacular view of the valley. _____

3. Barbara accepted Carol's offer, but Dan refused.   _____

4. The bank and the title company approved the sale
   of the property.   _____

5. The guard stopped the nervous young woman at
   the gate, and later he received praise for his
   action.   _____

C. Add commas (,) and semicolons (;) wherever they are needed in the following sentences. First, write V above each verb and NS above each subject in the sentence to help you find the independent clauses. Then, insert punctuation.
(20 points—2 points each)   (Lessons 28, 29, 30)   Score _____

1. Jerry was the youngest child in a family of ten consequently he never knew

   loneliness.

2. The college president spoke at two colleges attended a convention and talked

   with many outstanding educators.

3. Joan moved back into her parents' house but they wanted her to leave.

4. The radio equipment consisted of an amplifier a tuner and two speakers it was

   installed in the comfortable family room.

5. First the pilot wanted a well-trained crew second he needed a reliable plane third he wanted a safe cargo.

6. Furthermore Martin recognizes the seriousness of the council's decision.

7. The arrangement of furniture was uncomfortable in addition the furniture itself was poorly designed.

8. The contact lens irritated Gary's eye however the doctor was able to adjust it.

9. Barbara has found moreover the solution to the family's financial problems.

10. Spring rains melted much of the snow in the mountains as a result rivers and streams filled to the top of their banks.

D. In the following sets of sentences, you will find two or more nouns naming the same person or object. Combine the sentences by placing the noun (or nouns) and modifiers immediately after the noun it renames. The nouns that follow the first noun become appositives, nouns that rename another noun. Enclose the appositives in commas only if they add extra information.
(15 points—5 points each)   (Lesson 31)   Score _____

1. Sandra Holmes left for Europe today.
   She is the author of children's mystery stories.

2. The boat needs a new sail, a patch, and paint on the hull.
   Its name is *Sea Squirt.*

3. Most people remember the names of at least two former presidents of the United States.
   One is George Washington.
   The other is Abraham Lincoln.

E. Combine each of the following sets of sentences into one sentence. First, write NS above each subject and V above each verb to help you see the patterns of the sentences. Place X before the base sentence. Then draw lines through words to be deleted. Finally, combine the sentences. Add connectors and punctuation wherever they are needed.
(35 points—7 points each)   (Lessons 28–31)   Score _____

1.   X   Passengers visited nine ports in a two-week period / . /;/
                   ~~They were~~ on a cruise.
                   ~~The cruise was~~ in the western Mediterranean.
                   They traveled almost four thousand miles.

2.   X   Two hostesses on the Greek ship planned programs for the
                   passengers. /;/

/in addition,/ They spoke with individual passengers / .
             ~~They spoke~~ in English. /,/
             ~~They spoke~~ in French. /,/
             ~~They spoke~~ in German. /,/
             ~~They spoke~~ in Spanish. /,/
/and/ ~~They spoke~~ in Italian.

3.   One afternoon about a hundred passengers played Bingo.
           The passengers were in the lounge.
           The hostesses gave directions in the five languages.
           The hostesses called numbers in the five languages.

4.   The stewards on the ship spoke Greek.
           The waiters on the ship spoke Greek.
           The stewards spoke several other languages.
           The waiters spoke several other languages.
           They were able to speak to most of the passengers.

5.   Many of the passengers took guided tours.
           The tours were at each of the ports.
           Some of the passengers bought souvenirs.
           Later they returned to their "floating hotel."

PART II

A. Write sentences according to the directions given. Write NS above each subject and
   V above each verb.
   (50 points)   (Lessons 28–32)   Score _____

  1. Write a sentence with a compound direct object. (5 points)

  2. Write a sentence with a compound predicate. (5 points)

  3. Write a compound sentence with a coordinating conjunction such as *and, but, or,*
     or *for.* (5 points)

4. Write a sentence with a transitional expression such as *however, as a result,* or *in addition.*   (5 points)

5. Write a sentence with three independent clauses.   (15 points)

6. Write a sentence with three or four independent clauses. To show the order in which something happened, use *first, second,* and *third* or *first, next,* and *finally.* (15 points)

B. Write five sentences about ONE topic. Make at least three of them compound. Use connectors and punctuation wherever they are needed.
   (50 points)   (Lessons 28–32)

   1.

   2.

   3.

   4.

   5.

Unit Eight

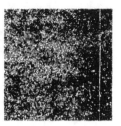

Subordination: Dependent Clauses

You have practiced combining two related ideas by writing a compound sentence, which consists of two independent clauses joined by *and* or other connectors. In the following example the two ideas receive equal emphasis:

> Clara took photographs, **and**
> Sharon developed and printed them.

Now you will learn that you may also combine ideas by emphasizing one idea and relating others to it. The idea to be emphasized appears in an independent clause, and the related, or subordinate, idea appears in a dependent clause:

> DEPENDENT CLAUSE: After Clara took photographs,
> INDEPENDENT CLAUSE: Sharon developed and printed them.

The dependent clause about Clara cannot stand alone as a sentence because it is a fragment, a part of a sentence. It must be connected to the independent clause about Sharon. The whole dependent clause functions as an adverb that tells *when*. Other dependent clauses may function as adjectives or nouns.

In this unit you will learn to write the three kinds of dependent clauses and to use them in **complex** sentences, sentences which consist of at least one independent clause and one or more dependent clauses.

Lesson 33

Adverbial Clauses

As you reread an essay or report you have written, you may feel that your writing style is monotonous because all the sentences follow the same pattern. This monotony may result if you have given equal emphasis to all the ideas you have expressed by writing only simple and compound sentences.

To show a difference in emphasis and to add variety to your writing, you can use another connector, called a **subordinating conjunction** (SC), to introduce some of the ideas. *Subordinating* means *placing at a lower level.* First, decide how the ideas are related to one another just as you did to choose suitable connectors for compound sentences. You might find a time order, a cause and an effect, a comparison, or other relationships. For example, the following set of sentences shows a time order: first, Doan arrived; then the others left:

> NS   V   NS   V
> Doan arrived. The others left.

Next, place X before the base sentence. Then place the subordinating conjunction, such as *when, if,* or *because,* before the other sentence. The sentence then becomes a dependent (subordinate) clause, which must be attached to an independent clause. In the following example, place *when* before *Doan arrived.* The sentence becomes an adverbial clause with a subject and a predicate:

>   NS   V
> **When** Doan arrived, . . .

Finally, combine the sentences. In the following example, sets of simple sentences appear on the left, combined sentences in the middle, and the relationship the subordinating conjunction expresses on the right:

SINGLE SENTENCES		COMBINED SENTENCE	RELATIONSHIP
/when/ X	Doan arrived. /,/ The others left.	**When Doan arrived,** the others left.	Time (When)
X **/because/**	His friends / could not stay. they ~~His friends~~ were busy.	His friends, **because they were busy,** could not stay.	Cause (Why)
X **/as if/**	Doan worked. He could go on forever.	Doan worked **as if he could go on forever.**	Manner (How)

X	He continued.	He continued **where the**	Place (Where)
/where/	The others had left off.	**others had left off.**	

You can see from the examples above that the dependent clauses function as adverbs in the sentences just like the single words and word groups you studied in Lessons 6, 19, and 20. You learned that single words may be *quickly* (how) and *now* (when), word groups may be *next door* (where) and *every day* (when), and prepositional phrases may be *under the table* (where), *because of his weight* (why), and *in the morning* (when). Dependent clauses that function in similar fashion are, therefore, called *adverbial clauses*.

Before you combine sets of sentences with subordinating conjunctions, you should study these connectors and the relationships they express. If you do not recognize the relationship of ideas and use the wrong connector, you might write a sentence that makes no sense, such as the following example:

NOT: **Although** the ancient ruins are ready to collapse, people must stay away.

If you write a sentence such as the one above, you can examine it by breaking it into two basic sentences:

The ancient ruins are ready to collapse.
People must stay away.

Next, examine the relationship of ideas. The first sentence about the ancient ruins tells why people must stay away; the first sentence expresses a cause, and the second sentence is a result. Therefore, you cannot use *although* to introduce the first idea. You must use *because* to show the reason why people must stay away:

SINGLE SENTENCES		COMBINED SENTENCE
/because/	The ancient ruins are ready to collapse. /,/	Because the ancient ruins are ready to collapse, people must stay away.
X	People must stay away.	

SUBORDINATING CONJUNCTIONS

The following words can function as subordinating conjunctions to introduce adverbial clauses. They are grouped according to the relationship they expressed. Notice that these relationships are some of the same that you can express with coordinating conjunctions and the transitional expressions given on pages 181–82.

RELATIONSHIP	SUBORDINATING CONJUNCTIONS (SC)	EXAMPLES
Time (when)	*after, as, before, now (that), once, since, till, until, when, whenever, while, as long as, as soon as*	**Before the students visited the art museum,** they studied the paintings of several artists.
Place (where)	*where, wherever*	Sandy went **where she could study quietly.**
Reason, cause, (why)	*because, since*	Homeowners are insulating their homes **because the charges for gas, oil, and electricity are sky-rocketing.**
Purpose (why)	*so that, in order that*	Dennis swam several hours daily **so that he could enter the state competition.**
Manner (how)	*as, as if, as though*	Maria looks **as if she has recovered completely from the surgery.**
Similarity	*as, as . . . as*	Tod is definitely **as** handsome **as his father (is).**
Contrast	*than*	No one is happier about winning **than Tina (is).**
Condition	*if, provided that, unless*	**If** (on condition that) **the athlete trains himself thoroughly,** he will qualify for the race.

The clause expressing condition indicates that something happening in the independent clause may be somewhat controlled by something expressed in the dependent clause. In the preceding example, whether or not the athlete qualifies for the race depends on whether or not he trains himself thoroughly.

A clause expressing condition may also suggest the conditions under which something may result:

> **If the athlete would train himself thoroughly,** he would (OR might) qualify for the race.

Concession	*although, though, unless, provided (that), providing (that)*	**Although the athlete trained himself thoroughly,** he will not win the race.

A clause expressing concession admits something that contrasts with or opposes the idea expressed in the independent clause. In the preceding example, the clause expressing concession shows that the athlete may have trained himself thoroughly, but the training alone will not guarantee that he will win the race.

ADVERBIAL CLAUSE OR PREPOSITIONAL PHRASE?

Included in the list of subordinating conjunctions are the words *as, before, after, since,* and *until,* which, you may recall, also appear in the list of prepositions on page 109. To decide whether these words are functioning as subordinating conjunctions (SC) or prepositions, label the sentence parts. If a subject and verb appear after any of these words, the word group is a dependent clause. If only a noun appears, the word group is a prepositional phrase:

```
                                    SC   NS  V       Adv
CLAUSE:   Bret has not been happy since he returned home.

                                    Pr       Nop
PHRASE:   Bret has not been happy since his accident.
```

Underline the adverbial clauses in the following sentences. Tell what relationship each adverbial clause has to the independent clause by writing one of the following in the blanks at the right: *time, place, cause, purpose, manner, condition, concession.*

1. If the injured child agrees to cooperate, I will help him.   _____

2. After their truck had a flat tire, the hijackers abandoned their loot.   _____

3. The old man yelled and cheered as if he had won the race.   _____

4. The helicopter frightened the horses because it landed on the racetrack.   _____

5. If the store would hire a detective, it would save money in the long run.   _____

6. Although the suit was expensive, it did not fit well.   _____

7. The volunteers worked where they had light and fresh air.   _____

8. Jerry, even though he had trained carefully, did not win the race.   _____

9. The young executive took the reading class so that he could improve his comprehension.   _____

10. Her dark brown eyes opened wide while she watched the horror movie.   _____

PUNCTUATION WITH ADVERBIAL CLAUSES

An adverbial clause *at the beginning* of the sentence is followed by a comma:

When you talk with Michael, you should explain his responsibilities.

An adverbial clause *within the independent clause* is enclosed in commas:

Michael, **though he is a good worker,** sometimes does not pay attention to detail.

An adverbial clause *at the end* of the sentence usually is not preceded by a comma:

He rushes through each step **because he wants to get to the next one.**

Underline each adverbial clause in the following sentences. Then add punctuation only if it is necessary.

1. The Wilsons after they had traveled all night found no place to stay.

2. Although Peter was engaged to Nan he really loved her sister.

3. The free-form statue in the park arouses a lot of comment because each person sees it differently.

4. While the young woman was waiting for the test results she paced back and forth nervously.

5. The window because it had a crack in it leaked cold air.

6. As soon as Celia saves enough money she will buy a new car.

7. The toolbox stayed where the carpenter had placed it two years before.

8. After Jed Walker retired the town's one taxi gave service only in the daytime.

9. If the accountant goes to the office early she avoids the rush-hour traffic.

COMBINING SENTENCES

At the beginning of this lesson you learned how sentences can be combined by using subordinating conjunctions as introductory words. After you decide how the ideas are related to one another, you choose a suitable subordinating conjunction to make one of the sentences a dependent clause. Then you attach the dependent clause to the independent clause. Here is further discussion about this process.

The following sentences tell about the things Kathy and Tim did:

```
                     NS    C    NS   V
SENTENCE:    Kathy and Tim spent less money for gasoline.

                     NS    V————
SENTENCE:    They had bought a small car.
```

If you want to show that one event happened before the other, you can combine the two sentences by placing the word *after* before the second sentence. The second sentence then becomes a dependent clause that functions as an adverb because it tells *when:*

```
                                NS    C    NS   V
INDEPENDENT CLAUSE:    Kathy and Tim spent less money for gasoline
                                SC   NS    V————
ADVERBIAL CLAUSE:      after they had bought a small car.
```

You may place the dependent clause first if you wish:

```
ADVERBIAL CLAUSE:      After Kathy and Tim had bought a small car,
INDEPENDENT CLAUSE:    they spent less money for gasoline.
```

If you change the introductory word to *because,* the adverbial clause tells *why:*

> INDEPENDENT CLAUSE: Kathy and Tim spent less money for gasoline
> ADVERBIAL CLAUSE: **because they had bought a small car.**

In the next example the two sentences tell about two things happening:

> The bank closed.
> The tellers counted their money.

However, readers cannot tell the exact relationship of the sentences unless the writer indicates when the counting took place. Subordinating conjunctions like *although* and *if* are not suitable, but *after, before, when,* and *as soon as* are because they indicate time (when):

> NOT: **If** the bank closed,
> the tellers counted their money.
> BUT: **After** the bank closed,
> the tellers counted their money.
> OR: **Before** the bank closed,
> the tellers counted their money.

The next example consists of three sentences in the set. The first sentence explains that the pears are ripe. Usually the owner picks ripe fruit before it spoils. However, the second sentence says the ranch owner will not harvest the pears. As a result, the idea in the second sentence is in contrast with the idea in the first sentence. The third sentence then explains why the ranch owner will not harvest the pears. To help readers understand this relationship quickly, you select *although* to show contrast between the first two sentences and *because* to explain the reason why harvesting will not take place:

SINGLE SENTENCES		COMBINED SENTENCE
/although/	The pears are ripe. /,/	**Although the pears are ripe,** the
X	The ranch owner will not harvest the pears.	ranch owner will not harvest them **because he has not hired the**
/because/	He has not hired the pickers.	pickers.

Essentially the same set of sentences with *not* deleted in the third sentence can be combined by using *until* before the third sentence to tell when:

/although/	The pears are ripe. /,/	**Although the pears are ripe,** the
X	The ranch owner will not harvest the pears.	ranch owner will not harvest them **until he has hired the pickers.**
/until/	He has hired the pickers.	

The same set of sentences with *not* deleted from the second sentence can be combined to show a time sequence:

/when/	The pears are ripe. /,/	**When the pears are ripe,** the ranch
X	The ranch owner will harvest the pears.	owner will harvest them **after he has hired the pickers.**
/after/	He has hired the pickers.	

EXERCISE 33C

Combine the following sets of sentences by making one an independent clause and the others adverbial clauses or by deleting repeated words and combining the remaining words with a clause. First, place X before the sentence that will become the independent clause. Then select the subordinating conjunction you intend to use before the remaining sentence(s). Draw a line through repeated words. Finally, write the combined sentence.

1. /when/   Tom was sixteen.   /,/
   X   He decided to study medicine.
   /because/   He wanted to help people.

2. /after/   He graduated from high school.   /,/
   X   He attended a four-year college.

3.   He studied hard the whole time.
   He took biology courses.
   He took chemistry courses.
   He took physics courses.
   He took required courses.

4.   In addition, he worked as an orderly in a small hospital.
   He wanted to get some practical experience.
   He wanted to earn money.

5.   Tom had sent applications to several medical schools.
   He waited for mail each day.

6.   He faced disappointment several times.
   The medical schools could not accept him.

7.   He became discouraged.
   He did not give up hope.

8.   He finally received a letter of acceptance.
He packed his belongings.
He moved to a large city.
He found an apartment.

9.   Medical school classes began.
He studied harder than ever before.

10.   He graduated from medical school.
He spent a year as an intern.
He spent four years as a resident in radiology.

EXERCISE 33D

Write five sentences with adverbial clauses. Use the subordinating conjunction following each number to introduce the adverbial clause. Write NS above each subject and V above each verb in your sentences to be sure you have written clauses and not phrases.

1. *(because)*

2. *(when)*

3. *(although)*

4. *(if)*

5. *(before)*

Show these sentences to your instructor or tutor.

Lesson 34

Adjective Clauses

Adjectives may be single words or word groups that modify nouns and pronouns and tell *which one* (Lessons 18 and 20). In the sentence "The sculptor gave the library a marble statue," the adjective *marble* describes the statue. You may also tell what the statue is made of by writing "a statue of marble." In this second example, the prepositional phrase *of marble* functions as an adjective to describe *statue.* A third kind of adjective modifier, the adjective clause, may be used to describe statue:

The sculptor gave the library a statue **that he had carved in marble.**

The adjective clause, like the adverbial clause you studied in Lesson 33, is a dependent clause with a subject and a predicate. However, it is different from the adverbial clause because it is formed differently and its relationship to the independent clause is different.

To write a sentence with an adjective clause, begin with two sentences that contain the same noun, or a noun and a pronoun that refers to the noun. In the following example *book* appears in both sentences:

Cindy read a **book.**
Her roommate recommended the **book.**

To avoid repeating *book,* change *book* in the second sentence to the relative pronoun *that,* and place *that* at the beginning of the second sentence, which then becomes a dependent adjective clause. Next, place the adjective clause immediately after *book* in the first sentence. The adjective clause functions as an adjective modifier that tells *which book:*

SINGLE SENTENCES		COMBINED SENTENCE
X	Cindy read a **book.**	Cindy read a book **that her room-**
/that/	Her roommate recommended that	**mate recommended.** (Which book?)
	~~the book.~~	

RELATIVE PRONOUNS

The following words can function as relative pronouns to introduce adjective clauses:

1. The relative pronoun *who* refers to people. It has three forms: *who,* used as a subject; *whom,* used as an object; and *whose,* used as an adjective within the clause. The following examples show the two simple sentences with a noun repeated, or a noun and a pronoun referring to it, and the combined sentence:

SINGLE SENTENCES		COMBINED SENTENCE

X	Gary took a rafting trip in Colorado. /,/	NS NS Vi Adv———— **Gary, who works in the library,**
	who	
/who/	~~Gary~~ works in the library. /,/	Vt Ndo Adv———— took a rafting trip in Colorado.

X	He went with some friends.	NS Vi Adv———— He went with some friends
	whom	
/whom/	He had known ~~them~~ for several years.	Ndo NS Vt——— Adv———— **whom he had known for several** ——— **years.**

X	Gary's sister was expecting them on Sunday. /,/	Adj NS Adj NS LV Adj **Gary's sister, whose home is a tiny**
	whose	
/whose/	~~Her~~ home is a tiny cottage. /,/	Nsc Vt———— Ndo Adv **cottage,** was expecting them on ——— Sunday.

2. The relative pronoun *which* refers to animals and objects:

X	Their camping gear / filled the car. /,/	NS Ndo NS Vt Their camping gear, **which they had**
	which	
/which/	They had bought ~~the camping gear~~ before the trip. /,/	Vt Adv———— **bought before the trip,** filled the Ndo car.

3. The relative pronoun *that* may refer to people, animals, objects, and ideas:

X	They left on a day.	NS Vi Adv——— NS LV Adj-c They left on a day **that was sunny**
	that	
/that/	~~The day~~ was sunny and warm.	C Adj-c **and warm.**

Sometimes the word *that* is not stated, but the relationship of the two parts stays the same:

Gary and his friends were excited about the trip **(that) they had planned for weeks.**

EXERCISE 34A

Underline the adjective clause in the following sentences. Write the noun or pronoun that *who, which,* or *that* refers to in the blanks at the right. Identify the adjective clause by locating *who, which,* or *that.* Remember that *that* might be understood in some sentences. Begin by writing V above each verb and NS above each subject.

```
            NS   NS   V   V
EXAMPLE:   The boxer who won received a prize.                        boxer
```

1. The radio that he bought two months ago will not operate.   _____

2. The child who was lost in the department store cried
   hysterically.   _____

3. He waited for the letter that would bring the contract.   _____

4. He directed his attack against those people whom he
   despised.   _____

5. The puppy Sue showed at school was her birthday present.   _____

6. The office manager ordered new furniture, which arrived
   after a long delay.   _____

7. The unusual jewel collection intrigued those who viewed it. _____

8. The young man whose fiancée cried at their engagement
   party became worried.   _____

ADVERBIAL OR ADJECTIVE CLAUSE?

The only similarities between adverbial and adjective clauses is that they are both
modifiers and they are added to sentences. Otherwise, they each have distinct
characteristics:

ADVERBIAL CLAUSE

1. Tells *when, where, why, how:*

   A flight attendant on a passenger
   jet demonstrates the use of the
   oxygen mask **before the plane
   takes off.**

2. Begins with a subordinating
   conjunction, such as *because, as,
   if, when, before, until, although,*
   and others, but it does not function within the dependent clause:

   ```
       SC        NS    V
   . . . before the plane takes off.
   ```

ADJECTIVE CLAUSE

Tells *which one* or gives extra information about a noun or pronoun:

The flight attendant **who demonstrates the oxygen mask** is calm
and efficient.

The oxygen mask, **which all com-
mercial airplanes must have,** drops
automatically during loss of cabin
pressure.

Begins with a relative pronoun
(who, which, that) that functions as
subject, direct object, object of the
preposition, or adjective within the
dependent clause:

```
         NS   V
. . . who demonstrates the oxygen
mask . . .
     Ndo                      NS
. . . which all commercial airplanes
V————
must have . . .
```

Underline the adjective or adverbial clause in each of the following sentences. Then write Adj or Adv in the blanks at the right.

EXAMPLE: <u>Although</u> <u>some</u> <u>people</u> <u>have</u> <u>a</u> <u>dog</u> or <u>cat</u> <u>as</u> <u>a</u> <u>family</u> <u>pet,</u> many prefer birds.   _____Adv_____

Birds, <u>which</u> <u>can</u> <u>stay</u> <u>in</u> <u>the</u> <u>house</u> or <u>apartment,</u> provide companionship.   _____Adj_____

1. Among the several kinds of birds that pet owners choose are canaries, parrots, and mynahs. _____

2. Although finches are about the same size as canaries, they need roomy cages. _____

3. One kind of bird that many people enjoy is the parakeet. _____

4. Parakeets, which are very affectionate, can develop extensive vocabularies. _____

5. Medium-sized parrots, which sometimes live twenty years, can be noisy and aggressive at first. _____

6. Some of the larger birds, such as macaws and cockatoos, are not good pets because they require a lot of attention. _____

7. Although most birds eat seeds, mynahs prefer meat, insects, fruit, and even dog food. _____

8. If owners let their birds exercise by flying about a room, the owners must be sure doors and windows are closed. _____

9. Most birds return to their cages themselves when they need food and rest. _____

PUNCTUATION WITH ADJECTIVE CLAUSES

NO COMMAS are used when the adjective clause is necessary to make a general term specific. In the following examples the adjective clauses tell *which bridge* and *which applicant:*

> The bridge **that crosses the river at Goldsport** collapsed suddenly for no apparent reason.
> The personnel manager hired the applicant **who had the best qualifications for the job.**

If you read the sentences without the adjective clauses, they are vague:

> The bridge collapsed for no apparent reason.   (Which bridge?)
> The manager hired the applicant.   (Which applicant?)

COMMAS ENCLOSE an adjective clause that gives additional information about a specific noun or pronoun it modifies. In the following sentence a particular bridge is named; therefore, the adjective clause gives additional information. Commas must be placed BEFORE and AFTER it:

> Mayer's Bridge, **which crosses the river at Goldsport,** collapsed suddenly for no apparent reason.

The adjective clause in the next sentence gives additional information about Rex Watson. Because the clause appears at the end of the sentence, only the comma before it is needed:

> The personnel manager hired Rex Watson, **who had the best qualifications for the job.**

An adjective clause may give extra information about a general term that has already been identified in a preceding sentence. In the following example, readers will know that *the bridge* in the second sentence refers to *Mayer's Bridge* in the first sentence:

> Mayer's Bridge, **which crosses the river at Goldsport,** collapsed suddenly for no apparent reason. Engineers have regularly checked **the bridge, which has carried heavy traffic every day for the last ten years.**

As you try to decide whether to use commas to enclose adjective clauses, you will find that clauses beginning with *that* are needed in the sentences (no commas), and that those beginning with *which* usually give extra information (enclose in commas).

EXERCISE 34C

Some of the adjective clauses in the following sentences are needed to make a general term specific. Others merely give additional information about the noun. Enclose in commas only those modifiers which give additional information.

1. Jeff Brown who owns the big yacht is the new bank president.

2. The dog that has brown spots caught a mouse.

3. Tod bought the car that Mr. Hansen had owned.

4. The teacher read stories that his students had written.

5. Janet Oakes' new play which began last week has received excellent reviews.

6. Warren Hill who owns the bakery is a candidate for city councilman.

7. Bennett Evans listened attentively to the mayor's speech which lasted two hours.

8. Blake who constantly repairs his house fell off the roof last weekend.

COMBINING SENTENCES

As you learned at the beginning of this lesson, you can combine two sentences by making one an adjective clause if both sentences contain the same noun, or a noun and a pronoun referring to it. You combine the sentences by substituting a relative pro-

noun *(who/whom/whose, which, that)* for the repeated noun or the pronoun referring to the noun. In the following example, *calculator* in the first sentence and *it* in the second sentence represent the same object. If you wish to emphasize the idea in the first sentence, that Dennis bought a calculator, the first sentence becomes the independent clause. Place X before it. Draw a line through *it* in the second sentence, and substitute *that* for *it:*

SINGLE SENTENCES	COMBINED SENTENCE
X Dennis bought a **pocket calculator.**	Dennis bought a pocket calculator **that fits into his shirt pocket easily.**
that	
/that/ ~~It~~ fits into his shirt pocket easily.	

If you wish to emphasize the idea in the second sentence above, you can write it as the independent clause and change the first sentence to an adjective clause:

SINGLE SENTENCES	COMBINED SENTENCE
that	
/that/ Dennis bought ~~a pocket calculator.~~	A pocket calculator **that Dennis bought** fits into his shirt pocket easily.
X **A pocket calculator** fits into his shirt pocket easily.	

In each of the preceding sentences, the adjective clauses make the general term *calculator* more specific by telling which calculator the sentence is about; therefore, the adjective clauses are necessary, and NO commas enclose them. In the next example, on the other hand, the adjective clause *which constantly needs repair* gives additional information about the car; therefore, the clause is preceded by a comma:

SINGLE SENTENCES	COMBINED SENTENCE
X Darlene drives her mother's **car.**	Darlene drives her mother's car, **which constantly needs repair.**
which	
/which/ ~~It~~ constantly needs repair.	

When you combine sentences in which the adjective clause refers to a person, you must be careful to choose the proper form of the relative pronoun *who.* In the following example, *Joyce* and *she* name the same person. To combine the two sentences, substitute *who,* the subject form for *she,* for the subject of the second sentence:

SINGLE SENTENCES	COMBINED SENTENCE
X **Joyce** makes jewelry. /,/	Joyce, **who recently collected unusual rocks in the desert,** makes jewelry.
who	
/, who/ ~~She~~ recently collected unusual rocks in the desert.	

To combine the next sentences use *whom*, the object form of the relative pronoun *who*, in place of *him*, the direct object in the second sentence. Notice that both object forms end in *m: him, whom:*

SINGLE SENTENCES	COMBINED SENTENCE
X Joyce gave some rocks to **Steve.** /,/	Joyce gave some rocks to Steve, **whom she had met in a jewelry design class.**
whom /whom/ She had met ~~him~~ in a jewelry design class.	

Use *whose*, the possessive form of *who*, in place of the possessive *her* to combine the next two sentences:

SINGLE SENTENCES	COMBINED SENTENCE
X **Joyce** sold most of the rings and necklaces. /,/	Joyce, **whose jewelry attracted many buyers,** sold most of the rings and necklaces.
whose /, whose/ ~~Her~~ jewelry attracted many buyers.	

If you find that one sentence in a set contains a form of the verb *be*, change that sentence to an appositive (Lesson 31) rather than to an adjective clause:

		Adj clause——————
	who	
NOT:	~~Joyce~~ is a jewelry designer.	Joyce, **who is a jewelry designer,** operates a successful business.
	Joyce operates a successful business.	

		Appositive——————
BUT:	~~Joyce~~ is a jewelry designer.	Joyce, **a jewelry designer,** operates a successful business.
	Joyce	
	~~She~~ operates a successful business.	

EXERCISE 34D

Combine the following sets of sentences. First, place X before the sentence that will become the independent clause. Next, find the noun that repeats a noun in the other sentence or the pronoun that refers to the noun, and draw a line through it. Write above the deleted noun or pronoun the relative pronoun *(who/whom/whose, which, that)* that you intend to use in its place. Finally, write the combined sentence, placing the adjective clause beginning with the relative pronoun immediately after the word it modifies in the independent clause. In combining some sets you may have to use other sentence-combining techniques you learned in earlier lessons.

EXAMPLE:

X	Jerry bought his guitar Saturday. /,/ who	Jerry, **who had finally earned enough money**, bought his guitar Saturday.
/, who/	~~He~~ had finally earned enough money.	
X	Jerry had finally earned enough money. /,/ which	Jerry had finally earned enough money, **which he used to buy a guitar Saturday**.
/, which/	He used ~~it~~ to buy a guitar Saturday.	

1. X
   /who/

   Five people devoted a year to organizing a new bank.
   They had known one another since high school days.

2. X
   /, who/

   Carrie Willett became president of the bank. /,/
   She had worked as a bank manager for five years.

3.

   Tom Fields became the head of the loan department.
   His real estate business had been extremely successful for twelve years.

4.

   Linda Carson took charge of the bank's hiring and supervising of employees.
   She gave up her position as personnel manager of a large department store.

5.

   The directors wanted Bryce Sutton as treasurer.
   Bryce Sutton's wife had inherited a large fortune.

6.

   Ted Weber handled public relations and advertising.
   People seemed to admire him.
   People seemed to trust him.

7.

   During the year the bank directors rented a small building.
   The bank directors kept working at their regular jobs.
   They moved furniture in.
   They hired the banking staff.

8.

   Ted Weber placed advertisements in newspapers in the surrounding area.
   The advertisements attracted widespread attention.

9.   He also developed radio announcements.
He also developed television announcements.
The announcements proved to be effective.

10.   During the first week the bank was crowded with customers.
The customers wanted to open accounts.
They wanted to arrange for loans.

11.   The bank directors were exhilarated by the response.
They had been slightly apprehensive before opening day.

POSITION OF ADJECTIVE CLAUSES

To keep the meaning of the sentence clear, place each adjective clause as close as possible to the noun it modifies. In reading the following sentence, readers might be temporarily confused until they examine the parts and realize that Mr. Brian is the one wearing the hearing aid:

Adj————————————————
NOT: Mr. Brian listened closely to the young men **who wears a hearing aid.**

Adj————————————
BUT: Mr. Brian, **who wears a hearing aid,** listened closely to the young men.

In the next sentence, readers might become confused because the adjective clause seems to modify *Forest*, the object of the preposition, instead of *cabin:*

NS   Pr   Nop   Adj————————————   LV   Nsc
Parker's cabin in the Trinity Forest **which burned last year** is a total loss.

The way to clarify the meaning is by rewriting the sentence:

NS   Vi   NS LV   Nsc
Parker's **cabin** in the Trinity Forest burned last year. It is a total loss.

You can see from the example above that you must use good judgment in combining sentences. Sometimes two simple sentences explain ideas more clearly than a single complex sentence.

You will find that some writers use *which* to refer to a whole idea rather than just one noun as in the sentence that follows:

Darlene did not come home last night, **which worried her parents.**

Review Lesson 26, Faulty Pronoun Reference, pp. 161–63.

A better way is to examine the relationship of ideas in the two sentences and write them to show this relationship. The second sentence about Darlene gives a cause and a result (or effect), which can be shown by using the subordinating conjunction *because* to combine the sentences:

Darlene worried her parents **because she did not come home last night.**

EXERCISE 34E

In the following sentences, the adjective clause may be misplaced, or the relative pronoun may not have a noun to refer to. First, underline the dependent clause. Then rewrite the sentence to correct the faulty relationship.

EXAMPLE: The sales representative received a large order for stationery, <u>which surprised him.</u>

CORRECTED: The sales representative received a large order for stationery. The size of the order surprised him.

EXAMPLE: The flowers bloomed early in the spring <u>that Amanda had planted in the fall.</u>

CORRECTED: The flowers that Amanda had planted in the fall bloomed early in the spring.

1. Some people avoid mowing their lawns for two or three weeks, which irritates their neighbors.

2. The promotion came after many years which she had earned.

3. The trip to Australia cost much more than Maria had expected, which disappointed her.

4. The *No Smoking* signs were fluorescent red that had been placed on the classroom walls.

5. The newsmagazine lay on the living room table that contained depressing reports.

6. Ken offered to lend Tom some money, which made Tom happy.

7. Everyone bet Barbara would marry Bill, not Ben, which made Bill nervous.

8. Mr. Hopkins had a toothache all night, which the dentist pulled it the next day.

Write five sentences with adjective clauses. Use the relative pronoun given after each number to introduce the adjective clause.

1. *(who)*

2. *(whom)*

3. *(which)*

4. *(that)*

5. *(whose)*

Show these sentences to your instructor or tutor.

Lesson 35

Noun Clauses

The third kind of dependent clause is the noun clause. Like the adverbial clause and adjective clause, the noun clause results when two sentences are combined.

	SINGLE SENTENCES	COMBINED SENTENCE
	I know ~~something.~~	I know **that I should finish my**
/that/	I should finish my assignment, but I feel ~~this.~~	**assignment,** but I feel **the teacher does not understand me.**
/that/	The teacher does not understand me.	

In the example above, the words in bold type in the combined sentence function as noun clauses. Both clauses are introduced by **that:** in the first one it is expressed; in the second one **that** is understood. Noun clauses may also begin with *who, whoever, which, what, whether, where, why, when, how, after,* and *before.* Here are examples with two of these introductory words:

What Marty has said should not upset us.
We know **why he is angry.**

Although noun clauses may look like adjective or adverbial clauses when they begin with *who, that, when,* or *why,* they are NOT additions to sentences as adjective and adverbial clauses are. They are a **necessary part of the sentence** because they function in one of the noun positions in the basic sentence. As a result, NO COMMAS enclose noun clauses. If you remove a noun clause from a sentence, you have only a part of a sentence left:

        NS   Vt   Ndo————————————————
The club members know ~~that Bob is building a sailboat.~~

    NS——————— LV Adj-c
~~Who will help~~ is uncertain.

If you cannot identify a noun clause immediately, use the Sentence Keys to locate it. First, find the verbs in the sentence. In the following example, *knows* and *will win* are the verbs. Then identify the subjects. In the example, *Nick* and *he* are the subjects:

    NS   V   NS V———
Nick knows that he will win the race.

The third step is to read the first subject-verb combination and ask *whom* or *what:*

    NS   V
Nick knows what?

The word group that answers the question is the direct object; it is a noun clause:

```
NS    Vt      Ndo
```
Nick knows **that he will win the race.**

The same steps will work if the noun clause appears first in the sentence. The verbs in the sentence below are *can win* and *is. He* is the subject of *can win.* When you ask *who* or *what is* to locate the subject of the verb *is,* you discover that the noun clause is the subject of the verb *is:*

```
      NS V                    V
```
Whether he can win the race is uncertain.

```
NS                          LV Adj-c
```
Whether he can win the race is uncertain.

In the following examples, the word groups in bold type are noun clauses. Notice that noun clauses may function in any noun position in a sentence:

SUBJECT:
```
NS                          LV Adj    Nsc
```
What each member will do is Bob's decision.

DIRECT OBJECT:
```
NS    Vt      Ndo
```
Nick asked **how he can help.**

INDIRECT OBJECT:
```
NS    Vt      Nio                    Adj   Adj   Ndo
```
Bob will give **whoever does the work** free sailing lessons.

OBJECT OF THE PREPOSITION:
```
NS Vi   Adv                  Pr    Nop
```
He talks enthusiastically with **whoever is interested.***

SUBJECT COMPLEMENT:
```
Adj  NS       LV Nsc
```
The question is **whether he can succeed.**

APPOSITIVE:
```
Adj  NS       NS
```
His suggestion **that everyone participate in the building**
```
Vt         Adj Adj   Ndo
```
pleased the club members.

Whoever is used in this sentence because it is the subject of the clause. The whole clause is the object of the preposition.

EXERCISE 35A

Underline the noun clauses in the following sentences, and indicate in the blank whether the clause is subject (NS), direct object (Ndo), indirect object (Nio), object of the preposition (Nop), subject complement (Nsc), or appositive (Appos). If there is no noun clause, write X in the blank. Begin by writing V above each verb and NS above each subject.

EXAMPLE:
$\overset{\text{NS}}{\text{The}}$ watch $\overset{\text{NS}}{\text{that}}$ Marilyn $\overset{\text{V}}{\text{selected}}$ $\overset{\text{V}}{\text{had}}$ a luminous dial.   ___X___

(Adjective clause: *that Marilyn selected* modifies *watch*)

$\overset{\text{Ndo}}{\underline{\text{What}}}$ $\overset{\text{NS}}{\underline{\text{she}}}$ $\overset{\text{V}}{\underline{\text{chose}}}$ was very attractive.   ___NS___

(Noun clause: *what she chose* is the subject of the verb *was*)

1. The old lady had a son whom she loved dearly. _____

2. The lumberyard owner said he would operate the mill next year. _____

3. Why the accident happened is still a mystery. _____

4. Jackson, who owned the livery stable, had a stroke yesterday. _____

5. The order was written by whoever signed it. _____

6. The picture you admired was sold yesterday. _____

7. He complains that he has no time for sleep. _____

8. Her excuse is that unexpected guests arrived last night. _____

9. Tell whoever calls the title of the movie. _____

10. The fact that he cannot dissect frogs is the reason for his failure. _____

COMBINING SENTENCES

When you separate an adjective or an adverbial clause from its dependent clause, you can change both clauses to individual sentences quite easily. However, when you remove a noun clause from a sentence, you can change the noun clause to a sentence, but the remaining part has to be filled in with a general term, such as *something, this,* or *that.* Given below is a combined sentence with a noun clause that functions as a direct object. It replaces *something,* the direct object in the first sentence on the left.

SINGLE SENTENCES		COMBINED SENTENCE
		$\overset{\text{NS}}{\text{The}}$ old man $\overset{\text{Vt}}{\text{learned}}$ $\overset{\text{Ndo———}}{\text{that his son}}$
X	The old man learned	
	$\overset{\text{Ndo}}{\text{something.}}$	**had had an accident.**
/that/	His son had had an accident.	

In the next example the noun clause, introduced by *that,* replaces *this* in the second sentence on the left and functions as the subject of the sentence:

SINGLE SENTENCES		COMBINED SENTENCE

NS————————————————————————
That Dan needs help with his home-
——— LV Adj-c
work is obvious.

/that/   Dan needs help with his homework.

            NS
X   ~~This~~ is obvious.

Knowing how noun clauses fit into sentences will help you to edit what you write. For example, you can sometimes combine a question with a statement by making the question a noun clause. In the following example, the question is rewritten as a statement, and it is introduced by *whether:*

SINGLE SENTENCES   COMBINED SENTENCE

                                    Ns   LV Nsc————————
X   The question is ~~this.~~   The question is **whether he will be**
                                             ——————————————
/whether/ Will he be ready for the   **ready for the test.**
           test?

Frequently the word beginning a question—*who, which, what,* and others—can become the introductory word for a noun clause:

SINGLE SENTENCES   COMBINED SENTENCE

                                    NS——————————————————— LV
/who/   Who will train the new   **Who will train the new employees** is
           employees?   Nsc
X   ~~This~~ is a decision for the   a decision for the supervisor.
           supervisor.

To combine the next pair of sentences you can begin the noun clause with *when* and omit *some time* in the second sentence:

SINGLE SENTENCES   COMBINED SENTENCE

                                    NS   Vt   Ndo———————
X   The salesclerk wonders   The salesclerk wonders **when she**
           ~~something.~~   ——————————————
                                             will get a pay raise.
/when/   She will get a pay raise
           ~~some time.~~

The phrase *in some way* in the second sentence on the left can be changed to *how* to introduce a noun clause:

SINGLE SENTENCES   COMBINED SENTENCE

                                    NS   Vt
X   The young woman asked   The young woman asked the credit
           the credit department   Nio   Ndo———————
           ~~something.~~   department **how she could pay for**
/how/   She could pay for the   ——————————
           furniture ~~in some way.~~   **the furniture.**

EXERCISE 35B

For further practice in understanding noun clauses, combine the following pairs of sentences by making one sentence a noun clause that becomes part of the other sentence. First, place X before the sentence that will be the independent clause. Second, draw a line through the words to be deleted. Third, use a subordinator to introduce the noun clause. Finally, write the combined sentence.

	EXAMPLE: SINGLE SENTENCES	COMBINED SENTENCE
X	Tina knew ~~this.~~	Tina knew **that Michael was having**
/that/	Michael was having serious financial problems.	**serious financial problems.**

1.　　　Mark decided ~~something.~~
  /when/　He would fly to Europe some time.

2.　　　Why did Glenn refuse the promotion?
  /why/　~~This~~ is a mystery.

3.　　　Millie knows this.
　　　　She will want a larger apartment soon.

4.　　　The committee knows something.
　　　　Who will receive the award?

5.　　　The well-trained athlete asked something.
　　　　Does he qualify for the football team?

EXERCISE 35C

Write four sentences with noun clauses. Have each noun clause function according to the label given after each number. Review the examples in this lesson if you need help.

1. Subject (NS)

2. Direct object (Ndo)

3. Subject complement (Nsc)

4. Object of the preposition (Nop)

Show these sentences to your instructor or tutor.

EXERCISE 35D

Draw a line above each dependent clause in the following sentences. Some sentences have more than one dependent clause. Then label each dependent clause N, Adj, or Adv. Review Lessons 33, 34, and 35 for examples.

1. Travelers who fly from California across the Pacific see unending stretches of ocean for at least 2,500 miles.

2. As they fly southwest toward the equator, they eventually find the Hawaiian Islands.

3. Passengers in a plane may wonder how the pilot can find the international airports on Oahu and Hawaii, two dots of land in the vast Pacific.

4. The 132 islands in the Hawaiian chain, which reaches across 1,600 miles of ocean, are actually the tops of volcanic mountains that began erupting 25 million years ago.

5. If the water of the Pacific Ocean were drained, the mountain Mauna Kea on the Island of Hawaii would be the tallest in the world because it stands almost 33,500 feet above the ocean floor.

6. Historians believe that Polynesians from other Pacific islands migrated to the Hawaiian Islands.

7. These explorers used their knowledge of the ocean currents, winds, and stars as they sailed northwest toward the Hawaiian Islands.

Lesson 36

Clauses Within Clauses

Each of the sentences you have studied and written in the first three lessons in this unit is made up of one independent clause and one dependent clause. However, sentences may contain several dependent clauses and more than one independent clause. Even though the structure of these sentences may seem to be complicated, the sentences are easily understandable if the ideas are carefully related. The sentence below, for example, is not extremely long, and it is easy to understand:

> Barbara thought Tom did not like the movie they say Thursday.

Yet when you examine the sentence, you find that it is made up of three sentences:

SENTENCES: Barbara thought something.
/that/   Tom did not like the movie.
/that/   They saw the movie Thursday.

COMBINED:

NS	Vt	Ndo		Adj
Barbara	thought	Tom did not like the movie		they saw

Thursday.

The next sentence consists of five sentences that can be combined into one. The diagram below shows how the clauses fit into one another. The subordinator that introduces each clause appears at the end of each line.

SENTENCES:

/before/   Work began one day.
        Baker told his employees this.
/that/   He believed something.
/that/   The employees could double production in a few months.
/if/   Each one must limit coffee breaks to fifteen minutes a day.

COMBINED:

Adv	NS	Vt	Nio	Ndo
Before work began one day,	Baker	told	his employees	that he believed

Ndo	Adv
(that) they could double production in a few months	if each one limited

coffee breaks to fifteen minutes a day.

COMPOUND-COMPLEX SENTENCES

The preceding sentences are complex sentences, which means that they consist of at least one independent clause and one or more dependent clauses. The next example is compound-complex because it contains two or more independent clauses as well as at least one dependent clause. First, the individual sentences that make up the longer sentence appear below. The combined sentence shows how they fit together into a single sentence:

SENTENCES:

Bob and Irene planned something.
/that/ They would go out for dinner on Saturday evening with Dick and Judy. (,)
But they were surprised.
/when/ Several friends arrived at their new home for a housewarming party.

COMBINED:

NS   C   NS   Vt————   Ndo————————————
Bob and Irene had planned │ that they would go out for

————————————————————————— C   NS   LV
dinner on Saturday evening with Dick and Judy, but they were

Adj-c   Adv————————————————————————————
surprised │ when several friends arrived at their home for a house-

————————
warming party.

SUMMARY OF PUNCTUATION WITH DEPENDENT CLAUSES

Dependent clauses need commas only in these places:

1. COMMA after an adverbial clause at the beginning of the sentence.
2. COMMAS before and after an adverbial clause within a sentence.
3. COMMAS before and after an adjective clause that gives extra information about specific terms.

Do not use commas with noun clauses.

EXERCISE 36A

Combine the following sentences into a single sentence. First, read all the sentences and place X before the sentence(s) you have chosen to be an independent clause. Next, delete unnecessary words. Then use connectors that you have studied in Units 7 and 8 to combine the sentences.

EXAMPLE:

SINGLE SENTENCES		COMBINED SENTENCE
/although/	Charles Taylor had found a new island in the Pacific. /,/	**Although** Charles Taylor found a new island in the Pacific, the newspapers did not carry the story; **however,** three magazines featured Taylor's discovery, **which** botanists and zoologists regarded as very important.
X	The newspapers did not carry the story. /;/	
X /**however,**/	Three magazines featured Taylor's discovery. /,/	
/**which**/	Botanists and zoologists regarded the discovery as very important.	

1. /, **who**/   Dennis attends a private school. /,/
   X   Dennis told his parents something.
   /**that**/   He will not go back.
   /**when**/   The fall semester begins some time. /;/
   X   He will look for a job instead.

2. /**after**/   Cleo had finished her father's portrait. /,/
   X   She decided something.
   /**that**/   She would paint a picture of a mountain cabin.
   /**that**/   She remembered the mountain cabin. /;/
   X   Later she would paint portraits of her children.

3.   The moon was full that night.
               The moon cast bright light on the mirror-smooth lake.
               The lake lay at the edge of town.
               No one knew something.
               A swimmer with scuba gear was crossing the lake under water.

4.   The weight lifter raised the three-hundred-pound weights to his shoulders.
               With a tremendous push he raised them above his head.
               He held them there for a moment.
               He dropped them to the floor.

EXERCISE 36B

On a separate sheet of paper write three sets of sentences. Each set should consist of three or four simple sentences. Combine each set into a single sentence, making at least one an independent clause and the others dependent clauses. (If you wish, you may write the combined sentence first and then break it into parts.) Label your sentences *Exercise 36B,* and show them to your instructor or tutor.

Lesson 37

Review of Phrases and Clauses

When you study details about the characteristics and function of language as you have in this text, a brief, comprehensive overview helps you understand how all the parts fit together and relate to one another. You had such an overview in Lesson 24 when you reviewed subjects and predicates and all the sentence patterns.

This lesson also provides an overview. This time you will reexamine the structure of the phrases and clauses you have studied to this point and review their relationship to one another in sentences, observing once again the flexibility of language. Knowing these relationships thoroughly is important in helping you gain control of language. Then you can write clear, understandable sentences. By understanding problems that might occur, you are able to analyze your problems and rewrite the confusing sentence by moving a word or word group to another position or rearrange the ideas without causing even greater confusion.

The following examples demonstrate the flexibility of language by showing how the same word group can function in a variety of ways:

Question:	**Who lives in the house next door?**
Noun clause:	Sandy does not know **who lives in the house next door.**
Adj clause:	Sandy met the man **who lives in the house next door.**
Adj clause:	Kevin, **who lives in the house next door,** manages a delicatessen.

In the next sentence *who lives in the house next door* is a misplaced modifier. Because you know that the adjective clause functions as a unit and must follow the noun it modifies, you can revise the sentence by placing the clause after *woman:*

NOT:	The woman owns a horse **who lives in the house next door.**
BUT:	The woman **who lives in the house next door** owns a horse.

When you studied prepositional phrases, you learned that moving a prepositional phrase from one position to another changes the meaning of the sentence:

The kittens **in the cardboard box** are asleep.
The kittens are asleep **in the cardboard box.**

The following outline summarizes the characteristics and function of phrases and clauses. The examples indicate where punctuation is to appear:

I. **PHRASE**—meaningful word group WITHOUT subject or verb

   A. **Prepositional Phrase**—preposition (Pr) + object of preposition—functions as adjective by telling *which one* or as an adverb that tells *when, where, why,* or *how* (Lesson 20):

NS Adj——— Vi   Adv———
The top **of the tree** swayed **in the wind.**

Adv——— Adj——— NS Adj——— Adj——— Adj——— Vt
At the end of the year each **of the people on the list of contributors** receives a

Ndo Adj——— Adv——— Adj——— Adj———
letter **of thanks from the dean of the medical school in Chicago.**

   B. **Appositive**—a noun and its modifiers—renames a noun in the sentence (Lesson 31):

NS   NS Appos V   Pr Nop   Nop Appos
The shepherd **Gino**   lived on Corsica, **an island.**

   C. **Verb Phrase**—auxiliary verbs + main verbs—functions as the verb in the sentence (Lessons 9–12):

should be completed   was being taken   have done
Verb phrase: Jack **had been asking** about you.

   D. **Verbal Phrase**—You will study verbal phrases in Unit 9.

II. **CLAUSE**—meaningful word group WITH a subject and verb

   A. **Independent Clause**—(NS V) CAN stand alone as a sentence.

     1. *Simple sentence*—one independent clause: NS V.   NS and NS V.   NS, NS, and NS V.   NS V and V.   NS V, V, and V.   NS, however, V.

     2. *Compound sentences*—two or more independent clauses: NS V, and NS V. NS V, NS V, and NS V.   NS V; NS V.   NS V; NS V; NS V.   NS V; however, NS V. NS V; NS, however, V.

       COORDINATING CONJUNCTIONS: *and, but, or, nor, for, yet*
       TRANSITIONAL EXPRESSIONS: *besides, consequently, however, as a result, furthermore, in addition, moreover, then*

   B. **Dependent Clause** (Sr NS V) begins with a subordinator (Sr), an introductory word, and CANNOT stand alone.

   Complex sentence—one independent clause and one or more dependent clauses.

   Three kinds of dependent clauses:

     1. *Adverbial (subordinate) clause* begins with *until, after, although, because, when, since, while, if* and others. It tells *when, where, why,* or *how.*

Adv-when————————————— NS   Vi
After Lloyd Brewster had resigned, a search began for a successor.

2. *Adjective (relative) clause* begins with *who, which,* or *that* and functions as Adj.
   It makes general terms specific and gives additoinal information about specific
   terms. It tells *which one.*

   NS   LV Nsc————————— Adj————————————————————
   The most likely choice is Gene Williams, **who prefers his present job.**

3. *Noun clause* begins with *who, which, that, how, when, why* and functions as NS,
   Ndo, Nio, or Nsc in sentences.

   NS————————————————— LV Adj-c
   Who will accept the job is debatable.

   NS   Vt   Ndo—————————————————
   Everyone knows **that the job is demanding.**

EXERCISE 37A

Read each of the following sentences, and write V above each verb and NS above each
subject. Then decide whether each word group in bold type is a phrase, a dependent
clause, or an independent clause. Write P for phrase, D for dependent clause, and I for
independent clause in the blanks at the right.

After Brenda and Paul had heard (1) **about three burglaries in their**

neighborhood, they decided that they needed a dog for protection.   1. _____

They celebrated (2) **because they had made their decision without an**

argument. However, they soon realized (3) **that their first decision was**   2. _____

only one of several that they had to make before they could actually   3. _____

purchase the dog. (4) **The second decision was the size of the dog.**   4. _____

Brenda, (5) **who weighed about a hundred pounds,** wanted a small dog;   5. _____

Paul, on the other hand, felt that only a large dog, such as a Doberman

or a German shepherd, (6) **could** really **offer** protection. Brenda in-   6. _____

sisted, however, (7) **that a small dog could make enough noise to scare**

possible intruders. The two of them argued about the size of the dog   7. _____

for quite a while, (8) **but they could not agree.** They talked instead   8. _____

about (9) **who would feed the dog.** Paul thought Brenda was the logical   9. _____

one (10) **because she cooked all the meals.** Brenda, in turn, suggested   10. _____

that Paul, (11) **a devoted jogger,** could exercise the dog every day.   11. _____

(12) **At the end of their discussion about care of the dog,** they (13) **had**   12. _____

each **accepted** specific responsibilities. They then turned back (14) **to**   13. _____

their discussion about the kind of dog they would buy, but they still   14. _____

(15) **could** not **agree.** (16) **Finally, they chose to install a burglar alarm**   15. _____

system.   16. _____

EXERCISE 37B

On a separate sheet of paper write nine sentences about one topic. Then identify three phrases, three dependent clauses, and three independent clauses in the sentences. Draw a line above the phrase or clause, and label it by writing P (phrase), D (dependent clause), or I (independent clause). Label the sentences *Exercise 37B,* and show them to your instructor or tutor.

Unit Eight Review

Practice Test

SCORE PART I (Total—100 points) _____
SCORE PART II* (Total—100 points) _____
TOTAL _____
AVERAGE _____

*Average scores for Part I and Part II only if the Part I score is 85 percent or more.

PART I

A. Write an X after each of the words that can be used to introduce a dependent clause.
   (12 points—1 point each)   (Lessons 33-35)   Score _____

1. when _____	5. in _____	9. although _____
2. however _____	6. but _____	10. under _____
3. if _____	7. as a result _____	11. because _____
4. that _____	8. who _____	12. then _____

B. Underline each dependent clause in the following sentences. Then label it N, Adj, or Adv.
   (18 points—sentences 1-5, 2 points each; 6 and 7, 4 points each)
   (Lessons 33-35)   Score _____

1. Mr. Finch, who owns the tailor shop, was robbed last night.

2. The children are restless because the movie has not begun.

3. He suddenly felt ill while he was eating lunch.

4. Whoever buys a car today will receive a 20 percent discount.

5. The actors left the theater after the play had ended.

6. People who spend time in Paris usually visit the Eiffel Tower, which was built

   for a world exposition in the early 1900s.

7. As slowly moving elevators carry tourists to the top of the Eiffel Tower, the view of

Paris widens until spectators can see the whole city.

C. In the following sentences, the words in bold type may be a phrase, a dependent clause, or an independent clause. Write P for phrase, D for dependent clause, or I for independent clause in the blanks at the right. Write V above each verb and NS above each subject.
(10 points—2 points each)   (Lesson 36)   Score _____

1. **After work** she bought groceries.   _____

2. The tables were piled with food **when the party began.** _____

3. The ocean liner docked **after a stormy Atlantic crossing.** _____

4. **While Marie sings,** she seems to have trouble breathing. _____

5. **He waited in vain at City Hall for his bride-to-be.**   _____

D. Some of the adjective clauses in the following sentences are needed to identify the nouns they modify. Others merely give additional information about the noun. Enclose in commas ONLY those adjective clauses that give additional information.
(10 points—2 points each)   (Lesson 34)   Score _____

1. Try to open the window that has a broken lock.

2. A man who devotes his life to perfecting precision tools should expect some failures.

3. The newspaper that the college students publish won an award.

4. Tracy Watson who lives in Oakland flew to Japan recently.

5. Cheryl's house which needs a coat of paint could be very attractive.

E. In the following sentences, the adjective clause may be misplaced or the relative pronoun may not have a noun to refer to. First, underline the dependent clause. Then rewrite the sentence to correct the faulty relationship.
(15 points—5 points each)   (Lesson 34)   Score _____

1. The artist contributed several of his paintings to the museum that he had completed in Europe.

2. The museum director accepted the paintings enthusiastically, which pleased the artist.

3. The board of directors sent a letter of appreciation to the artist, who valued the artist's contribution.

F. Combine the following sentences into a single sentence. First, read all the sentences and place X before the sentence(s) you have chosen to be an independent clause. Next, delete unnecessary words. Then use connectors that you have studied in Units 7 and 8 to combine the sentences.
(35 points—sentences 1–3, 5 points each; 4 and 5, 10 points each)
(Lessons 33–37)   Score _____

1.   Tourists plan a trip to California during the summer.
   /who/   Tourists may wonder this.
   /what/   What kinds of clothes should they take with them?

2.   Tourists discover something.
   /that/   A daytime temperature of 95 degrees in the inland valleys is hot. /;/
   /however,/   The heat is not extremely uncomfortable.
   /because/   It is dry heat.

3. /As/   The tourists travel west from the valleys to the coast.   /,/
                The temperature drops. /;/
   /in fact ,/ They may feel uncomfortably cool at 60 degrees. /,/
   /and/   They may reach for a sweater or a jacket.

4.   Tourists travel south along the Pacific Ocean.
                Tourists find the mornings cool and foggy until about 10 A.M.
                The sun finally emerges.

5.   Tourists can enjoy a pleasant day most of the summer.
                Almost no rain falls between May and September.
                The days are bright and warm.
                They enjoy their vacation in California.

PART II

Write sentences using each of the following words as a subordinator to introduce a dependent clause—adjective clause, adverbial clause, noun clause. Underline each dependent clause. Include punctuation wherever it is necessary.
(100 points—20 points each)   (Lessons 33–37)   Score _____

1. *(if)*

2. *(that*—noun clause)

3. *(who* or *whom)*

4. *(although)*

5. *(since)*

After you have received a passing score on this test, your instructor will give you the Unit Eight Writing Test.

Unit Eight

Practice Writing Test

(These are the instructions you will receive when you take the Unit Eight Writing Test. Write your paragraph on a separate sheet of paper.)

Write six to eight sentences (approximately 100 to 150 words) about a SINGLE topic. Try to write sentences of different lengths for variety. **Write at least two compound sentences and two sentences with dependent clauses.** Use connectors such as *but, or, as a result, however, if, although, when, who, which,* and *that.* Your sentences will be evaluated on their content, form, grammar, and punctuation.

You may use another sheet of paper to write your first and final drafts of the sentences. Be sure to attach your extra sheets to this test. Do all your writing during the class period. **Do not take the test home.**

Your instructor may assign a topic. Or you may write about any of the following topics: an accident, a disagreement or conflict, observations about current events, housing, social customs and folklore, working conditions, entertainment, recreation, alternative life styles, computers, energy, hazards, or any other topic that **your instructor approves.** Choose a topic that you understand well. Base it on your own experience, but write it in **third person.**

EVALUATION

Content—all sentences about one subject	50 points	_____
Form—variety of length; 2 compound, 2 with dependent clauses	50 points	_____
	Total	_____

Points taken off for the following:

Fragments, run-ons, comma splices	Minus 20 each	_____
Misused semicolon or comma	Minus 5 each	_____
Sentence style errors, awkward wording, PA agr, Ref, SV agr, DM, MM, Shift, Tense	Minus 3 each	_____
Spelling, comma omitted, capitalization	Minus 1 each	_____
	Total	_____
	TOTAL	_____

Show your paragraph to your instructor.

Unit Nine

Subordination: Verbal Phrases

In Unit Eight you practiced relating ideas by making some of them into dependent clauses:

> Sid and Gale, **who were standing at the bus stop,** saw a three-car collision in the intersection.

Often, however, you do not need the entire dependent clause to convey your ideas. In the preceding sentence, for example, you can omit *who were:*

> Sid and Gale, **standing at the bus stop,** saw a three-car collision in the intersection.

The word *standing* in the sentence above appears without the auxiliary verb *were.* A verb form used in this way is called a **verbal.** It may be used by itself or in a phrase and functions as a noun or a modifier. The use of verbals allows you to write a compact and meaningful sentence that makes its point effectively and economically. In the lessons that follow, you will learn about the characteristics and functions of verbals and verbal phrases.

To understand how some verbals are formed, you will learn about a verb pattern you have not studied up to this point—passive voice—the subject of the next lesson.

Before you begin the first lesson in this unit, you may find it helpful to review verbs in Units Two and Three.

Lesson 38

The V-ing Verbal Phrase

You learned to show that an event or an action continues over a period of time when you studied the progressive tenses in Lesson 11. To form the progressive tenses, you use a form of the verb *be (am, is, are, was, were, been)* together with a main verb ending in *-ing*. The combination forms a **verb** phrase that functions as the verb in the sentence:

Charles **is building** a cabin cruiser in his backyard.
His friends **have been watching** his progress for three years.
Soon Charles **will be taking** the cruiser to the river for a tryout.

Now you will learn that most V-ing forms can be used without the auxiliary verb as nouns, adjectives, or adverbs. Compare the following sentences. The verb in each sentence on the left consists of an auxiliary verb and the V-ing form, for example, *was running*. The verb becomes a verbal by dropping the auxiliary verb—*is, was,* or *had been*. Then the verbal functions as an adjective, adverb, or noun in sentences such as those on the right:

VERBS	VERBALS
The water **was running**.	Adj: The **running** water sounded peaceful.
Carl **was packing** the dishes.	Adv: Carl spent an hour **packing**.
The gardener **is watering** the plants.	Noun: The **watering** takes two hours.
The man **has been arguing** all day.	Noun: The man's **arguing** angered the neighbors.

EXERCISE 38A

All of the following sentences contain verbs, and some of them also contain V-ing verbals. Underline the verb or verb phrase in each sentence. Then write the verb in the first blank. If you also find V-ing verbals in the sentences, underline the verbals, and write them in the second blank.

	VERB	V-ING VERBAL
EXAMPLE: Kyle is chopping wood.	is chopping	
Greta is tending the roaring fire.	is tending	roaring

1. The whole group is going fishing. _____ _____

2. The girl was holding the crying child. _____ _____

3. Flying insects have been swarming outside. _____ _____

4. The art classes are beginning today. _____ _____

5. The two friends had been going shopping twice a week. _____ _____

V-ING VERBAL PHRASES

A **verbal phrase** is the verbal and the words that complete and modify it. Like verbals, verbal phrases may function as adjectives, adverbs, and nouns. The following examples show sentences with verbal phrases, and the labels before the sentences identify how each phrase functions:

	SENTENCE	VERBAL PHRASE
Adj:	The Nubian goat walks about,	**sampling leaves and blossoms.**
Adv:	Marilyn, her owner, spends time each day	**caring for the goat.**

The following examples show verbal phrases functioning as nouns:

Subject: **Running and suddenly leaping in the air** please the goat.
Direct object: Marilyn enjoys **watching the goat's antics.**
Object of Prep: Marilyn keeps the goat healthy by **feeding her carefully.**

The following sections explain how you can combine sentences by changing one sentence to a verbal phrase and inserting it in the base sentence.

V-ing as Adjectives

You may combine sentences by changing one sentence to a verbal phrase with the following steps:

1. Read the sentences. Place X before the base sentence.

> X   The firefighters fought a raging blaze in a large warehouse.
>   They **were shivering** with the cold.   /, V-ing,/

2. Delete unnecessary words, and change the verb to a verbal.

> The firefighters fought a raging blaze in a large warehouse.
> ~~They were~~ **shivering** with the cold.

Shivering with the cold is a verbal phrase. Because *they were* has been deleted, the word group is no longer a sentence; it is a fragment, only a part of a sentence. It has been transformed into a phrase that must be inserted in a sentence.

3. Insert the verbal phrase in the base sentence.

> **Shivering with the cold,** the firefighters fought a raging blaze in a large warehouse.   OR
> The firefighters, **shivering with the cold,** fought a raging blaze in a large warehouse.

The verbal phrase in the sentence above functions as an adjective, telling more about the firefighters. An adjective verbal phrase, like any other adjective modifier, should be placed immediately before or after the noun it modifies. However, an adjective verbal phrase that modifies the subject can appear at the end of the sentence if there is no other noun in the sentence:

> The firefighters worked hard, **operating the equipment and rescuing people.**

In the following example, you can change the verb *climbed* in the first sentence to the verbal *climbing* in order to combine the sentences:

>   climbing
> X   ~~One firefighter climbed~~ the slippery ladder.   /V-ing,/
> X   /One firefighter suddenly dropped his axe.

The verbal phrase *climbing the slippery ladder* can be placed before or after *one firefighter,* but probably not at the end of the sentence because it seems to modify *axe:*

> **Climbing the slippery ladder,** one firefighter suddenly droped his axe.
> One firefighter, **climbing the slippery ladder,** suddenly dropped his axe.
> NOT: One firefighter suddenly droped his axe, **climbing the slippery ladder.**

You could also combine the preceding pair of sentences in the following way:

> One firefighter, **who was climbing the slippery ladder,** suddenly dropped his axe.

However, there is no advantage in using *who was;* the meaning is clear without the extra words, and the sentence is more readable with the verbal phrase.

When you read the following set of sentences, you note that they are short and choppy. However, if you change four of them to verbal phrases and insert them in the base sentence, you have improved the presentation of the information greatly. Before you change verbs to verbals and combine the sentences, you have to consider carefully what the set of sentences is saying. In reading the sentences that follow, you could determine that the second sentence about the three food experts provides focus for the other sentences. The second sentence, therefore, becomes the base sentence, and the other sentences are inserted in it:

> ~~Three food experts were judging~~ the student chefs' final exam.   /, V-ing/
> X   / Three food experts walked about /.
> ~~They were~~ tasting small samples.   /, V-ing,/
> ~~They were~~ smelling the aroma.   /, V-ing,/
> ~~They were~~ examining the appearance of the food.   /, V-ing/
>
> **Judging the student chefs' final exam,** three food experts walked about, **tasting small samples of each entree and dessert, smelling the aroma, and examining the appearance of the food.**

Punctuation with Verbal Phrases

Commas enclose verbal phrases that modify specific terms:

> Master chef Pierre Blanc, **walking with the three experts,** appeared very pleased with the display.

No commas enclose verbal phrases needed to identify a general term:

> The food expert **licking his lips and smiling** has been a chef in large hotels in Paris and New York. (Which expert? The expert licking his lips and smiling . . .)

V-ing as Nouns

The adjective verbal phrases in the preceding examples modify nouns and tell which one. Verbal phrases can also function as nouns in sentences. In the following examples the V-ing verbals function as subject, object, object of the preposition, and appositive. If you read two or three sentences you have written and believe that the relationship of ideas is closer than the sentences would indicate, think about combining the sentences. In the first example below, the two sentences on the left are satisfactory, but the combined sentence helps the readers see more quickly and directly that the dripping of the water caused Jennifer to be uncomfortable. You will note a similar result in the other sentences that follow:

SINGLE SENTENCES	COMBINED SENTENCES	
The water was dripping. This made Jennifer uncomfortable.	Subject:	The **dripping of the water** made Jennifer uncomfortable.
The organist enjoyed something. She played her pipe organ for friends.	Object:	The organist enjoyed **playing her pipe organ for friends.**
The attorney fulfilled his obligations. He worked late every day.	Object of preposition:	The attorney fulfilled his obligations by **working late every day.**
The gardener liked his work. He maintained flower beds in public parks.	Appositive:	The gardener liked his work, **maintaining flower beds in public parks.**

EXERCISE 38B

Combine the following sets of sentences by changing one or more sentences to verbal phrases and inserting them in the base sentence.

```
                                    wanting
EXAMPLE:    The college student wanted a vacation after final exams.   /V-ing,/
        X   The college student traveled west to the Rocky Mountains.
```

> **Wanting a vacation after final exams,** the college student traveled west to the Rocky Mountains.

1. The college student was gazing at the towering mountain before her.
   She wanted an exciting adventure.

2. The college student tried something.
   She climbed the mountain.

3. She was carrying heavy equipment.
   This tired her quickly.

4. She rested occasionally.
   She sat on a ledge.

5. She spent her resting time in this way.
   She looked out over the green valley below.

6. She was feeling hungry.
   She ate a granola bar.
   She drank hot chocolate.

7. Her goals were these.
   She was trying to reach the top before noon.
   She was trying to return to the valley before nightfall.

V-ing as Adverbs

The V-ing verbal can be used as an adverb following the verbs *go* and *spend:*

> Vassily went **looking for a job.** . . . went where? **looking**
> He spent many hours **waiting for job interviews.** . . . spent hours how? **waiting**

V-ing can also be a part of an adverbial modifier that begins with the connectors *while, before, after, since,* and *when.* This modifier can develop by combining sentences if the subject of two sentences is the same:

> The pilot was flying over tree-covered mountains to Spokane.
> X   He noticed a fire in the wilderness below.

One way you have studied to combine the set is to make the second sentence an adjective clause:

> The pilot, **who was flying over tree-covered mountains to Spokane,** noticed a fire in the wilderness below.

A second way is to change the adjective clause to an adjective verbal phrase by deleting **who were:**

The pilot, **flying over tree-covered mountains to Spokane,** noticed a fire in the wilderness below.

A third way is to change the second sentence to an adverbial clause by use of the connector *while* before it:

While the pilot was flying over tree-covered mountains to Spokane, he noticed a fire in the wilderness below.

The fourth way is to change the adverbial clause to an adverbial phrase by deleting *they were.* The modifier can appear before or after the base sentence:

While flying over tree-covered mountains to Spokane, the pilot noticed a fire in the wilderness below.

The pilot noticed a fire in the wilderness below **while flying over tree-covered mountains to Spokane.**

EXERCISE 38C

Combine the following sentences. If the *subjects of both sentences are the same,* and the sentences show a time relationship, change one of the sentences to a V-ing adverbial modifier. Follow these steps. First, change one of the sentences to a dependent clause by using connectors such as *while, since, when, before,* and *after.* Then delete the subject of the dependent clause, and change the verb to a V-ing verbal. Finally, combine the sentences. If the subjects of the two sentences are not the same, combine them by using the techniques you have learned in earlier lessons.

EXAMPLE: X   ALAN seemed to fall behind schedule on the job.
     /after/ HE had experienced a number of personal problems.

Adv. clause   ALAN seemed to fall behind schedule on the job **after HE had experienced a number of personal problems.**

Adv. V-ing   Alan seemed to fall behind schedule on the job **after experiencing a number of personal problems.**
OR: **After experiencing a number of personal problems,** Alan seemed to fall behind on the job.

EXAMPLE: X   The company manager wanted to fire Alan immediately.
   /because/ He had no patience with inefficient employees.

COMBINED: The company manager wanted to fire Alan immediately because he had no patience with inefficient employees.

1.   X   However, Alan's supervisor, Celeste, refused.
   /because/ Alan had been a valuable employee for several years.

2.   /after/ Celeste had attended a conference about employee-assistance programs. /,/
            Celeste believed something.
    /that/ Alan could be helped.

3.   Celeste prepared a proposal for an employee-assistance program.
                  Celeste talked with the company manager.

4.   Celeste pointed out something.
                  The program would save the company money.
                  Training a new employee would cost more than helping Alan.

5.   The company manager talked with other managers and supervisors.
                  The company manager tried the program.

EXERCISE 38D

Connect and combine the following sentences. In some cases you will be able to combine the sentences by changing verbs to verbals that modify nouns. In other cases you will use ways that you have studied in preceding lessons. First, read the sentences in the set. Second, place X before the sentence or sentences that you choose for the base sentence. Third, cross out unnecessary words. Fourth, change the verbs to verbals wherever you can. Fifth, add connectors, or make any other appropriate changes. Finally, combine all the sentences in a set into a single sentence.

EXAMPLE: ~~People~~ bathe for cleanliness.   /V-ing/
           X ~~This~~ / has become a daily activity for people.
      /who/ ~~People~~ have modern plumbing.   **/and/**
          ~~People have~~ automatic water heaters.

COMBINED: Bathing for cleanliness has become a daily activity for people who have modern plumbing and automatic water heaters.

1.   X Bathing was an important ritual among early Egyptians.   **/and/**
           ~~It was also important among~~ other ancient peoples.   **/;/**
           Ancient Greeks, for example, provided heated water.

2.   X Bathing was also popular among early Romans.
    /who/ ~~The Romans~~ built luxurious public baths.
  /where/ People could talk with others.   **/,/**
       ~~People could~~ enjoy works of art.   **/, and/**
       ~~People could~~ listen to music.
  /while/ ~~People were~~ bathing.

3.   The Romans brought water by aqueducts.
              The Romans stored the water in reservoirs.
              They later heated the water to various temperatures.
              Then they distributed it by pipes to bathing areas.

4.   In later centuries some people took very few baths.
They believed something.
Baths were bad for them.

5.   They used perfumes.
They tried to cover up unpleasant odors.

6.   By the 1700s doctors were encouraging people to bathe.
The doctors were telling people something.
Cleanliness promoted good health.

7.   People today provide relaxation for themselves.
They soak in hot tubs.
They enjoy the massaging action of water in spas.
They swim in heated indoor and outdoor pools.

Lesson 39

Active and Passive Verbs

The second kind of verbal you will learn to use in combining sentences is the V-ed (past participle) form. In Lesson 10 you learned that you use the auxiliary verbs *have* or *has* with V-ed to form the present perfect tense and *had* with V-ed to form the past perfect tense. The following sentences give examples of each one:

> New Englanders **have preserved** picturesque covered bridges.
> Many bridges **have existed** for at least a hundred years.
> The roofs **had been built** to keep heavy snow off the bridges.

In the next lesson you will learn to use V-ed as a verbal, but first you will study active and passive verbs because the V-ed verbal is derived from passive verbs. You may have observed that sentences consisting of the subject, transitive verb, and direct object, represent a common—probably the most common—sentence pattern in English. Such sentences show that the subject affects or does something to the direct object. The verb is **active.** In the example below Jack, the doer, does something to the car, the receiver of the action:

```
NS     Vt       Adj Ndo
Jack repairs the car.
```

The same idea can be expressed in a different way by using a **passive** verb instead of the active verb. To make this change, follow these steps, using the sentence above:

1. Place the word *car,* which is the receiver of the action, in the subject position in the sentence.
2. Change the active verb *repair* to the passive (PV) form by using a form of the verb *be* with Part 4 of the verb: *is repaired.*
3. Make the subject *Jack* the object of the preposition *by: by Jack.*

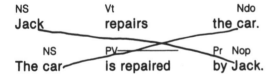

If the readers do not have to know who repaired the car, you can omit *by Jack.* The sentence then reads:

> The car is repaired.

One point to remember is that *passive* does NOT mean *past tense.* Passive verbs may be written in the present, past, future, perfect, and progressive tenses. The examples that follow show both active and passive verbs in several tenses:

	DOER (NS)	ACTIVE VERB (Vt)	RECEIVER (Ndo)
ACTIVE VERBS:	The plane	will transport	the jewel collection.
	The pilot	has completed	his assignment.
	The museum director	complimented	the pilot.

	RECEIVER (NS)	PASSIVE VERB (PV)	DOER (BY Nop)
PASSIVE VERBS:	The jewel collection	will be transported	by the plane.
	The assignment	has been completed	by the pilot.
	The pilot	was complimented	by the museum director.

Use passive verbs sparingly. Keep your readers interested and involved in what you are saying by focusing on the subject of your sentence doing something:

NOT: The movie was enjoyed by Joe and Kim.
BUT: Joe and Kim enjoyed the movie.

EXERCISE 39A

Underline the verbs or verb phrases in the following sentences. Decide whether each one is an active verb or passive verb. Write A for active and P for passive in the blanks at the right.

1. Diving deep into the ocean gives people a thrill. _____

2. A competent diver must be trained mentally as well as physically. _____

3. Varying qualities of instruction are offered in diving schools all over the world. _____

4. Some schools sell a poorly trained diver a ticket to suicide. _____

5. Others provide a full thirty-hour course and, eventually, certification. _____

6. For a long time diving was taught by the fear technique. _____

7. Nowadays good diving techniques are emphasized. _____

8. A diver must have reliable equipment. _____

9. The well-equipped, well-trained diver plunges into the water eagerly. _____

10. For safety, the diver never travels alone. _____

EXERCISE 39B

Rewrite each of the following sentences, making the verb passive. Use the verb form given in parentheses following each sentence.

1. Edmund Hillary and Tensing Norgay conquered Mount Everest in 1953.
   (was conquered)

2. Towers of ice surrounded the climbers.   (were surrounded)

3. The men wore goggles, padded clothes, and oxygen masks.   (were worn)

4. On the way up the mountain the climbers set up camps.   (were set up)

5. Hillary, Norgay, and other men erected the last camp at 25,850 feet.   (was erected)

6. Hillary and Norgay spent a stormy night in a tent 1,200 feet from the peak.   (was spent)

7. They climbed the steep slopes in the morning.   (were climbed)

8. At one point a ridge of ice stopped them completely.   (were stopped)

9. Fortunately they found a passage to the top.   (was found)

10. They finally reached the top just before noon.   (was reached)

Read the ten sentences once again as a story. Next read the sentences you have written. Notice that the passive verbs change the tone of the story.

EXERCISE 39C

Rewrite each of the following sentences, making the verb active.

1. Video games are being played by thousands of children and adults.

2. Many players who play regularly are no longer challenged by the games.

3. In another five years games will be made more realistic and complex by designers.

4. Scenery for war games and adventures may be provided by videodiscs.

5. A player in one city may be challenged by a player in another city by using computers connected with telephone lines or cable television.

6. People in several locations may be pitted against one another by complex war games.

EXERCISE 39D

Write two sentences with active verbs.

1.

2.

Write two sentences with passive verbs.

1.

2.

Show these sentences to your instructor or tutor.

Lesson 40

The V-ed Verbal Phrase

Now that you have studied passive verbs, you will learn how many of them can be changed to V-ed verbals. The V-ed verbals were also mentioned in Lesson 18, where you learned that they may be used alone as adjectives:

Adj   Adj
The **trusted** housekeeper carefully polished the highly **valued** silverware.

V-ED VERBALS

If you have a passive verb in a sentence, you can change it to a V-ed verbal by deleting the auxiliary verb. Then you can use the verbal as an adjective to modify a noun in a second sentence. You can study the process, which is similar to what you learned in Lesson 21, by examining the following sentences. Place X before the base sentence. Then delete unnecessary words from the other sentence. Finally, combine the sentences by inserting the verbal in the base sentence:

SINGLE SENTENCES	COMBINED SENTENCE
~~Walt's camera was~~ **broken.** Walt quickly repaired his camera.	Walt quickly repaired his **broken** camera.
~~The door was~~ **closed** and **sealed.** It hid family secrets for fifty years.	The **closed** and **sealed** door hid family secrets for fifty years.

A few V-ed verbals such as *injured, wounded,* and *forgotten* can be used as nouns:

VERB	VERBAL AS A NOUN
Several drivers **were injured.**	The **injured** were taken to the hospital.
Two people **had been wounded** during the shooting.	The **wounded** received first aid.
Old people **are** sometimes **forgotten** by family and friends.	The **forgotten** lead lonely lives.

EXERCISE 40A

All of the following sentences contain verbs, and some of them also contain verbals. Underline the verb or verb phrase in each sentence. Then write the verb in the first blank. If you also find a V-ed verbal in the sentence, underline it, and write it in the second blank.

	VERB	V-ED VERBAL
EXAMPLE: The <u>torn</u> coat <u>had been placed</u> in the closet.	had been placed	torn
The water <u>is frozen</u> in the pail.	is frozen	

1. The job applicant is required to take a test. _____ _____

2. The injured man was carried to the hospital. _____ _____

3. His bruised hand had been fractured in two places. _____ _____

4. Stanley has been asked to get authorized signatures on the documents. _____ _____

5. The hidden money has been located recently. _____ _____

V-ED VERBAL PHRASES

When you combine sentences by changing the verb to a V-ed verbal, the process is the same as combining sentences with the V-ing verbal. The V-ed verbal, functioning as an adjective, should either come before or follow the noun it modifies to keep the meaning of the sentence clear. Commas enclose the verbal phrases because they give extra information about specific terms:

X   The young tennis player / won the last two sets.
~~He had been~~ **defeated** in the first game.   /, V-ed,/

The young tennis player, **defeated in the first game,** won the last two sets.

~~The crowd was~~ **pleased** with his game.   /, V-ed,/
X   The crowd / cheered loudly.

The crowd, **pleased with his game,** cheered loudly.

V-ed verbals following verbs such as *become, remain,* and *feel* can sometimes be taken from one sentence and placed in the base sentence to tie the ideas together more closely:

The young tennis player ~~felt~~ **exhilarated** after the game.   /, V-ed,/
X   He / wanted to celebrate all night.

The young tennis player, **exhilarated after the game,** wanted to celebrate all night.

Sometimes you can change an adverbial clause beginning with *although, when, once,* and *unless* to an adverbial phrase if the subject of both the independent and adverbial clauses is the same. In the following example, *Akiko had been* is deleted from the adverbial clause, and *Akiko* replaces *she* in the independent clause:

Akiko
Although ~~Akiko had been~~ trained as a model, ~~she~~ preferred to work as a dress designer.

Although **trained** as a model, Akiko preferred to work as a dress designer.

When ~~David was~~ hired by the international airline, he moved to Minneapolis.
When **hired** by the international airline, David moved to Minneapolis.

Occasionally you can combine sentences in more than one way. For example, by using the following sentences about a California city, you can emphasize the city's location by making the second sentence the independent clause and the first sentence the adjective verbal phrase. Or you can emphasize the city's reputation by making the first sentence the independent clause and the second sentence the adjective verbal phrase. In each sentence the verbal phrase is placed immediately after *Gilroy*, the noun it modifies:

SINGLE SENTENCES	COMBINED SENTENCES
Gilroy is the garlic capital of the nation.	Gilroy, **called the garlic capital of the nation,** is located seventy miles south of San Francisco.
Gilroy is located seventy miles south of San Francisco.	Gilroy, **located seventy miles south of San Francisco,** is called the garlic capital of the nation.

PUNCTUATION WITH VERBAL PHRASES

Commas enclose adjective verbal phrases that give extra information about a specific term. If the verbal phrase begins the sentence, only the comma following it is written:

Wrecked beyond repair, Brian's car became rusted and corroded.

If the verbal phrase appears within the sentence, two commas enclose it:

Brian's car, **wrecked beyond repair,** became rusted and corroded.

If the verbal phrase appears at the end of the sentence, a comma comes before it:

No one wanted Brian's car, **wrecked beyond repair.**

No commas enclose the verbal phrase that is needed to identify a general term:

The cabin **situated near Rattlesnake Bar** does not belong to Gordon.

EXERCISE 40B

Connect and combine the following sentences. In some cases you will be able to combine the sentences by changing verbs to verbals. In other cases you will use ways to connect and combine sentences that you have studied in preceding lessons. First, read the sentences in each set. Second, place X before the sentence you choose for the base sentence. Third, cross out unnecessary words. Fourth, change the verbs to

verbals wherever you can. Fifth, add connectors, or make any other appropriate changes. Finally, combine all the sentences in a set into a single sentence.

EXAMPLE: X   A new food processing technique / helps preserve food for long periods without canning or freezing.
~~The technique is~~ **called** irradiation.   /, V-ed,/

COMBINED: A new food processing technique, **called irradiation,** helps preserve food for long periods without canning or freezing.

1. X   Potatoes, for example, have been stored for seven months in Japan.
~~The potatoes have been~~ irradiated.   /V-ed/

2.   In experiments meats, fish, and poultry have been stored up to fourteen months.
The meats, fish, and poultry appear to be fresh.

3.   Irradiation is praised by scientists.
It is an effective weapon against insect infestation such as the Medfly.

4.   Irradiation can replace chemicals.
Chemicals are currently used to fumigate food.

5.   These chemicals are suspected of causing cancer.
These chemicals may be harmful to humans.

Lesson 41

The Infinitive Verbal Phrase

The infinitive, like V-ing and V-ed, functions as a verbal in sentences. It expresses action or existence, and it shows tense just as the verb does. However, it is different from the verb because it does not function as the predicate in a sentence and it does not indicate person (first, second, third) or number (singular, plural):

> Verbs, third person singular: Sandra **helps** George. George **rebuilds** cars.
> Infinitive: Sandra helps George **to rebuild** cars.

The infinitive consists of a form of the verb preceded by *to,* which serves as a marker of the infinitive. Here are the forms of the infinitive:

ACTIVE	PASSIVE
to invite	to be given
to be thinking	
to have chosen	to have been appointed
to have been working	

Every sentence must include at least one verb, but it may or may not include infinitives. Yet infinitives are used extensively. If you examine what you say and write, you will find that many of your sentences contain one infinitive, sometimes more.

Infinitives may appear after a large number of verbs. Here is a partial list of these verbs: *begin, continue, like, shock, need, deserve, want, decide, expect, find, urge, force, be, cause, advise, appoint, allow, ask, choose, claim, teach, permit, order, like, require,* and *tell.* Each of the following sentences has at least one verb, and all but one of the sentences have infinitives:

> A tightrope walker decided **to perform** a spectacular feat. He planned **to walk** on a wire between the twin towers of the World Trade Center in New York City. Knowing that he could not get permission **to perform** his stunt, he sneaked past the guards in one of the towers and went to the top of the building 110 stories above the ground. He used a bow and arrow **to shoot** his wire from one building to the other. Then he walked to the other tower on the wire.

The infinitive may appear in sentences without *to* if the following words are the verbs: *hear, watch, see, help, let, make:*

> A crowd saw the tightrope walker **make** his way to the other tower.
> They watched him **advance** slowly but surely.

All of the following sentences contain verbs, and some of them also contain infinitive verbals. Identify the verb in each sentence by writing the verb in the first blank. If you also find an infinitive verbal in the sentence, write it in the second blank.

	VERB	INFINITIVE VERBAL
EXAMPLE: Sam advised Stefanie to wear a dress for the interview.	advised	to wear
1. Monica urged her husband to buy a new car.	_____	_____
2. Paolo decided not to travel this year.	_____	_____
3. The riverboat captain was eager to please the passengers.	_____	_____
4. John heard the baby cry several times during the night.	_____	_____
5. The rock stars appeared willing to sign autographs.	_____	_____
6. Kevin made the small boys follow him in the woods.	_____	_____
7. Burt told Steven to cancel the order for film.	_____	_____

INFINITIVE PHRASES

Infinitives may function as adjectives, adverbs, and nouns in sentences. Like the other verbals, they may be completed by modifiers, objects, and complements. The following examples show infinitives and infinitive phrases:

ADJECTIVE:	The trees **to save from cutting** are near the mountain road. The worker avoids listening to the instructions **to be followed**.
ADVERB:	The parents were eager **to hear from their son.** The crowd waited impatiently **to learn the final score.** The meal is easy **to make.** The drivers wait **to cross the one-lane bridge.**
NOUN SUBJECT:	**To travel around the world** is Jeremy's main goal.
OBJECT:	Jeremy hopes **to have enough money for his trip soon.** He finally decided **to try to borrow** a fourth of the money.
COMPLEMENT:	The reason is **to be ready to leave in a month.**

The examples above show infinitives with modifiers, objects, and complements. Infinitives may also have subjects:

> The mayor chose **Bessie to represent the city at the conference.**
> Bessie wants **her husband to accompany her.**
> The mayor advised **Bessie to go to the conference alone.**

CHANGING DEPENDENT CLAUSES TO INFINITIVES

The infinitive, like other verbals, enables you to make sentences more compact. By being aware of infinitives, you can sometimes change dependent clauses to infinitive phrases by deleting unnecessary words:

SENTENCES WITH DEPENDENT CLAUSES	SENTENCES WITH INFINITIVE PHRASES
Mary hopes ~~that she can~~ finish the cocktail dress by Tuesday.	Mary hopes **to finish the cocktail dress by Tuesday.**
Her daughter decided ~~that she would~~ model the cocktail dress in the fashion show.	Her daughter **decided to model the cocktail dress in the fashion show.**
Mary has orders for two more cocktail dresses ~~that must be~~ completed by Tuesday.	Mary has orders for two more cocktail dresses **to be completed by Tuesday.**

EXERCISE 41B

You will find a dependent clause in each of the following sentences. Rewrite the sentence by changing the dependent clause to an infinitive phrase.

EXAMPLE: Dependent clause: The people voted **that farmers stop burning rice fields.**
            Infinitive phrase: The people voted **to stop burning rice fields.**

1. The old lady pretended that she was a cousin of the president.

2. The teacher hopes that she will convince the principal to add more basic writing classes.

3. Melody told her fiancé that he should find an apartment downtown.

4. The doctor needed a small car that he can drive around town.

5. Elaine's plan is that she will buy several acres of land near her home.

COMBINING SENTENCES WITH INFINITIVES

You may combine sentences by using infinitives in three ways. One is to use an infinitive to express purpose (or tell *why*):

> Spiros needs help. ~~Spiros wants~~ to build a house.
> Spiros needs help **to build a house.**

> Tom is collecting and growing house plants.
>   to open   to sell
> ~~Tom's purpose is opening~~ a nursery. ~~Tom's purpose is selling~~ the plants.
> Tom is collecting and growing house plants **to open a nursery and to sell the plants.**

The infinitive phrase may also tell *how*:

>   to learn
> The physical therapist helped George. ~~He learned~~ to live with his disability.
> The physical therapist helped George **to learn to live with his disability.**

A third way is to use the infinitive as a noun:

>   to complete
> The motion picture ~~must be completed. Completion~~ requires additional financial backing.
> **To complete the motion picture** requires additional financial backing.

>   to
> The producer expects ~~something. She will~~ receive offers during the next week. ~~She will be able~~ to continue with the filming.
> The producer expects **to receive offers during the next week and to continue with the filming.**

When you combine the following sentences, you have to supply a subject for the infinitives by changing *he* to *him*:

>   him to lose   him to feel
> Don's constant complaining caused ~~this. He lost~~ friends. ~~He felt~~ lonely and depressed.
> Don's constant complaining caused **him to lose friends and to feel lonely and depressed.**

EXERCISE 41C

Combine the following sets of sentences in these steps: Place X before the base sentence; then change the other sentence(s) to infinitive phrases and attach them to the base sentence.

EXAMPLE: X   The police sergeant received orders.
                ~~He was~~ to send the prisoner to the county jail.   /Inf/

                The police sergeant received orders **to send the prisoner to the county jail.**

EXAMPLE: **to feed**

                  The animals in the zoo ~~needed more food.~~
          X   ~~This~~ required additional funding.

                  To feed the animals in the zoo required additional funding.

1. X Giovanni worked hard all day.
        ~~He wanted~~ to complete the concrete sidewalks.   /Inf/

2.   The interior decorator helped Theo.
        He chose wallpaper and upholstery fabric for his apartment.

3.   The author was disappointed.
        She had received a rejection slip from the editor.

4.   The company president expected this.
        She was to open a new plant in Georgia.
        She was to spend six months there herself.

5.   The new owners of the house immediately painted all the walls.
        They wanted to cover fingerprints, crayon marks, and splotches of paint.

6.   Craig Hudson was eager to do something.
        He wanted to show everyone his completed house plans.
        He wanted to begin building immediately.

Lesson 42

Misplaced and Dangling Modifiers

A verbal phrase must be related to something in the sentence. If the verbal phrase seems to modify the wrong word or if it has nothing to modify, the meaning of your sentence will not be clear. You can eliminate these problems by following the suggestions in this lesson for rewriting sentences.

MISPLACED MODIFIERS

When you studied adjectives (Lesson 18) and adjective clauses (Lesson 34), you learned that these modifiers must be placed as close to the noun that they modify as possible because adjectives tend to modify the nearest noun. If the adjective modifiers are misplaced, the meaning of the sentence may be unclear. The only way to clarify meaning is to rewrite the sentence, placing the modifier where it belongs. The correction symbol MM is often used to indicate a misplaced modifier.

Misplaced Verbal Phrases

When verbal phrases function as modifiers, you must also take care to place them as close to the word they modify as possible. If you do not, the sentence may be wrongly interpreted. For example, if you combine the sentences on the left in the usual way, you then have a combined sentence like the one on the right. The most likely interpretation is that Don was driving to work with a new friend when Karen saw him. The sentence does not indicate clearly whether Don or the friend was driving:

Karen saw Don.
~~Don was~~ with a new friend.
~~They were~~ driving down the street.

Karen saw Don with a new friend, driving down the street.

By placing *driving* next to *Don,* you can indicate much more clearly that he was the driver:

Karen saw Don, ~~who was~~ driving down the street with a new friend.
Karen saw Don, driving down the street with a new friend.

However, if you want to say that Karen was the one driving to work, you can rewrite the sentence in these ways:

While driving to work, Karen saw Don with a new friend.
Karen, driving to work, saw Don with a new friend.

If you find a sentence that seems confusing in a paragraph you have written, you can examine it by breaking it into its basic parts. In the first example, the V-ed verbal phrase *confused by the vague directions* does not seem to belong at the beginning of the sentence:

Confused by the vague directions, the party had ended before Tim arrived.

To decide where the V-ed verbal phrase belongs, write the verbal phrase down:

confused by the vague directions

Then ask who was or were confused by the vague directions. Write the answer before *confused.* You now have a sentence:

Tim was confused by the vague directions.

Then write the second part of the sentence as a separate sentence:

The party had ended before Tim arrived.

Finally, combine the two sentences in the usual way, and you will be able to place the verbal phrase after *Tim;* however, you will have to change the relationship of the last two sentences. *Tim arrived* becomes the base sentence, and *the party had ended* becomes a dependent clause beginning with *after:*

	~~Tim was~~ confused by the vague directions. /V-ed,/ ~~The party had ended.~~	**Confused by the vague directions,** Tim arrived after the party had ended.
X	/ Tim arrived.	
/after/	The party had ended.	

See Lesson 20 for a discussion of misplaced prepositional phrases and Lesson 34 for misplaced dependent clauses.

DANGLING MODIFIER

A modifier "dangles" because it has no noun in the independent clause to modify. Sometimes a dangling modifier results if you leave out words needed to explain something clearly. In the following example, the verbal phrase *seeing the sign* does not explain who was seeing the sign, and the independent clause does not give this information either. Because of its position at the beginning of the sentence, the verbal phrase seems to modify *the town:*

NOT: **Seeing the sign,** the town was only a few miles away.
(The town, which was seeing the sign, was only . . .)
BUT: **Seeing the sign,** *we* realized that the town was only a few miles away.
(We, who were seeing the sign, realized . . .)

In the next example, *looking at the unusual scenery* has no noun to modify; therefore, it is a dangling modifier:

NOT: **Looking at the unusual scenery,** the car went into the ditch.
(The car, which was looking . . .)

If you tell who drove the car as subject of the independent clause, your readers then understand who was looking at the scenery:

> BUT: **Looking at the unusual scenery,** *Tom* drove the car into a ditch.
> (Tom, who was looking...)

Dangling modifiers may also result when the verb in the independent clause is passive (*be* + Part 4) and the doer is not included in the sentence:

> NOT: **Glancing at her watch,** no time was lost in leaving for the airport.
> (Who was glancing at her watch? Who was leaving for the airport?)
> NOT: **Glancing at her watch,** it was decided to leave immediately for the airport.
> BUT: **Glancing at her watch,** *Terri* lost no time in leaving for the airport.

A verbal phrase may also be a dangling modifier if the word it should modify is a possessive modifying the subject of a sentence. In the next sentence, *wearing old clothes and a big hat* cannot modify *woman's,* a possessive that modifies *garden.* The sentence has to be rewritten with *woman* as the subject:

> NOT: **Wearing old clothes and a big hat,** the woman's garden needed weeding.
> BUT: **Wearing old clothes and a big hat,** the *woman* weeded her garden.

EXERCISE 42

Revise the following sentences to eliminate dangling or misplaced modifiers. Suggestion: If the verb in the independent clause is passive (*be* + Part 4), make the verb active. The verbal phrase should then modify the subject of the verb.

1. Looking out the window, the mysterious object was seen by three curious people.

2. Lapping water eagerly from the mud puddle, Joan's uncle waited for the thirsty dog.

3. Upset by the decision, it was decided by the woman to look for another job.

4. The tall, blonde woman held a small poodle wearing a red bikini.

5. Standing on the beach, three sharks were watched not far from shore by frightened swimmers.

6. While painting the wall, the ladder slipped, and Jane fell to the floor.

7. Running to catch the train, Ted's suitcase was dropped, and his clothes scattered everywhere.

8. Shining brightly through the window, the room was lighted by the sun.

9. Sitting in the doctor's office for an hour, the magazine was read from cover to cover.

10. After opening the package, the frozen vegetables should be placed in boiling water for four minutes.

11. The boy gently stroked the soft, fluffy kitten carrying a BB gun.

Lesson 43

Absolute Phrases

The adverbial, adjective, and noun verbal phrases you studied in lessons in this unit function as nouns or modifiers within an independent clause. Another kind of phrase with a verbal in it is the **absolute phrase.** It must be attached to an independent clause, but it does not function within the independent clause as a noun or modifier. It contains an idea closely related to the idea in the independent clause.

A second difference between the two kinds of phrases is that the absolute phrase has a subject, but the adverbial, adjective, and noun phrases usually do not have subjects. These differences are illustrated in the examples that follow. The first example shows three sentences with the same subject—*dog.* The combined sentence shows two of the sentences changed to *adjective verbal phrases:*

SINGLE SENTENCES

The huge black *dog* watched two men near the high fence.
The *dog* growled viciously.
The *dog* snapped his teeth menacingly.

COMBINED SENTENCE

The huge black dog, **growling viciously, snapping his teeth menacingly,** watched two men near the high fence.

The next example shows three sentences, each with a different subject—*dog, teeth,* and *body.* The combined sentence shows two of the sentences changed to *absolute phrases:*

SINGLE SENTENCES

The huge black *dog* growled viciously.
His white *teeth* snapped menacingly.
His *body* was positioned to attack.

COMBINED SENTENCE

The huge black dog growled viciously, **his white teeth snapping menacingly, his body positioned to attack.**

In the next example, the absolute phrase appears at the beginning of the sentence:

The steering pin broke.
The car plunged off the mountain road into a ravine.

The steering pin having broken, the car plunged off the mountain road into a ravine.

Notice that commas enclose absolute phrases.

Combine the following sets of sentences by making one sentence an independent clause and the others absolute phrases. First, underline the words that will make up the absolute phrase. Then change the verb to a verbal. Finally, attach the absolute phrase to the independent clause and write the combined sentence.

1. The young woman prepared the dinner automatically.
   Her mind was fixed on the events of the day.

2. The mission was accomplished.
   The astronauts were able to return to earth.

3. He relaxed in his large chair.
   The fire was blazing in the fireplace.
   The wind was blasting the trees and shrubs outside.

4. The new owners moved eagerly into the old house.
   Its rooms were newly painted and carpeted.

5. The heir had been located.
   The attorney was able to settle the old man's estate.

6. The best-selling novel lay in the rubbish.
   Its cover was badly stained.
   Its pages were torn.

Lesson 44

Combining Phrases and Clauses

The phrases and clauses you have studied in this unit and in Unit Eight suggest ways you can write tightly constructed sentences, each containing several ideas. The following examples show some of the possibilities using just verbal phrases:

SINGLE SENTENCES

        managing
~~The president managed~~ the business.
X The president spent many hours.

X The president's secretary could not cope with the details.
      lacking
~~He lacked~~ the necessary experience.

~~The president was~~ exhausted by all the work.
X The president called a consultant.
~~The consultant was~~ well-qualified and highly trained.
         to examine
~~The consultant examined~~ the business procedures.

X The consultant agreed.
          to make
~~The consultant would make~~ a detailed study.
    to recommend
~~She would recommend~~ a plan.
        to increase
~~The plan would increase~~ business efficiency.

COMBINED SENTENCES

The president spent many hours, **managing the office.**

The president's secretary, **lacking the necessary experience,** could not cope with the details.

Exhausted by all the work, the president called a **well-qualified and highly trained** consultant **to examine the office procedure.**

The consultant agreed **to make a detailed study** and **to recommend a plan to increase office efficiency.**

In the process of combining sentences you may want to change the order of the words, placing a word from one sentence next to a word in another sentence. Such rearranging works effectively as long as you keep the ideas expressed in the original sentences. In some cases omitting one idea might change the meaning of the combined sentence.

EXERCISE 44A

Combine the following sets of sentences by making one sentence the base sentence and the other a phrase—verbal phrase, appositive (Lesson 31), prepositional phrase (Lesson 20), absolute phrase, or a compound construction. Begin by placing X before the base sentence. Then draw a line through words to be deleted. Finally, combine the sentences into a single sentence, using punctuation wherever it is needed.

EXAMPLE:
          Looking
    ~~Henry looked~~ out the window. /V-ing,/
    X / Henry saw an / ambulance next door.
    /and/ ~~He saw~~ a police car next door.

COMBINED:
    Looking out the window, Henry saw an ambulance and a police car next door.

1. X   Barbara's aunt / puffed nervously on the cigarette.
    /,/ ~~She is~~ a little old lady. /,/
           trying
    ~~She tried~~ hard to look sophisticated. /, V-ing/

2. X   The airplane / barely missed the treetops at the end of the runway.
       The airplane was overloaded with cargo. /, V-ed,/

3.   The young man wanted to appear well informed.
       The young man used words he could scarcely pronounce.

4.   The girl is Dave's friend.
       She is the one combing her hair.

5.   Barbara was sobbing uncontrollably.
       Barbara paid no attention to the strolling musicians.
       They were singing beneath her window.

6.   Michael awoke suddenly.
       He was in his hotel room.
       He saw two men.
       They were looking out the door.
       They were looking down the hall.

7.   Many students have been able to pay college tuition.
They receive scholarships.
The scholarships are donated by business people in the community.

8.   Marcia typed the letters rapidly.
She was efficient.
She was well trained.
Her fingers moved quickly over the keys.

RELATIONSHIP OF VERBAL PHRASES AND DEPENDENT CLAUSES

The next examples show the complex relationship of verbal phrases and dependent clauses in a single sentence. One verbal phrase may complete another, a prepositional phrase may modify a verbal, or a dependent clause may either modify or complete verbals. The symbols immediately above the words identify each word's function or form. The top rows of symbols identify the function of the phrase or clause:

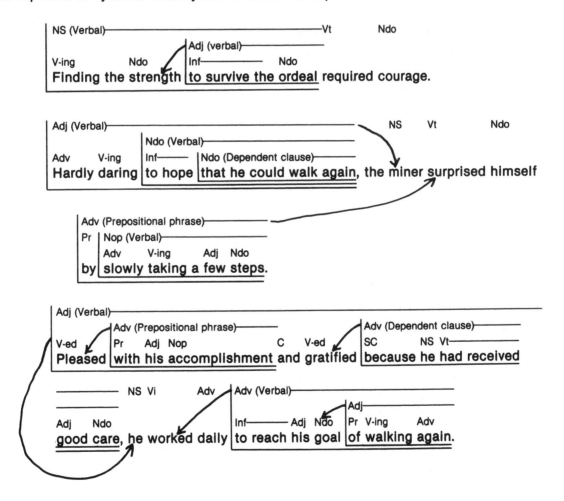

Combine the following sets of sentences by making one sentence the independent clause and the others phrases or dependent clauses. Begin by underlining the words you will use in each phrase or clause. You may find more than one way to combine each group of sentences.

1. The man sat at the desk.
   He was young.
   He was blond.
   He was typing a letter very rapidly.
   He was typing a letter to the mayor.

2. He burned with anger because of the damage.
   Damage had been done to his new green sports car.
   Damage had been done the night before.

3. He was lying in bed about midnight.
   He heard a car.
   The car raced wildly down the street.
   The car sideswiped the left side of his car.
   It dented the door.
   It dented the fender badly.

4. The letter was completed.
   He read it once again.
   He corrected two typing errors.

5. He asked the mayor something.
   Why did the police not patrol the streets more closely?

6. He drove to the post office.
   He stopped to the right of a late model black sedan.
   It was waiting for the traffic light to change.

7. He immediately noticed long scratches and dents.
   They were along the right side of the car.
   They matched those on his car.

8. The light changed.
   The black car raced across the intersection.
   It raced down the crowded street.

9. The young man pursued the black car as closely as he could.
   He helped to catch a glimpse of the license plate.

10. He managed to see three numbers.
    He repeated them over and over to himself.
    He followed the car.

11. The black car turned a corner.
    It disappeared down a side street.

12. The young man heard a siren behind him.
    He pulled over to the curb.
    He stopped.

13. The police officer noted the dents on the side of the young man's car.
    The officer said something.
    The police had been looking for the person.
    The person had sideswiped the mayor's car the night before.

14. The officer was pleased about something.
    He had found the person.

EXERCISE 44C

On a separate sheet of paper write three sets of simple sentences about a single topic. Each set should contain three or four sentences. Then combine each set into one sentence containing phrases and clauses. See Exercises 44A and 44B for examples. Label your sentences *Exercise 44C,* and show them to your instructor or tutor.

Lesson 45

Fragments: Nonsentences

As you write several sentences about a topic, you may discover in rereading the passage that some of the word groups are not sentences. They are parts of sentences, called **fragments**. They occur because you sometimes concentrate so hard on the idea you are expressing that you pay little attention to sentence structure. This experience is not at all unusual, and it should cause no problems if you are able to go back later and examine each of the word groups to be sure they are sentences.

In many cases you may find that the fragment should be connected to the preceding sentence, or you may prefer to add or change words to make the word group a sentence. You should be able to recognize the fragments discussed below because they are phrases and dependent clauses, constructions you have been studying in this text. If you find that you have punctuated a fragment as if it were a sentence, decide whether it can be attached to the sentence just before or after it or whether you should add or change words to make it a sentence. As you read the fragments in the following examples, try to decide how you would change them before you check your revision with the one given. The correction symbol for fragments is **Frag**.

Prepositional Phrase

NOT: The man keeps coming back. **In spite of all the trouble he has caused.**
BUT: The man keeps coming back in spite of all the trouble he has caused.

Adjective with Modifiers

NOT: The mother of a five-year-old spends her mornings at the elementary school. **Ready to help children who need attention.**
BUT: The mother of a five-year-old spends her mornings at the elementary school, ready to help children who need attention.

Appositive

NOT: The runner won seven races in the competition. **A record few others could match.**
BUT: The runner won seven races in the competition, a record few others could match.

Verbal Phrase

NOT: The old man searched for food constantly. **Wondering where he would find his next meal.**
BUT: The old man searched for food constantly, wondering where he would find his next meal.
OR: Wondering where he would find his next meal, the old man searched for food constantly.

NOT:	Some people now ride the bus to work. **To save gasoline and parking fees.**
BUT:	Some people now ride the bus to work to save gasoline and parking fees.

Dependent Clause

NOT:	**Even though George did not like the people there.** He went to the party.
BUT:	Even though George did not like the people there, he went to the party.
NOT:	Several guests spoke to George. **Which surprised him.**
BUT:	Several guests spoke to George. Their unexpected friendliness surprised him.
OR:	Several guests spoke to George, who was surprised by their unexpected friendliness.

A fragment like the one below needs rethinking to focus on the point to be made. The writer begins with one idea—television programs—and then becomes involved in discussing disabled viewers. The revision limits the discussion about disabled people and focuses on television programs:

FRAGMENT:	The television programs that appeal to people who watch television several hours a day because they are physically disabled and cannot go out by themselves.
SENTENCE:	Television serials and game shows seem to appeal especially to disabled people confined to their rooms.

Fragments like those shown above are not acceptable. However, you will find that experienced writers can use fragments skillfully, sometimes to emphasize a point or to comment on it:

People who overcome their fear of flying sometimes experience a great sense of relief. **For a very good reason.** They no longer feel trapped in a "flying coffin." **Quite the opposite.** They feel free, capable of conquering anything.

Sometimes fragments are used to set a mood, especially in stories:

A starlit night. Waves breaking on the beach. The two of them were oblivious to everything except this moment.

Until you gain writing experience, you probably should change fragments that you write to sentences. If you believe a fragment is appropriate and effective, talk with your instructor about the fragment. You will gradually develop a sense of judgment that will enable you to write acceptable fragments.

EXERCISE 45A

Decide whether each of the following groups are sentences or fragments. Write S for sentence and F for fragment in the blanks at the right.

1. the heart is a hollow, muscular organ   _____

2. divided into four chambers   _____

3. the heart is a double pump   _____

4. the first pump receives blood containing carbon dioxide   _____

5. pumping the blood to the lungs   _____

6. oxygen enters the bloodstream in the lungs   _____

7. the blood returns to the heart   _____

8. the second pump receiving the oxygenated blood   _____

9. which is pumped through the aorta   _____

10. the heart pumps the blood to all parts of the body   _____

EXERCISE 45B

Some of the following word groups are independent clauses, and others are fragments.
Read all the word groups first. Then decide which ones can be sentences and which
ones can be combined to make a sentence. Finally, rewrite the combined sentences,
beginning each sentence with a capital letter and placing a period after it. Add commas wherever they are needed.

the duckbill platypus, a strange creature that
lives in Australia and Tasmania

the platypus seems to be both a waterfowl and
animal

although the platypus is a mammal

its young hatch from eggs

its body looks like that of an otter

yet it has a ducklike bill

used for finding worms in the mud

and feeding on tadpoles and small fish

and it has broadly webbed feet

used for swimming

the male platypus has a poisonous spur on his
hind foot

used for self-defense

The following word groups are fragments. Make them sentences by adding words or by changing words and using punctuation as needed.

1. At the time of his departure for the Orient.

2. Which resulted in his being dismissed.

3. Being the last person to leave the meeting.

4. While he could not manage his own affairs.

5. The scientific experiment being conducted in the laboratory.

6. History reports reviewed at the end of the semester.

7. Hoping to find at least one friend in Europe.

8. Magnificent view from every room in the house.

9. Unlike any other play he had ever seen.

10. Not wanting to appear overly inquisitive.

Show these sentences to your instructor or tutor.

Unit Nine Review

Practice Test

SCORE PART I (Total—100 points) _____
SCORE PART II* (Total—100 points) _____
TOTAL _____
AVERAGE _____

*Average scores for Part I and Part II only if the Part I score is 85 percent or more.

PART I

A. Rewrite the following sentences, and make the verbs active. Write basic sentence patterns above YOUR sentences.
(6 points—3 points each)   (Lesson 39)   Score _____

1. The auditorium was dedicated by the mayor last Sunday.

2. The building was illuminated by several hundred ceiling lights.

B. Rewrite the following sentences, and make the verb passive. Write basic sentence patterns above YOUR sentences.
(6 points—3 points each)   (Lesson 39)   Score _____

1. The movers carried the furniture into the new apartment.

2. The biologist placed the test tubes in the incubator.

C. Underline the entire verbal phrase in each of the following sentences. In the blanks at the right write *V-ing, V-ed, Inf,* or *Absolute* to identify each phrase.
(20 points—2 points each)   (Lessons 38, 40, 41, 43)   Score _____

1. The passengers, recovered from their seasickness, enjoyed the cruise. _____

2. Dave helped by carrying the furniture into the apartment. _____

3. The prizewinner having arrived, the awards banquet began. _____

4. Mary was ready to take the history exam. _____

5. The lawmakers hoped to pass the tax relief legislation. _____

6. Holding a job and taking five courses became increasingly difficult for the college sophomore. _____

7. Dale found writing essays to be a challenge. _____

8. To hope for success is not enough. _____

9. Opening the refrigerator door, Susie saw the custard cream pie. _____

10. Jim completed the job by working twelve hours a day for two weeks. _____

D. In the following sentences you will find dangling or misplaced modifiers. If the modifier is dangling, rewrite the sentence and add words if necessary to clarify the meaning. If the modifier is misplaced, rewrite the sentence to correct the faulty relationship.
(20 points—4 points each)　　(Lesson 42)　　　　　Score _____

1. While washing the car, the bucket turned over accidentally.

2. Unhappy with the apartment, it was agreed to find another place.

3. Sam filled the copper kettle with vegetables, which he kept polished.

4. Reaching the amusement park, a ride was taken on the roller coaster.

5. Sitting on his perch, Bob was amused by the parrot.

E. Combine the following sets of sentences by making one sentence the independent clause and the others phrases or clauses. First, place X before the base sentence. Then draw lines through words to be deleted. Finally, combine the sentences, and add punctuation where it is needed.
(48 points—8 points each for sentences 1-3; 12 points for 4-5)
(Lessons 40, 41, 43, 44)　　　　　　　　　　　Score _____

1.　　　　　The restaurant manager works constantly.
　　/Inf/　~~He tries~~ to provide appetizing menus.　/and/
　　　　　~~He tries to provide~~ a relaxed atmosphere in the restaurant.

2.　　　　　Brett Weaver represented the Star Corporation.
　　/who/　Brett Weaver could scarcely lift his heavy brown leather suitcase.
　　　　　It was filled with samples of attractive upholstery material.　/, V-ed/

3. The woman waited apprehensively for her friend to arrive.
   She feared anyone who approached her.

4. Wayne likes helping physically disabled people.
   This gives Wayne great satisfaction.

5. The news reporter examined her odd assortment of clothes.
   The news reporter decided this.
   She would throw everything away.
   She would invest in a few coordinated skirts, blouses, and jackets.

PART II

A. Write sentences with verbal phrases. Use the kind of verbal indicated in the parentheses after each number. Underline each verbal phrase.
(60 points—15 points each)   (Lessons 38, 40, 41, 43)   Score _____

   1. (V-ing)

   2. (V-ed)

   3. (*to* + verb)

   4. (*having* + Part 4)

B. Change the following fragments to sentences in either of these ways:
   (a) Add words to the fragments.   (b) Change words within the fragment.
   (40 points—10 points each)   (Lesson 45)   Score _____

   1. Leaving home for the first time.

   2. Although the tourist had brought seven hundred dollars.

   3. Packed tightly in the small car.

   4. The nurse being a kind person.

Unit Ten

Punctuation and Capitalization

This unit is mainly a review of punctuation you have already studied, but it is a very important unit because it brings together the patterns of sentences you have studied and the punctuation used within sentences. You have seen that punctuation is usually orderly and consistent in the sentences you have been writing. The marks of punctuation serve as signals: sometimes a period or semicolon may tell readers to stop and then begin the reading of another idea. Or two commas may enclose a word group that gives extra information about a word in the sentence. In this unit you will review these uses along with certain conventional uses of punctuation, such as the colon after the salutation in a business letter.

The marks of punctuation are an attempt in written English to indicate the pauses, stress, and rising and falling pitches in spoken language; however, the uses of punctuation do not match the spoken signals consistently. *You should not use commas to indicate every pause you make in spoken language.* You use commas in certain ways with particular grammatical constructions.

You will find that punctuation varies in different kinds of writing. A technical or legal report may contain more detailed punctuation than a newspaper or magazine article. The punctuation you have been studying is suitable for the reports and papers you will write for college and for business.

In the first two lessons you will see that punctuation either separates specific kinds of words or word groups from others or encloses a word group within a sentence or within another word group. The third lesson discusses marks of punctuation used in conventional or generally accepted ways. Finally, the fourth lesson discusses the conventions for capitalizing words in English.

For more details about the grammatical constructions named in this unit, refer to the index at the end of this book or to the lessons noted in parentheses following the name of the grammatical construction.

Lesson 46

Punctuation to Separate

Three marks of punctuation—period, question mark, and exclamation point—signal the end of sentences and separate one sentence from another. Frequently these end marks are the only ones needed for short, uncomplicated sentences; but you learned in other lessons in this book that sentences can be combined and that you usually must use punctuation to separate the parts.

PUNCTUATION TO SEPARATE SENTENCES

1a. The PERIOD (.) is placed at the end of a declarative statement:

> The newlyweds made plans for a European trip.
> They read travel books and studied maps.

1b. The PERIOD is also used after commands:

> Call the travel agent tomorrow.

2a. The QUESTION MARK (?) indicates the end of a direct question:

> Did they really want to travel?
> What kinds of clothing should they take?

2b. It is not used after an indirect question, a sentence in which the question is a part of a declarative statement:

> They asked themselves why they wanted to see Europe.
> They wondered how much money they would need.

3. The EXCLAMATION POINT (!) appears after words, phrases, or clauses expressing shock or excitement:

> For fun!   The opportunity of a lifetime!

PUNCTUATION TO SEPARATE INDEPENDENT CLAUSES

When you combine two sentences with related ideas to form a compound sentence, you have to show where one ends and the other begins. Commas, semicolons, and colons are used in the following ways:

4a. Two independent clauses (word groups with subjects and predicates) joined by coordinating conjunctions, such as *and, but, or, nor,* and *for,* in a compound sentence (Lesson 28) are generally separated by a COMMA (,). The comma comes before the coordinating conjunction:

> The newlyweds talked about their European trip for several weeks, **but** they could not decide how long to stay.

NOTE: NO COMMA separates a subject and its verb because these are not coordinate (equal to one another); each serves a different function in the sentence (Subject and Predicate, Lesson 1):

> NOT: Tod and Ellen, planned an exciting trip.
> BUT: Tod and Ellen planned an exciting trip.

4b. If each independent clause is short, NO COMMA is needed:

> They talked **and** they thought.

4c. If either of the two independent clauses contains commas, a SEMICOLON (;) is used before the coordinating conjunction. In some cases, the semicolon helps readers see the beginning of the second independent clause, which could be hidden because of the commas in the first independent clause:

> Ellen and Tod wanted to see Michelangelo's *David* in Florence, his *Pietà* in Rome, and his *Pietà* in Milan; **but** they could visit only two of the cities, not three.

5a. Two independent clauses with closely related ideas are separated by a SEMICOLON alone:

> They planned to visit Italy; Rome, Florence, and Venice captured their interest.

5b. If the second independent clause is an explanation that is closely related to the first independent clause, a COLON (:) is used to separate the two clauses:

> Ellen had a good reason for visiting Italy: She wanted to see the small town where her grandparents had lived.

6a. When a transitional expression *(however, furthermore, for example)* comes immediately after the SEMICOLON in a compound sentence (Lesson 29), a COMMA follows the conjunctive adverb to separate it from the second independent clause:

> Tod wanted to travel Venice's Grand Canal in a gondola; **however,** Ellen was afraid she would become seasick.

6b. Transitional words or word groups, such as *that is* and *namely,* used to introduce an independent clause that explains a preceding independent clause, follow the semicolon and are set off by a comma:

> They decided to begin their tour in northern Europe; **that is,** they planned to visit England and Scotland.

7a. Three or more independent clauses in a series are separated by COMMAS:

>They had their pictures taken for passports, they applied for passports, **and** they bought traveler's checks.

7b. If the independent clauses in a series are long or contain commas, they are separated by SEMICOLONS:

>Tod and Ellen loaned their car to a friend for three months; they decided to find an apartment to rent after they returned from their trip; **and** they stored their wedding presents, furniture, and clothing in a huge locker.

EXERCISE 46A

Numbers appear at various points in the sentences below. Corresponding numbered blanks appear at the right. Add punctuation at these points wherever it is needed in the sentences by writing the NAME of the mark of punctuation in the first blank at the right. In the second blank write the number of the rule you find in the lesson to tell why you have used the punctuation. If no punctuation is needed, write X in the first blank and the number of the rule in the second blank. Begin by writing V above each verb and NS above each subject to identify the independent clauses.

Marks of punctuation: Comma (,)   Semicolon (;)   Colon (:)

NS   V

EXAMPLE: The Louvre in Paris houses famous

1. _____semicolon_____   ___5a___

paintings and sculptures for example
                             1   **2**

2. _____comma_____   ___6a___

NS   V———
visitors can see the *Mona Lisa* and *Winged Victory.*

Notre Dame Cathedral was built on an island in

1. _____   _____

the Seine River in Paris but it is easily accessible
                        1

2. _____   _____

because of bridges from both banks. The Cathedral

3. _____   _____

is old and it is beautiful. Gargoyles project out on
     2   **3**

4. _____   _____

all parts of the outside walls of the Cathedral. The

gargoyles are carved statues and they look like hor-
                        4

rible demons one sees in bad dreams. Some are

winged creatures with claw feet others have gro-
5

5. _____ _____

tesque, satanic faces with huge, bulging eyes and

6. _____ _____

sharp teeth and still others are unreal combinations
6

7. _____ _____

of different kinds of animals. However, gargoyles

8. _____ _____

serve a practical purpose hollows in their backs car-
7

9. _____ _____

ry rainwater away from the ornate building walls to

10. _____ _____

prevent erosion. The water trickles through their

11. _____ _____

open mouths and it falls to the streets.
8

12. _____ _____

Another attraction most visitors to Paris see is the

13. _____ _____

Eiffel Tower it was built for the 1903 World Exposi-
9

tion. The Eiffel Tower is impressive   the massive
10

network of metal rises almost four hundred feet into

the air. People beneath the Eiffel Tower   feel very
11

insignificant. Slow-moving elevators carry hundreds

of people to the four levels   consequently   the
12   **13**

lines of people waiting often become very long.

PUNCTUATION TO SEPARATE WORDS AND PHRASES

Punctuation, especially commas, separates words or word groups of equal rank (coordinate) that appear as a list or as a series. The words in the list are the essential elements of a series of sentences that have been combined:

SINGLE SENTENCES	COMBINED SENTENCE
Tod and Ellen bought **airline tickets.** Tod and Ellen bought **luggage.** Tod and Ellen bought **clothes.**	Tod and Ellen bought **airline tickets, luggage,** and **clothes.**

Word groups at the beginning and end of a sentence, such as absolute phrases and questions, are separated by punctuation because they do not function within the sentence. Details about each of these uses of punctuation follow.

8a. COMMAS separate three or more nouns in a compound subject (Lesson 29):

Friends, relatives, **and** travel agents had suggested places to visit.

8b. NO COMMA appears before *and* when it joins just two subjects:

Tod and Ellen listened to everyone.

9a. COMMAS separate three or more verbs and their objects or complements in a compound predicate (Lesson 30):

The newlyweds picked a date to travel, chose countries to visit, **and** made airline and hotel reservations.

9b. NO COMMA appears before *and* when it joins two predicates:

They had talked with airline representatives and discussed plans with friends.

10a. A COMMA is used between items in a series—words, phrases, or clauses—including the word before *and:*

Ellen packed dresses, shoes, sweaters, **and** skirts.

10b. NO COMMA appears before *and* if it joins two words that form a unit:

Tod had sports coats with **coordinated shirts and trousers,** three pairs of shoes, and five bottles of aspirin.

10c. A SEMICOLON separates word groups in a series when the word groups have commas within them:

They carried the addresses of Joan Mason, Tod's mother; Tom and Betty Parker, Ellen's parents; **and** Virginia Gilbert, Ellen's married sister, to notify in case of an emergency.

11a. When a list or series follows a COLON at the end of an independent clause, COMMAS are used to separate the words or word groups:

Tod and Ellen wanted to visit four other countries: Czechoslovakia, Hungary, Italy, **and** France.

11b. When expressions such as *the following* or *as follows* and a colon introduce a list or series, COMMAS are used to separate the words or word groups:

In Prague they would travel with the following guides: the escort from Vienna, the guide representing the country of Czechoslovakia, **and** the guide for the city of Prague.

11c. NO COLON separates a verb and the nouns following it:

NOT: Their bus would carry: the passengers, the guides, and the luggage.
BUT: Their bus would carry the passengers, the guides, and the luggage.

12a. A COMMA separates adjectives if *and* has been omitted between them (Lesson 18):

smiling **and** enthusiastic travelers	smiling, enthusiastic travelers
noisy **and** fretful **and** dark-haired baby	noisy, fretful, dark-haired baby

12b. In some cases *and* cannot appear between adjectives; therefore, NO COMMA is used between them:

NOT:	crowded and airline terminal		NOT:	brown and leather suitcase
BUT:	crowded airline terminal		BUT:	brown leather suitcase

13. A question attached to the end of a sentence is set off by a COMMA and ends with a question mark:

The date for the trip seems far away, **doesn't it?**

14. The DASH, approximately twice as long as the hyphen, indicates a break in thought when the sentence is interrupted by a comment or question. (In typing use two hyphens together for a dash):

I am tired of—no, I must be patient and calm.

15. A COMMA may be used in places it usually does not appear if it is needed to separate words to prevent confusion in the reading of a sentence:

CONFUSING:	In the lead-lined bag Tod carried extra film for his camera.
CLEAR:	In the lead-lined bag, Tod carried extra film for his camera.
OR:	In the lead-lined bag Tod carried was exta film for his camera.

16. An absolute phrase (Lesson 43) is separated from the beginning or end of a sentence with a COMMA:

The day for departure having arrived, Tod and Ellen went to the air terminal. Ellen waited nervously in the boarding area, **her hand trembling slightly as she held her ticket.**

EXERCISE 46B

Numbers appear at various points in the sentences below. Corresponding numbered blanks appear at the right. Add punctuation at these points wherever it is needed in the sentences by writing the NAME of the mark of punctuation in the first blank at the right. In the second blank write the number of the rule you find in both parts of the lesson to tell why you have used the punctuation. If no punctuation is needed, write X in the first blank and the number of the rule in the second blank. Begin by writing V above each verb and NS above each subject to identify the independent clauses.

Marks of punctuation: Comma (,)   Semicolon (;)   Colon (:)   Dash (—)

Venice and a few other cities have no streets and
    1   2

no cars. The famous Italian city was built on more
                      3

than a hundred small islands, formed by deposits of

silt at the mouths of four rivers emptying into the

Adriatic Sea. Twelfth and thirteenth century Vene-

tian merchants built their warehouses at the water's

edge and their houses on top of the warehouses.
     4

The unusual magnificent city has not changed
        5

much in several hundred years. Today Venetians
                              6

and visitors may go from one building or apartment
                            7

to another on stone walks or travel from one place
                   8

to another in water taxis water buses or private
                 9   10

motorboats. Even the police travel in boats. The

city offers a different way of living doesn't it?
                  11

1. _____ _____
2. _____ _____
3. _____ _____
4. _____ _____
5. _____ _____
6. _____ _____
7. _____ _____
8. _____ _____
9. _____ _____
10. _____ _____
11. _____ _____

EXERCISE 46C

Write sentences according to the directions given below. If you need help, refer to the examples in this lesson.

1. Write a sentence in which a comma (,) and coordinating conjunction (*and, but, or, for*) are used between two independent clauses.

2. Write a sentence that requires one or more semicolons (;).

3. Write a sentence in which commas are used to separate words or word groups in a series.

Show these sentences to your instructor or tutor.

Lesson 47

Punctuation to Enclose Extra Information

The basic sentence consists of a subject and a predicate, but words or word groups may be added to either part. As you practiced combining sentences in earlier lessons in this text, you often used clauses or phrases as modifiers that needed to be enclosed in commas:

SINGLE SENTENCES

Ellen was eager to see Europe.

/who/ Ellen had never traveled outside the United States.

COMBINED SENTENCE

Ellen, **who had never traveled outside the United States,** was eager to see Europe.

Punctuation marks that enclose word groups are used in pairs, one at the beginning and the other at the end of the word group. As you go through the uses of punctuation discussed in this lesson, you will see two commas or two dashes enclosing a word group within a sentence; but if the word group comes at the beginning or at the end of the sentence, only one mark of punctuation appears. Two other marks of punctuation—parentheses ( ) and brackets [ ]—are always used in pairs to enclose additional information.

1a. COMMAS appear before and after an appositive (Lesson 31) if it gives extra information about a specific noun it renames:

Ellen and Tod boarded a plane, **a Boeing 747,** that carried more than 300 passengers and twenty crew members.

1b. If the appositive is needed to make a general noun specific, NO COMMAS enclose it:

The Shakespearean actor **Dudley Hanes** came aboard.

1c. Two DASHES set off an appositive that has commas within it:

One passenger must have tried a variety of cosmetics—**bright red lipstick, frosted blue eye shadow, and white nail enamel**—but she looked more like a circus clown than a glamorous woman.

2a. COMMAS enclose an adjective clause (Lesson 34) if it gives additional information about the specific noun it modifies:

The chief flight attendant, **who spoke French, German, and Spanish in addition to English,** explained safety precautions in all four languages.

2b. If the adjective clause is needed to make a general noun specific or tell which one(s), NO COMMAS enclose it:

During the eleven-hour flight passengers **who had rented earphones** listened to music and later watched a movie.

3a. A COMMA follows an introductory adverbial clause, which begins with words like *because, although, if,* and *as* (Lesson 33):

As the giant plane flew northeast at more than five hundred miles an hour, Ellen saw the night sky on the right of the plane and daylight on the left.

3b. NO COMMA is used before an adverbial clause at the end of the sentence when it modifies the verb in the sentence:

In a short time the night sky was on the left of the plane, and brilliant layers of yellow, orange, and red appeared in the eastern sky **before the sun rose.**

3c. COMMAS enclose an adverbial clause within a sentence:

The plane, **before it landed in London,** flew over Greenland and Scotland.

4. NO COMMAS separate a noun clause (Lesson 35) from the rest of the sentence:

Tod and Ellen decided **that they would take a walking tour of London.**

5a. A COMMA sets off a verbal phrase modifier (Lesson 38) at the beginning or at the end of the sentence:

Waiting to cross London streets, Ellen and Tod became confused by traffic traveling on the "wrong" side of the street.
They hurried across, **holding hands tightly.**

5b. COMMAS enclose verbal phrase modifiers that give additional information:

During a visit to the Tower of London, they climbed the narrow, winding stairways in the White Tower, **built by William the Conqueror,** to examine suits of armor and weapons.

5c. NO COMMAS enclose the verbal phrase modifier when it is needed to identify the noun or make it specific:

The suit of armor **worn by Henry VIII** stood at least six feet tall.

5d. NO COMMAS enclose the verbal phrase when the verbal phrase is the subject, object, or complement:

Riding a double-decked bus in London was a new experience.
The young couple enjoyed **attending several plays in London theaters.**

6. COMMAS enclose modifiers following nouns (Lesson 18):

On a Sunday, **cold, foggy, and damp,** Ellen and Tod took a boat trip up the Thames River to Windsor Castle.

7a. A COMMA follows a noun of direct address and expressions such as *yes, no, well,* and *now* at the beginning of the sentence:

> **Yes,** the trip was thrilling and satisfying.
> "**Tod,** when will we arrive in Vienna?"

7b. Two COMMAS enclose a noun of direct address within the sentence:

> "I think, **Ellen,** that the flight from London takes about two hours."

8a. A COMMA follows transitional words, such as *moreover* and *finally,* when these words begin a sentence:

> **Finally,** they landed in the airport outside Vienna.

8b. Two COMMAS enclose transitional expressions *(however, in addition)* and parenthetic word groups *(I believe, it seems, of course, by the way)* within sentences:

> Vienna, **it appeared,** was built around St. Stephen's Cathedral, which dominated the skyline.

9a. A COMMA follows prepositional phrases (Lesson 20) at the beginning of the sentence if they are long or if they act as connectors with the preceding sentence:

> **During the tour through the Summer Palace on the outskirts of Vienna,** Ellen tried to imagine what life was like when the royal family lived there.

9b. NO COMMA follows prepositional phrases at the beginning of the sentence if they are short or if the verb follows them:

> **In the corner of each room** stood a huge porcelain stove for winter heating.

9c. NO COMMAS enclose prepositional phrases within sentences when they modify particular words in sentences:

> Tod and Ellen climbed to the top **of the cathedral spire** and looked out over the city.
> Ellen went **into several pastry shops** and sampled the delicacies.

9d. COMMAS enclose prepositional phrases used as transitions:

> Tod, **on the other hand,** tried the beers and wines.

10. Coordinate elements that show contrast are enclosed in COMMAS:

> They were finding it difficult, **but not impossible,** to buy souvenirs for everyone.

11. A phrase beginning with *such as* is usually enclosed in COMMAS if it adds extra information. (The first comma appears before *such*):

> Ellen chose small gifts, **such as brooches, earrings, and perfume,** for her mother and friends.

Although words and word groups added to a sentence are enclosed most frequently in commas, you may also use dashes and parentheses in certain cases. You have learned to use dashes to enclose appositives that have commas within them (Lesson 31):

12a. DASHES may also enclose parenthetic elements that comment on something in the sentence:

> Their suitcases—**each had brought two**—soon became tightly packed as they added the gifts.

12b. PARENTHESES, always used in pairs, enclose parenthetic elements that should be isolated from the sentence because they are not needed to understand the sentence; they are a temporary move away from the point being discussed:

> They spent three days in Czechoslovakia **(a republic formed after World War I of Bohemia, Moravia, Silesia, and Slovakia)** and then traveled to Hungary.

12c. PARENTHESES enclose numerals or letters in a series:

> The young couple had three choices: **(1)** they could spend all their time in Budapest; **(2)** they could take a two-day cruise on the Danube; **(3)** they could explore the Roman ruins in the area.

13a. BRACKETS, also always used in pairs, enclose information in a quoted passage, such as the name of a book, the writer's personal comment about the quotation, or words and dates inserted by an editor:

> "Twelve years later **[1541]** the greater part of Hungary became a Turkish province."

13b. BRACKETS may be used within PARENTHESES:

> Ellen kept sending postcards to her family (her parents, her two uncles **[one lives in Canada],** and five cousins).

Punctuation Within Parentheses and Brackets

NO PERIOD appears within the parentheses or brackets unless the sentence is completely set apart from other sentences:

> Tod sent cards only to his mother. **(He also wrote her long letters about the trip.)**

If COMMAS, PERIODS, and other marks of punctuation are part of the main sentence, they are placed outside the parentheses and brackets:

> Ellen and Tod had felt very much at home in England, but they really enjoyed Italy **(their favorite),** Austria, Czechoslovakia, and Hungary.

Numbers appear at various points in the sentences below. Corresponding numbered blanks appear at the right. Add punctuation at these points wherever it is needed in the sentences by writing the NAME of the mark of punctuation in the first blank at the right. In the second blank write the number of the rule you find in the lesson to tell why you have used the punctuation. If no punctuation is needed, write X in the first blank and the number of the rule in the second blank. Begin by writing V above each verb and NS above each subject to identify the independent clauses.

Marks of punctuation: Comma (,)   Dash (—)   Parentheses ( )

A.   Tod and Ellen enjoyed Budapest the capital
                                  1

1. _____ _____

of Hungary situated on both sides of the Danube
         2   **3**

2. _____ _____

River. The city Buda is one one side of the river; on
             4   **5**

3. _____ _____

the other side is Pest. The white stone castle that
                                          6

4. _____ _____

looks like something out of a fairy-tale kingdom
                                            7

5. _____ _____

was built by the Fisherman's Guild on one side of
       8

6. _____ _____

the river. The lacy Gothic-style Parliament building
                                                9

7. _____ _____

it still bears the World War II scars of bullets and

8. _____ _____

bomb fragments   lends its magnificence to the
              10

9. _____ _____

other side of the river. The fairylike atmosphere is

10. _____ _____

heightened   moreover   when these and other
         11   **12**

11. _____ _____

decorative buildings are bathed in soft yellow lights

12. _____ _____

at night.

B. Tod and Ellen began to feel a link with the
                                    1

1. _____ _____

ancient world as they walked among Roman ruins.
          2

2. _____ _____

The Colosseum a tremendous Roman amphi-
          3

theater had been stripped of its metal and marble
        4   5

by Christians to build their churches. It was a dimly

lit, quiet ruin overrun by hundreds of cats at night.
                6

C.   Other relics of the past were catacombs long
                                              1   2

low narrow passages burrowing hundreds of miles
    3   4

on three and four levels below the earth's surface.

The Catholic Brother who served as a guide ex-
                     5

plained, "The Christians it appears probably did not
                         6   7

live in the catacombs to escape the Romans as

many people have thought. First no air passages
                                8

lead to the lower levels and second   no evidence of
                             9   10

household articles exists." Most of the visitors

(Ellen and Tod included   were happy to get back to
                        11

daylight.

3. _____ _____

4. _____ _____

5. _____ _____

6. _____ _____

1. _____ _____

2. _____ _____

3. _____ _____

4. _____ _____

5. _____ _____

6. _____ _____

7. _____ _____

8. _____ _____

9. _____ _____

10. _____ _____

11. _____ _____

EXERCISE 47B

Write sentences according to the directions given below. If you need help, refer to the examples in this lesson.

1. Write a sentence in which commas enclose a word group.

2. Write a sentence in which NO commas are used with an appositive or a dependent clause.

3. Write a sentence with a noun of direct address or an expression such as *well, yes,* or *no.*

4. Write a sentence in which a parenthetic element is enclosed in parentheses.

5. Write a sentence in which a transitional expression appears at the beginning or within a sentence.

Show these sentences to your instructor or tutor.

Lesson 48

Conventional Uses of Punctuation

Certain marks of punctuation are used according to general agreement among writers to help readers move through reports and stories easily. Quotation marks, for example, enclose words that another person has spoken or written, but quotation marks also have other uses. Another mark, the ellipsis (. . .) tells readers a sentence may be incomplete if the ellipsis appears at the end or that a part of a sentence has been omitted in quoted material. You will study these marks of punctuation and others in this lesson.

CONVENTIONAL USES OF QUOTATION MARKS

1. DOUBLE QUOTATION MARKS (" . . . ") enclose the actual words of a speaker of passages quoted from a publication:

> The decorator wrote, "Deep colors make the walls of a room seem heavy."

2. DOUBLE QUOTATION MARKS enclose titles of short stories, poems, songs, articles, television programs, and other short works:

> "The End of Something"   "A Very Precious Love"   "Masterpiece Theatre"

3. DOUBLE QUOTATION MARKS are used to indicate a shift in usage or to suggest irony:

> The young executive tried to be a "cool cat."
> His friend, on the other hand, always used "correct" English.

4. SINGLE QUOTATION MARKS (' . . . ') enclose a second quotation or a title within a first quotation:

> "Tell him to begin his story with 'Once upon a time . . . ' to catch their attention," the writer said wryly.
> "Have you read 'Neighbour Rosicky' by Willa Cather?"

Punctuation with Quotation Marks

1a. A COMMA is used to separate the main part of the sentence from the direct quotation enclosed in quotation marks:

> The historian wrote, "In the early days travel was difficult because of poor roads."

1b. NO COMMA is used when the direct quotation is a question at the beginning of the sentence:

"Would you want to return to the early days?" he asked his readers.

2. COMMAS are used to separate a broken quotation, enclosed in quotation marks, from the main part of the sentence:

"Most frequently," the historian continued, "they used waterways."

Although the practice is not completely uniform, the following punctuation is usually acceptable:

3. Place all periods and commas within the quotation marks.

4. Place question marks and exclamation points within the quotation marks if they are a part of the quotation, or place them outside the quotation marks if they terminate the sentence in which the quotation appears.

"No!" they shouted.
Did John say, "I agree"?

5. Semicolons and colons, which almost never appear as part of quoted material, are placed outside quotation marks.

CONVENTIONAL USES OF PERIODS, COMMAS, AND COLONS

1. The PERIOD is used after initials:

T. E. Mason   R. E. M.   Susan L. Milton

2. The PERIOD is used after abbreviations:

Dr.   Mrs.   Jan.   Wed.   N.Y.   P.M.

3a. COMMAS are used in dates to enclose the year when the date appears in a sentence:

July 4, 1776, marks the signing of the Declaration of Independence.

3b. If only the month and year are given, NO COMMA is required between them:

The Wright brothers demonstrated the first motor-driven airplane in December 1903.

4. COMMAS enclose parts of addresses—town or city, county, state, and country:

The first flight took place at Kitty Hawk, North Carolina, U.S.A.

5. COMMAS enclose degrees and titles that follow the name:

George Talbot Hunt, Ph.D., Professor of History, Western Reserve University

6. A COMMA follows the close in a letter:

> Sincerely,   Fondly,

7a. A COMMA follows the salutation in a personal letter:

> Dear Bob,   Dear Mother and Dad,

7b. The COLON follows the salutation in a business letter:

> Dear Mr. Mason:
> All your reservations have been confirmed . . .

8. The COLON separates hours and minutes in writing time:

> Departure time is 12:30 P.M., and arrival in London is 6:15 A.M.

CONVENTIONAL USES OF ELLIPSES, ITALICS, AND HYPHENS

9a. The ELLIPSIS is used to indicate something omitted, either a single word or several sentences. It is a series of three periods (. . .), used especially in quoted material:

> Let me give you some indication of what he said: "I stand firm in my belief that this country cannot survive . . . unless everyone sets himself the task of making it the strongest country in the world."

9b. If the omitted material comes at the end of the author's sentence, a fourth period is added to end the sentence:

> I believe that he substantiates what I have felt when he says in part that we can "win only by full cooperation . . . . Everyone must be willing to do his part."

ITALICS are printed letters that slant to the right. They are used in the ways listed below. To show italics in handwritten or typed manuscripts, UNDERLINE the words.

10a. Italicize (or underline) titles of books, magazines, newspapers, operas, motion pictures, plays, and other long works: *Newsweek, The New York Times, Slaughterhouse Five.*

> | Use quotation marks for chapters, short stories . . . | | Use italics for books, magazines . . . |
> |---|---|---|
> | "Carbon and Its Oxides" | in | *General Chemistry* |
> | "The Prophet" | in | *Moby Dick* |
> | "Thrill Seekers" | in | *Hot Rod Magazine* |

10b. Italicize (or underline) foreign words or phrases if they are likely to be unfamiliar to readers:

> | *persona non grata* | *coup d'etat* |
> |---|---|
> | BUT: à la carte | vice versa |

10c. Italicize (or underline) words that are being discussed:

> The word *maximum* comes from the Latin words *magnus* and *maximus.*

10d. Italicize (or underline) words for emphasis:

> He *did* agree with me.

11. The HYPHEN may be used as a separator between syllables. When a word of more than one syllable at the end of a line has to be divided and carried to the next line, the hyphen appears after a syllable, and the remainder of the word is carried to the next line. Only words of more than one syllable can be hyphenated and *only between the syllables.* Check your dictionary for syllables in a word:

> The court questioned his *judg-*
> *ment* in releasing the prisoner.

12. The hyphen may be used in compound words:

> Thirty-four   self-confidence   Franco-American

See your dictionary for details about using hyphens in compound words.

EXERCISE 48A

Numbers appear at various points in the sentences below. Corresponding numbered blanks appear at the right. Add punctuation at these points wherever it is needed in the sentences by writing the NAME of the mark of punctuation in the blank. If you find that no punctuation is needed, write an X in the blank. This exercise covers all the lessons in this punctuation unit.

Marks of punctuation:

Colon :	Hyphen -	Question mark ?
Comma ,	Italics—underlining	Semicolon ;
Dash —	Parentheses ( )	Double quotation marks " . . . "
Exclamation point !	Period .	Single quotation marks ' . . . '
Brackets [ ]		

A. "Tod the Colosseum must be down there where the   1. _____
      1   **2**

bright lights are shining   Ellen said as she and Tod walked   2. _____
                        3 4

hesitatingly on cobblestone pavement down a curved   3. _____
                                                5

4. _____

5. _____

narrow dark street in Rome. As they walked into the flood-
      6

lighted area Tod explained excitedly "It's a movie set We're
            7   **8**   **9**

on a movie set. The cameraman is over there.   Tod   and
                                          10 **11**

Ellen joined the watching crowd   at the other end of the
                          12

narrow street   and marveled that they were in Rome
         13   **14**

Italy   on a movie set on a warm July night.   I'll have to
   15   **16**

write Mother and Dad   " Ellen said excitedly   " and tell
                    17   **18**

them all about this."

Dear Mother and Dad
            19

   You'll never guess what Tod and I saw tonight . . .

. . . The trip is fabulous. Why don't you plan a second honey-

moon
20

            Love from both of us
                          21

            Ellen

B.

a. The Times-Herald is published daily.
   ------------- **1** -------------

b. The columnist wrote in part   The new television situation
                           2 3

comedies offer little that is new this season.
                                      4

6. _____	
7. _____	
8. _____	
9. _____	
10. _____	
11. _____	
12. _____	
13. _____	
14. _____	
15. _____	
16. _____	
17. _____	
18. _____	
19. _____	
20. _____	
21. _____	

1. _____

2. _____

3. _____

4. _____

c. When the telephone rang It seemed to ring constantly
                    5   **6**

the fat little man scowled, then answered it.

5. _____

6. _____

d. He thought the word libel was the same as liable.
        --7--   **---8---**

7. _____

8. _____

e. Mark Hudson wrote sentimentally about his boyhood   I
                                              9 10

9. _____

grew up in a small town   Editor's note: Medina   Ohio
                11   **12**   **13**

10. _____

where everyone knew everyone else.
                        14

11. _____

f. "Hamlet's soliloquy   To be, or not to be . . . ' is still my
        15

12. _____

favorite,   said the stooped   gray-haired actor.
    16   **17**

13. _____

14. _____

g.   The song   Happy Days Are Here Again   seemed to
    18   **19**   **20**

15. _____

give us hope   when we had very little,   Tom's grandmother
            21   **22**

16. _____

recalled.

17. _____

18. _____

19. _____

20. _____

21. _____

22. _____

h. Have you heard   I really should not say this   that Jane
              23   **24**

had another argument with Dick
                            25

i.   When will the tenth volume of History of the World be
    26   ---------- **27** ----------

published   the book reviewer asked the editor.
           28 29

j. The origin of the Greek word biblos, meaning book, is
                    ---**30**---   --**31**--

from the Egyptian word for papyrus.

23. _____

24. _____

25. _____

26. _____

27. _____

28. _____

29. _____

30. _____

31. _____

EXERCISE 48B

Write sentences, using punctuation according to the directions given after each number.

1. Write a sentence that requires double quotation marks (" . . . ")

2. Write a sentence that requires single quotation marks (' . . . ') within double quotation marks.

3. Write a sentence that requires one or two dashes (—).

4. Write a sentence that requires parentheses ( ).

5. Write a sentence that requires italics (underlining).

Show these sentences to your instructor or tutor.

Lesson 49

Capitalization

To show that a word represents a particular person or thing, capitalize the first letter of the word. Use capital letters in titles, at the beginning of a sentence, and in some abbreviations. Here is a summary of capitalization in expository writing.

1. Capitalize the first word of the following:
   a. Sentence:

   The well-known track star broke his leg.

   b. Lines of poetry:

   "For thy sweet love remembered, such wealth brings
   That then I scorn to change my state with kings."

   Exception: Some poets disregard this usage in order to create special effects.

   c. A direct quotation:

   He asked, "When will the plane arrive?"

   Exception: When partial quotes are given, the first word may not be capitalized:

   When he refers to the "land of the free and the home of the brave," everyone knows what nation he means.

2. Proper names, abbreviations of proper names, and words derived from proper names:
   a. People:

   Henry Robinson, Jos. Griffin

   Names of relatives:

   Mother (when it is used as a substitute for her given name), Uncle John, Aunt Mary

   Exception: Do not capitalize when the word is preceded by a determiner:

   my mother, his uncle

   b. Places:

   New York City, N.Y., Europe

   c. Races and other groups of people:

   Caucasian, Negro, Indian, Protestant

d. Languages and their abbreviations:

      English, Russian, German, Spanish, (Span.)

e. Days of the week and their abbreviations:

      Sunday, Monday, (Mon.)

Exception: The word *tomorrow* refers to any day of the week.

f. Months of the year and their abbreviations:

      January, February, (Feb.)

g. Points of compass to denote a specific region:

      North, West, Pacific Northwest

Exception: Do not capitalize when they indicate direction or a general region:

      She turned west at the corner.   They visited the south of France.

h. Armed forces when they refer to forces of a particular country:

      United States Air Force, British Navy

i. Reference to deity:

      God, Jesus, Zeus, Jehovah

Exception: The word *god* is not capitalized when it refers to a nonspecific deity.

j. Derivatives formed from proper names:

      Shakespeare—Shakespearean drama; Victoria—a Victorian lamp;
      England—English literature

Exceptions occur for commonly used derivatives:

      Pasteur—pasteurized milk; China—chinaware

3. The first and last word in all titles; all major words in titles, including verbs like *is* and *be,* except articles *(a, an, the),* conjunctions, and prepositions less than five letters in length.
   a. Books, articles, songs, etc.:

      The Old Man and the Sea   *Fate Is the Hunter*

   b. Organizations and historical events:

      Boy Scouts of America   The Battle of Bunker Hill

   c. Positions of importance (whether they are used as the name or following the name):

President of the United States
the Chief Justice of the Supreme Court

BUT: the president of the company

4. Specific courses but not areas of study. Names of languages are capitalized:

He has enjoyed History 17A better than any other history course he had previously taken.
He also studied French and Spanish.

5. Nouns which are part of names made up of two or three words when they are used as a substitute for the complete name:

When Californians say they are going to the Lake for the weekend, they mean Lake Tahoe.

6. Abstract nouns when they are personified or refer to ideals or institutions:

the Church   the State   the North Wind

7. *Street, River, Park,* etc., when they follow a proper name:

Sacramento River   Market Street

EXERCISE 49

Capitalize all words that should be capitalized in the following sentences:

1. juan garcia speaks spanish fluently.

2. harold radcliff wrote *car repair is a challenge.*

3. last sunday bob visited his mother.

4. his uncle lives on wild oak street.

5. people from new york city visited lake tahoe.

6. last march terry moved to eugene, oregon.

7. jeff enrolled in life science 2a.

8. martha did not take english or psychology.

9. the french play pleased the mayor.

10. judge walters greeted council members.

Unit Ten Review

Practice Test

PART I

Indicate the punctuation and capitalization to be used at each numbered point in the following sentences by writing the name of the mark of punctuation or the word *capital* in the corresponding blank at the right. If no punctuation or capital should be used, write X in the blank.
(100 points—2 points each)   (Lessons 46–49)   Score _____

Marks of punctuation:

Colon :	Hyphen —	Question mark ?
Comma ,	Italics—underlining	Semicolon ;
Dash —	Parentheses ( )	Double quotation marks " . . . "
Exclamation point !	Period .	Single quotation marks ' . . . '

EXAMPLE: "Gay Paree!" Ellen said happily. She and Tod   1. _____colon_____

had arrived in Paris about 7 30 A.M. after racing   2. _____X_____
                    1   **2**

through the french countryside on a midnight   3. _____capital_____
                3

train from Basel, Switzerland.

A. Score _____

"Let's have dinner at the french restaurant   1. _____
                    1

near Notre Dame Cathedral " Tod suggested to   2. _____
                              2

Ellen. "I'll find out how much French I remember.
                                    3

3. _____

They walked down the dark narrow, shop-lined street.
                            4

4. _____

Finally they found the entrance to the restaurant.
   5   6

5. _____

Seated on benches at a rustic table in the crowded
                                              7

6. _____

dimly lit room they waited for the waiter to bring
              8

7. _____

the menu but he set a large basket of bread   on the
        9   10

8. _____

table without saying a word.

9. _____

10. _____

B. Score _____

A short time later he brought another basket to the

1. _____

table this one was filled with raw unpeeled vegetables
   1   2   3

2. _____

tomatoes, peppers, onions, cucumbers, cauliflower, and

3. _____

celery. Again he said nothing "I wonder what we'll get
                              4

4. _____

next " Ellen said as she chewed on a stalk of celery
   5   6

5. _____

while Tod cut a tomato and a pepper into pieces. They
                      7

6. _____

did not have to wait long the waiter brought a third
                        8

7. _____

basket and it was filled with a large assortment of
      9

8. _____

sausages. He smiled   as he watched Ellen's surprised
                   10

9. _____

expression.

10. _____

C. Score _____

"Tod, I don't believe it " Ellen exclaimed. "Which one
                        1

1. _____

should I try first ” A short time later the waiter brought
      2

the menu. When he returned to take their orders Tod
                             3

quickly discovered that he had to order in French because
                             4

the waiter knew no English. After Tod and Ellen had finished

the main course the waiter brought a large basket of
              5

cheeses and then he brought the menu for dessert. As
     6

they left the restaurant at 11 15 P M , Ellen asked Tod
                 7   **8 9**

plaintively, "Do you suppose you could take me back to

the hotel in a wheelbarrow   I'm not sure I can walk."
           10

2. _____

3. _____

4. _____

5. _____

6. _____

7. _____

8. _____

9. _____

10. _____

D. Score _____

a. The whole class will read Hemingway's short story   The
                                     1 2

End of Something and his novel For Whom the Bell Tolls.
       3   **4** --------------**5**--------------

b. The Wall Street Journal gives daily stock market reports
--------------**6**--------------   **7**

and other financial news that businesspeople want.
            8

c. Her gross inefficiency what else can he call it   cost the
                  9   **10**

company five hundred dollars.

1. _____

2. _____

3. _____

4. _____

5. _____

6. _____

7. _____

8. _____

9. _____

10. _____

E. Score _____

d. "Pretend that you are your father   the counselor told

                   1   **2 3**

the young man. Try to show us how you think he acts.

        4   **5**

e. Ben tried to find the words whether and weather in the

                             6   **7**

dictionary.

f. Employees concerned about their new assignments

            8   **9**

crowded into the manager's office on wednesday

                                10

morning.

1. _____
2. _____
3. _____
4. _____
5. _____
6. _____
7. _____
8. _____
9. _____
10. _____

PART II

Write sentences, using punctuation according to the directions given after each number.

(100 points—10 points each)   (Lessons 46–49)   Score _____

1. Write a sentence in which a comma (,) and coordinating conjunction *(and, but, or, for)* are used between two independent clauses.

2. Write a sentence that requires one or more semicolons (;).

3. Write a sentence in which commas are used to separate words or word groups.

4. Write a sentence in which commas are used to enclose words or word groups.

5. Write a sentence that requires a colon (:).

6. Write a sentence that requires double quotation marks (" . . . ").

7. Write a sentence that requires one or two dashes (—).

8. Write a sentence that requires parentheses ( ).

9. Write a sentence that requires italics (underlining).

10. Write a sentence that requires an exclamation point (!).

Unit Eleven

Refining Sentences

A piece of jewelry, a chair, a vase—anything made from a variety of materials—gradually take shape as a person constructs them. When the general construction is completed, the maker may find that the object needs refinement—polishing to smooth rough surfaces or tighter bonding where two pieces of material come together. These final touches bring about a smoothness of design and completeness that make the objects distinctive and appealing to others.

You have reached the point now in your study of sentence writing where you should learn ways to refine your sentences. Among these are maintaining consistent point of view, using appropriate words, making comparisons logical and structures parallel, and editing and combining sentences. Each one of these writing techniques will be discussed in the lessons that follow.

Lesson 50

Point of View

In writing sentences, you sometimes use simple, informal language and perhaps address your readers directly by using *you.* In other sentences you perhaps use less familiar, more abstract words because your subject demands a certain vocabulary, and you do not address the reader. Whatever approach you use, you should maintain the same point of view in tone, person, number, and tense throughout.

TONE

Tone in writing refers to the total effect brought about by the choice of words and use of simple or complicated sentence structure. To help you understand tone, study the characteristics of different kinds of language outlined below under two headings—Standard English and Nonstandard English—and the examples that follow each kind. Standard English, sometimes called Edited American English, is generally the language of educated people, and Nonstandard English is the spoken language of people who have had relatively little formal education. Although you see only four headings, you should be aware that people use many variations of these kinds in speaking and writing. The outline neatly shows four kinds of language merely to help you understand tone.

I. Standard English—written and spoken language

    A. Formal English—used for sermons, ceremonials, public addresses, lectures to certain professional groups, and academic writing
        1. Large vocabulary containing specialized terms from scholarly fields
        2. Long, elaborate sentences with parallel structures and unusual word order because of use of constructions found only in writing
        3. No contractions

> "Cane" is not to be classified in terms of the ordinary literary types, for the genius of creation is evident in its form. Verse, fiction, and drama are fused into a spiritual unity, an "aesthetic equivalent" of the Southland. It is not a book to be intellectually understood; it must be emotionally, aesthetically felt. One must approach it with all of his five senses keenly alive if appreciation and enjoyment are to result. No previous writer has been able in any such degree to catch the sensuous beauty of the land or of its people or to fathom the deeper spiritual stirrings of the mass-life of the Negro. "Cane" is not **of** the South, it is not **of** the Negro; it **is** the South, it **is** the Negro—as Jean Toomer has experienced them.
>
> Montgomery Gregory, "A Review of *Cane,*"
> *The Merrill Studies in Cane*

B. General English—used for business conversations, class discussions, most correspondence, college and business papers, magazines, newspapers, and books.

  1. Specific, concrete vocabulary containing words in current use
  2. Sentences of moderate length that may follow speech patterns but also contain constructions used only in writing
  3. No contractions

  > Since the astronauts were being guarded against infection, they were seen next behind the protection of a glass wall in the visitors' room at the Lunar Receiving Laboratory. An entire building had been constructed to quarantine them on their return, a species of hospital dormitory, galley, and laboratory for the moon rocks. Since for twenty-one days after their return they would not be able to be in the same room with their families, or with the NASA technicians and officials who would debrief them, a chamber like the visitors' room in a prison had been built with a plate-glass partition hermetically sealed from floor to ceiling running down the middle. Dialogue through the glass wall proceeded through microphones.
  >
  > Norman Mailer, "The Psychology of Astronauts,"
  > *Of a Fire on the Moon*

C. Informal English—used in conversations with friends, casual talks, and personal letters
  1. Vocabulary containing colloquial expressions, newly coined words, and terms used in certain occupations
  2. Short, uncomplicated sentence structures that reflect daily spoken language
  3. Frequent use of contractions and informal *you*

  > Most stories about the animals, snakes, spiders, and nameless terrors of the jungle are pure bunk. You probably will never see a poisonous snake or a large animal. What may scare you the most are the howls, screams, and crashing sounds made by noisy monkeys, birds, night insects, and falling trees. The real dangers of the tropics are the insects, which may pass on diseases and parasites.
  >
  > "Survival on Land—Tropics," *AOPA Handbook for Pilots, 1975*

II. Nonstandard English—primarily a spoken language

  A. Vocabulary containing slang expressions and terms used only in particular areas, and nonstandard forms of verbs
  B. Short or run-on sentences and sentence fragments
  C. Frequent use of contractions and double negatives, and misuse of pronouns and verbs according to Standard English patterns

  > Seth Green was prob'ly the pick of the flock; he married a Wilkerson—Sarah Wilkerson—a good cretur, she was—one of the likeliest heifers that was ever raised in old Stoddard, everybody said that knowed her. She heft a bar'l of flour as easy as I can flirt a flapjack. And spin? Don't mention it! Independent? Humph! When Sile Hawkins come a-browsing around her, she let him know that for all his tin he couldn't trot in harness alongside of *her*.
  >
  > Mark Twain, *Roughing It*

PERSON AND NUMBER

To maintain consistent point of view in person and number, you should use the same person, singular or plural, in all your sentences. For example, if you write about a personal experience, use first-person pronouns *(I, me)* to refer to yourself:

> NOT: I went for a physical examination, and **you** get pinched with needles and attached to all kinds of machines.
>
> BUT: I went for a physical examination, and **I** was pinched with needles and attached to all kinds of machines.

The writer should not have used *you* in the second part of the original sentence because the experience was the writer's, not the reader's.

If you are writing directions, however, use the second person throughout because you are addressing the reader. You may use the pronoun *you* or the command form of the verb with *you* understood:

> **You** need mainly sports clothes for the trip, but **(you)** pack at least one suit.

For most college and business writing use nouns and third-person pronouns *(he, she, it, they)*. Remember to use pronouns that agree in person, number, and gender with their antecedents (Lesson 26). If you use a singular noun or pronoun, such as *person, student,* or *everyone,* that may refer to either a man or a woman, you may want to acknowledge both sexes by using *he or she, him or her,* or *his or her* to refer to the singular noun. You can avoid the awkwardness of repeating both pronouns several times by using a plural noun and referring to it with *they, them,* or *their:*

> ACCEPTABLE: The **person** who travels frequently should invest in a strap to hold **his or her** suitcase closed. Then **he or she** will not have to face an open suitcase coming down the airport baggage ramp.
>
> BETTER: **People** who travel frequently should invest in a strap to hold **their** suitcases closed. Then **they** will not have to face an open suitcase coming down the airport baggage ramp.

One is another word that sometimes causes awkwardness. Again, using plural nouns and plural third-person pronouns eliminates the problem:

> AWKWARD: **One** sometimes hesitates to try something new, but **one** must take some chances, especially if **one** does not put **oneself** in danger.
>
> IMPROVED: **People** sometimes hesitate to try something new, but **they** must take some chances, especially if **they** do not put **themselves** in danger.

TENSE AND NUMBER

Another way to keep point of view consistent is to use the same tense for all the verbs in a sentence:

> NOT: Many people **ate** (past) at the restaurant and **enjoy** (present) the food.
>
> BUT: Many people **eat** at the restaurant and **enjoy** the food.
>
> OR: Many people **ate** ate the restaurant and **enjoyed** the food.

If, however, you write about a sequence of events in a sentence or two, you will probably have to use more than one tense to show in what order the events happened. (For more details, review Lesson 10):

> Although Jon Karney **had won** many new friends while he **campaigned** for the state senator's seat, he **lost** to his opponent who **seems** to have great strength in the urban areas. Nevertheless, Karney **has said** he **will be** a candidate in the next general election.

In summarizing a plot or telling about an event as if it is happening now, you might use the historical present tense:

> The gladiator **is entering** the arena, and all eyes **are** on him as he **bows** and **pays** homage to the dignitaries present.

You should avoid using a sentence containing both active and passive verbs:

> NOT: The movie **was seen** (passive) by Barb and Ken, but they **did** not **enjoy** (active) it very much.
>
> BUT: Barb and Ken **saw** the movie, but they **did** not **enjoy** it very much.

Remember to use appropriate forms of the verbs with singular and plural subjects so that subjects and verbs agree. Review subject-verb agreement in Lesson 27.

EXERCISE 50A

Revise the following sentences to make them consistent in tone, person, and number. Cross out words to be changed and write revisions above them.

1. The artist should clean his brushes each time he finishes painting. You will find the brushes ready to use the next time you decide to paint.

2. Americans must vote for the people they want to run their government. We have no one to blame but ourselves if we get officials whom we don't want.

3. When preparing to write an essay, I try to select a topic which I understand thoroughly. If you have only general information, you can't write a convincing paper.

4. The newspaper is sometimes considered to be the voice of the people. But when they contain news stories against the best interests of the people, you begin to wonder whether they speak for the people or for their own personal interests.

5. If everyone wants to do their part to help others, they should work with volunteer service organizations and not expect to get paid for every minute they spend working.

6. A person who buys this car receives a guarantee which says you will not be charged for parts which have to be replaced, but you will be charged only for the labor for replacing them.

7. When a person fills out an application for a position, they should try to fill out every blank to indicate to the interviewer that they have tried to give all the information requested.

EXERCISE 50B

Revise the following sentences to make them consistent in tone, tense, and number. Cross out words to be changed and write revisions above them.

1. Quite unexpectedly the homeowners returned to their house and find someone searching through their belongings for valuable items.

2. There is at least thirty people at the intersection when the two cars collided.

3. A person may enjoy eating olives, but they refuses to try snails.

4. The photograph of the bride's aunts and uncles were copied and sent to each of them.

5. Travelers in several countries in Europe sees storks' nests built on top of chimneys.

6. As the four-course meal was served by the clumsy waitress, she drops bits of food on each of the diners.

EXERCISE 50C

Revise the following paragraph to make point of view consistent in tone, person, number, and tense.

Most people is interested in sports. You can enjoy sports by watching events on television or attending games. We also enjoy reading about them in the newspaper. Other people wants to participate in sports. If we're serious about the sport, we gotta join a team at school or in the community. You might prefer instead a friendly game with the neighbors on the weekend. One doesn't ever get enough exercise, you know.

Lesson 51

The Appropriate Word

Writing an effective sentence depends not only on your knowing the basic sentence patterns and the functions of words in sentences but also on your knowing how to choose the appropriate words to express what you want to say. The type of writing you do determines the tone of language you use. If you write a college or business paper, for example, you should avoid using words or expressions that may be more appropriate for informal conversations or letters.

In this lesson you will learn to substitute appropriate words for informal expressions, to distinguish between words that are similar in meaning or spelling, and to be aware of certain idiomatic expressions.

INFORMAL EXPRESSIONS

To maintain consistent tone in written language you should be aware of the current usage of words and phrases. Some are appropriate for both written and spoken language, others only for spoken language. Knowing when to use them has to be learned. Even as you learn them, you should be aware that language changes and that you should watch for these changes. Here is a partial list of words and phrases and notes about their usage. Others are listed in dictionaries. The labels *Informal* or *Colloq.* or *Slang* suggest that they may not be suitable in essays. Not all informal expressions are entirely inappropriate, but the discerning writer usually chooses the more formal expressions in preference.

All the farther—The preferred form in written English is *as far as.*

        NOT: This is all the farther he can travel.
        BUT: This is as far as he can travel.

As—Overworked word used instead of *that, whether, who, because,* and *since.*

        NOT: I don't know as I can come.
        BUT: I don't know whether I can come.

Awful, terrible—Overworked words used colloquially to mean *ugly, bad,* or *very.*

        NOT: That is an awful assignment.   NOT: We had a terribly good time.
        BUT: That is a difficult assign-   BUT: We had a very good time.
                   ment.

Being as, being that—Nonstandard substitutes for *because* or *since.*

    NOT: Being as how the project is complete, they can begin the new one.
    BUT: Since the project is complete, they can begin the new one.

Broke—Informal expression for *bankrupt* or *without funds.*

    NOT: The new business is broke.
    BUT: The new business is bankrupt.

Could of, should of, would of—In written English these are not substitutes for *could have, should have,* or *would have.*

    NOT: They could of gone to the meeting.
    BUT: They could have gone to the meeting.

Disremember—Nonstandard expression for *do not remember,* not used in written English except to indicate dialect in conversation.

    NOT: He disremembers the incident.
    BUT: He does not remember the incident.

Enthuse—Informal for *to be enthusiastic.*

    NOT: They were enthused about the new recording.
    BUT: They were enthusiastic about the new recording.

Expect—Informal when used as a substitute for *suppose* or *suspect.*

    NOT: I expect you are not able to operate the duplicator.
    BUT: I suppose you are not able to operate the duplicator.

Fix—Used as a noun, *fix* is informal for *predicament.* As a verb, it is colloquial for *punish.*

    NOT: She is in a fine fix.   NOT: The father fixed his son for
    BUT: She is in a serious predica-   lying.
           ment.   BUT: The father punished his son
                                     for lying.

Guess—*Guess* is not a substitute for *believe.*

    NOT: I guess you are right.
    BUT: I believe you are right.

Heap—Informal spoken word for *amount.*

    NOT: That is a heap of work to do.
    BUT: That is a large amount of work to do.

Invite—*Invite* used as a noun is an informal word for *invitation.*

    NOT: The invite came in the mail.
    BUT: The invitation came in the mail.

Kind of, sort of—Informal expressions.

> NOT: They kind of want to have a party.
> BUT: They are undecided about having a party.

Lots—Informal for *many.*

> NOT: Lots of people want new cars.
> BUT: Many people want new cars.

Mad—Informal for *angry* or *annoyed* and slang for *enthusiastic.*

> NOT: They are mad at John for no reason.
> BUT: They are angry with John for no reason.

O.K. or okay—Used as a noun, *okay* is informal for *endorsement* or *approval.* As a verb, it is informal for *endorse* or *approve.*

> NOT: She okayed the purchase.
> BUT: She approved the purchase.

Pretty—Informal for *moderately* or *fairly* or *almost.*

> NOT: The report is pretty complete.
> BUT: The report is fairly complete.

Shape—Informal for *condition.*

> NOT: They are in no shape to travel.
> BUT: They are in no condition to travel.

Show up—Informal for *appear.*

> NOT: She did not show up for the hearing.
> BUT: She did not appear for the hearing.

Take and, try and, up and—Usually *take and* and *up and* can be omitted entirely from a sentence without losing meaning. *Try to* should be substituted for *try and,* which is colloquial.

> NOT: He should not try and influence his friend.
> BUT: He should not try to influence his friend.

Used to, didn't use to, used to could—Informal expressions.

> NOT: He didn't use to come to meetings.
> BUT: He did not usually come to meetings.

Wait on—Dialectal for *wait for.*

> NOT: Do you want me to wait on you?
> BUT: Do you want me to wait for you?

Want in, out, off—Informal expressions which can be made general by inserting an infinitive.

> NOT: The dog wants out.
> BUT: The dog wants to go out.

EXERCISE 51A

Rewrite the following sentences, eliminating all informal usage.

1. Being as how the chairman is sick, the meeting has been canceled.

2. They were enthused about the invite they had received from William.

3. Jim could of done a heap of work with help.

4. Ted Jones was mad because his son got himself in a fine fix.

5. Jane should take and decide what is best and not wait on Tom to help her.

6. The manager wants out of the contract, but he has pretty much given up hope of getting an okay.

7. The football player was in bad shape for the game and did not show up that day.

8. He guessed she disremembered the date they had.

9. This is all the farther the bus goes.

WORD USAGE

Usage is the way people use language. Educated people may use it in certain ways and uneducated people in other ways. People who are educated tend to use Standard English in writing, and the following list of words and their usages reflect the preferences in Standard English.

Accept, except—*Accept* means *to receive; except* means *to omit.*

> I accept your kind offer.
> Everyone agrees except Tom.

Advice, advise—*Advice* is a noun; *advise* is a verb.

> Joe gave me valuable advice in this mattter.
> Perhaps he will advise you too.

Affect, effect—*Affect* is a verb meaning *to influence; effect* can be used as a verb meaning *to bring about* or as a noun meaning *result.*

> Will the news affect her decision?
> What effect will the news have on her decision?

All right—The spelling shown here is the only acceptable spelling. *Alright* is not yet accepted as a spelling variation.

A lot—Although pronounced as one word, *a lot* is written as two words.

Already, altogether—*Already* and *altogether* are adverbs, and *all ready* and *all together* are adjective phrases which indicate that all participants are ready or together.

> The tour group has already left.
> The tour members are all ready to leave.

Amount, number—*Amount* refers to quantity, and *number* is used for groups, the individual members of which can be counted.

> The amount of work to be done is overwhelming.
> The number of participants totals one hundred.

Apt, liable, prone—Frequently all three words are used to mean *likely;* however, each has its own meaning. *Apt* means *suitable, appropriate,* or it may mean *skilled* or *quick to learn; liable* suggests that a person is responsible for his actions; *prone* means that he is predisposed to something inevitable.

> He is likely to arrive tomorrow.
> The group has chosen an apt slogan.
> She is liable for the success of the enterprise.
> He is prone to have automobile accidents.

Balance, remainder—*Balance* is used in accounting, but it is not a substitute for *remainder.*

> The balance in their account is five hundred dollars.
> They will use the remainder of the supplies for the new project.

Beside, besides—*Beside* means *by the side of,* and *besides* means *in addition to.*

> The dog sat beside his bone.
> He had a large bowl of meat besides.

Between, among—*Between* shows difference between two people or things, and *among* shows difference among three or more.

> The house was built between two elms.
> The house stood among several large elms.

Disinterested, uninterested—*Disinterested* means *impartial, objective; uninterested* means *lacking interest.*

> Mr. Hopkins can offer a disinterested viewpoint.
> Mr. Hopkins is uninterested in the project.

Elicit, illicit—*Elicit* means *to draw out; illicit* means *not permitted.*

> He could elicit no complaint from her.
> He engaged in illicit drug trade.

Farther, further—*Farther* refers to measurable distance; *further* refers to degree, time, or quantity.

> He traveled farther than I did.
> Think further about the problem.

Formally, formerly—*Formally* means in a formal manner; *formerly* means *previously.*

> They have been formally initiated into the organization.
> They were formerly members of another organization.

Height, heighth—The first spelling is acceptable; the second is obsolete.

Infer, imply—*Infer* means *to draw a conclusion from evidence given; imply* means *to indicate* or *suggest.*

> He implied that Ruth is not welcome.
> He inferred that she has not been telling the truth.

Leave, let—*Leave* should not be used for *let* to mean *allow* or *permit. Leave* means *depart from.*

> Let him do what he wants.
> He will leave for Oregon today.

Less, fewer—*Less* shows extent, amount, degree, but *fewer* refers to numbers.

> There is less milk in this glass than in that one.
> There are fewer cookies on this plate than on that one.

Like, as if—*Like* is a preposition, and *as if* is a conjunction.

> Debbie looks like her mother.
> Debbie looks as if she is happy today.

Loose, lose—*Loose* is usually an adjective; *lose* is a verb.

> The bolt is loose.
> The wagon may lose its wheel.

Quiet, quite—*Quiet* means *silent; quite* means *completely, entirely.*

> The countryside is quiet.
> They are not quite finished with the mowing.

Suspicion, suspect—*Suspicion* is a noun; *suspect* is a verb.
> My suspicion was correct.
> I suspect he is guilty.

IDIOMS

Idioms are word combinations that convey meaning but usually cannot be analyzed according to the rules of the language. They are the most difficult part of the language for a nonnative speaker of English to learn; even native speakers sometimes have difficulty with them. Expressions like *drink up, get a move on, strike a bargain,* and *make no bones about it* convey meanings difficult to put into other words. Some idioms have synonyms: *pull through* for *recover, come up* for *approach,* and *put down* for *land* (an airplane) or *degrade.* Also the use of certain prepositions after particular verbs is idiomatic:

abide by	collide with	infer from	rejoice at
abstain from	comply with	insist on	resolve on
agree with	confide in or to	interfere with	secede from
alarmed at	deprive of	object to	succeed in
attend to	different from	part with	threaten with
charge with	disappointed in	plan to	wait for

If you are not sure how to write an expression that seems to be idiomatic, look it up in the dictionary. You might also use one of the many dictionaries of idioms, some of which are paperbacks.

EXERCISE 51B

Underline the words or phrases that are incorrectly used. In the blank at the right write the word or phrase that is appropriate for written English. If you believe that no change should be made, write A in the blank.

1. Are you going to leave him go out of town alone? _____

2. College students should plan on a lot of hard work before they get their degrees. _____

3. Students should be quite in the library. _____

4. The Martins are liable to think Jan does not like them if she does not attend the party. _____

5. Tim has less arithmetic problems to do than his sister. _____

6. The detective suspected that the old man had stolen the money. _____

7. It seems to be alright for him to use the car. _____

8. What affect did the rain have on the tomato crop? _____

9. The amount of people coming will have to be determined today. _____

10. Mrs. Hudson formally lived in Wichita. _____

11. Susan must travel further than I do to get to work. _____

Lesson 52

Comparison

When you compare two or more people, ideas, or objects, you examine the ways in which they are similar and different:

SIMILARITY	DIFFERENCE
This can of fruit weighs as much as that one,	but there is less fruit and more syrup in this one than in that one.

In some cases you may want to discuss only the similarities or the differences:

SIMILARITY	DIFFERENCE
This football team has won as many games as today's opponent.	The head cheerleader is at least four inches taller and ten pounds heavier than the other cheerleaders.

To show comparison, use one of the three forms or degrees of an adjective or an adverb: **positive, comparative,** or **superlative.** To form the comparative degree of most one-syllable words functioning as adjectives or adverbs, add -er to the positive degree; to form the superlative degree, add -est:

POSITIVE	COMPARATIVE	SUPERLATIVE
hard	harder	hardest
fast	faster	fastest

If the adjective has two or more syllables or the adverb ends in -ly, you generally use *more* or *less* before the word for the comparative degree and *most* or *least* for the superlative degree:

	POSITIVE	COMPARATIVE	SUPERLATIVE
Adjective:	intelligent	more intelligent	most intelligent
Adverb:	smoothly	more smoothly	most smoothly

However, two-syllable adjectives accented on the first syllable can take the -er and -est suffixes, or they may be preceded by *more/less* or *most/least*:

wealthy/wealthier/wealthiest   OR   more wealthy/most wealthy
gentle/gentler/gentlest   OR   more gentle/most gentle
handsome/handsomer/handsomest   OR   more handsome/most handsome

Some of the most frequently used adjectives and adverbs do not follow the usual pattern for forming the comparative and superlative degrees:

	POSITIVE	COMPARATIVE	SUPERLATIVE
Adjective:	good	better	best
	bad	worse	worst
		less	least
Adverb:	well	better	best
	badly	worse	worst
		less	least
	far	farther	farthest
	far	further	furthest

SHOWING SIMILARITIES WITH THE POSITIVE DEGREE

You can show that two things are similar by using *as* and the positive degree of an adjective or adverb followed by an adverbial clause beginning with *as*. Frequently the predicate of the adverbial clause is not expressed:

Adj Adj———————— NS LV Adj-c Adv————————————
The twelve-year-old boy is **as tall as his father** (is tall).

Or a form of the verb *do* stands in place of the repeated predicate:

NS Vt Ndo   Adv Adv————————————————
He lifts weights **as easily as his older brother does.**

SHOWING DIFFERENCES WITH COMPARATIVE AND SUPERLATIVE DEGREES

To show differences between two persons or things, use the comparative degree of an adjective as a modifier of the noun:

Adj   Adj   NS   Vt   Adj   Ndo
Martha's **younger** daughter won a music scholarship. (Martha has two daughters.)

Use the superlative degree to compare three or more:

Adj Adj   NS   Adj——————— LV Adj Nsc
The **tallest** man in the room is her husband. (There are several men in the room.)

You may also show differences by using the comparative degrees of an adjective or an adverb followed by an adverbial clause beginning with *than*. **The comparison must be completed:**

NOT: Today Dale worked **less energetically.**

Adv   NS   Vi   Adv Adv   Adv———————————————
BUT: Today Dale worked **less energetically than** (he worked) **yesterday.**

NOT: Sally is more considerate.

NS   LV Adv   Adj-c   Adv————————————————
BUT: Sally is **more considerate than Joan** (is considerate).

A pronoun following *than* may be either the subject or the direct object in the clause beginning with *than,* depending on the meaning:

> Jim knows Harold better than I (. . . better than I know Harold.)
> Jim knows Harold better than me. (. . . better than Jim knows me.)

If you compare three or more, use the superlative degree and a prepositional phrase beginning with *of:*

> The ocean liner is the **largest** (ship) **of the ships in the harbor.**

LOGICAL COMPARISONS

To make a comparison logical, you must compare things that have similar characteristics. For example, you can compare cars and airplanes if you discuss different kinds of transportation, but you cannot compare wages with office equipment or a color with china or wood. The following examples show sentences with faulty comparisons and the ways they may be revised:

NOT: The pink rose is more attractive than red.
            (*Rose* is a flower and *red* is a color. The comparison must be made
            between two flowers or two colors.)
BUT: The pink rose is more attractive than the red one.

NOT: Mary's purse is much larger than Jane.
            (The comparison here is between *purse* and *Jane.*)
BUT: Mary's purse is much larger than Jane's (or Jane's purse).

NOT: Mary is a better accountant than any employee in the office.
            (Mary is also an employee in the office. She cannot be compared with
            herself and should be excluded from the comparison by using *any
            other.*)
BUT: Mary is a better accountant than any other employee in the office.

Comparison among three persons or items must be made clear by completing the comparison:

NOT: Mary liked Ruth better than Molly.
            (This can be interpreted two ways.)
BUT: Mary liked Ruth better than she liked Molly.
OR: Mary liked Ruth better than Molly did.

EXERCISE 52

Rewrite the following sentences to make comparisons logical. Add, omit, or change words wherever necessary.

1. Dick is the tallest of my two sons.

2. Mrs. Smith hates weddings more than her husband.

3. A light blue dress is more becoming than yellow.

4. Martha says that her frog can jump farther.

5. Jim is a more powerful weight lifter than any man in the neighborhood.

6. Jerry already weighs more than him.

7. Brad's camping equipment is more complete than Tom.

8. Mr. Hollis says that Meg is the better musician of his four piano students.

9. I do believe that this new armchair is comfortable than the old one.

10. Does a pound of potatoes weigh more than feathers?

Lesson 53

Parallelism

When you repeat the same pattern of words within a sentence or in two or more sentences, the patterns are **parallel** with one another. For example, *student,* the appositive in the following sentence, is parallel with *Brian,* which it renames, because both are nouns:

> The counselor talked with **Brian,** a very troubled **student.**

The next example shows two sentences that are parallel because they each contain an independent clause and a dependent clause:

> Jim, who lives in an apartment, hates the noise. Annette, who lives in a single house, feels isolated.

Frequently the repeated patterns are joined by *and* or other coordinating conjunctions. As you learned in Unit Seven on coordination, compound subjects, compound predicates, compound sentences, and words in a series are repeated patterns. In the following sentence, the parts of the compound subject are parallel because the three nouns form a repeated pattern:

> N   N   C N
> **Trustees, managers,** and **employees** attended the opening of the space museum.

In the next example the two independent clauses in the compound sentence are parallel:

> Independent clause————— C   Independent clause——————
> **Norman studied hard,** but **he could not pass the test.**

CORRECTING FAULTY PARALLELISM

If you do not repeat a pattern following *and,* the sentence lacks parallelism and should be revised. One of the most frequent problems inexperienced writers seem to have is shown in the following sentence. The writer begins a series with the verbs *argues* and *hates,* then switches to an independent clause instead of completing the series with the verb *works.* The resulting pattern is NS V, V, and NS V. It should be NS V, V, and V:

>   Parallel————————————————————
>   NS————— V   V
> NOT: Brad Collins **argues** constantly with everyone, **hates** his job, and his
>   NS   V
>   work is unsatisfactory.

BUT: Brad Collins **argues** constantly with everyone, **hates** his job, and

      works unsatisfactorily.

In the next sentence the writer has written two adjectives that describe the physical characteristics of the subject *Bill* and then has added a noun that renames the subject. Because *driver* cannot be changed to an adjective, the writer can use *race car driver* as an appositive that renames Bill and keep the adjectives as complements that describe the subject:

                  Parallel─────────

      NS   LV Adj-c Adj-c   Nsc

NOT: Bill is **tall, muscular,** and a race car driver.

      Parallel─────────────   Parallel─────────

      NS   NS (Appos) LV Adj-c   Adj-c

BUT: **Bill,** a race car **driver,**   is **tall** and **muscular.**

In the next sentence the writer has used *and* between a noun and an adjective clause, two constructions that are not parallel. By removing *and,* the adjective clause follows the word it modifies:

      NS──────   NS (Appos)   Adj──────────────────

NOT: Farley Fox, the actor,   and who has visited us several times, will appear in a new movie.

BUT: Farley Fox, the actor who has visited us several times, will appear in a new movie.

The writer of the next sentence has switched from infinitive verbal phrases to a V-ing verbal phrase in the next example. The series can be made parallel by changing *enameling* to *to enamel:*

NOT: The art students wanted **to sketch** outdoor scenes, **to paint** still lifes, and **enameling** copper jewelry.

BUT: The art students wanted **to sketch** outdoor scenes, **to paint** still lifes, and **to enamel** copper jewelry.

PAIRED CONNECTORS

Other connectors that join repeated patterns are **correlative conjunctions,** which are used in pairs:

both . . . and	either . . . or	neither . . . nor
not only . . . but also	whether . . . or	

The pattern that follows the first correlative conjunction in a sentence must also follow the second one:

NOUNS:	He bought **not only** the boat	C Ndo
	but also the boat trailer.	C Ndo
ADJECTIVES:	She was **both** sensitive	C Adj-c
	and responsive.	C Adj-c
PHRASES:	They had to decide **whether** to rent an apartment	C Inf Ndo
	or to buy a house.	C Inf Ndo
CLAUSES:	**Either** she arrives on time,	C NS Vi Adv,
	or we will leave without her.	C NS Vi Adv

No punctuation is needed between the words or phrases joined by correlative conjunctions. Use a comma before the seond correlative conjunction that connects the second independent clause to the first, as in the last example above.

EXERCISE 53A

In the following sentences there may be a structure which is not parallel with other elements in the sentence. Underline it, and write the revised parallel form in the blank. If no revision is needed, write A for Acceptable in the blank. Begin by writing NS above each subject, V above each verb, and C above each conjunction. Then examine word groups joined by the conjunctions and determine whether they are parallel.

1. Jed sat there all day smoking and having a

   conversation.   _____

2. Mary can either wash the car, or she can repair

   the window.   _____

3. Ms. Nelson is a teacher and who writes stories.   _____

4. She traveled in Europe not only to see the sights

   but also to study art.   _____

5. The art course included drawing, to paint, and

   sketching.   _____

6. The building designed by the architect and

   which John built has large cracks in the walls.   _____

7. The class has three projects: writing a term

   paper, to read three novels, and attending two

   plays.   _____

8. Liz is not only sensible but also an intellectual. _____

9. That painting is gaudy and without meaning. _____

10. His suggestion is brilliant, original, and will

    work. _____

EXERCISE 53B

Combine the following pairs of sentences by inserting correlative conjunctions: *either . . . or, neither . . . nor, not only . . . but also, both . . . and, whether . . . or.* You may omit words or add words. Be sure that the construction following one connector is parallel with the construction following the other. Begin by writing NS above each subject, V above each verb, and C above each conjunction.

EXAMPLE: Charles will buy a horse.
            Charles will buy a sports car.

            NS   C   Ndo   C   Ndo
            Charles will buy **either** a horse **or** a sports car.

            C   NS   Vt———   Ndo   C NS Vt———   Ndo
      OR: **Either** Charles will buy a horse, **or** he will buy a sports car.

1. Sarah and Tom will buy the large white house in the center of town.
   They will consider living on her father's ranch.

2. He is a karate expert.
   He is an excellent wrestler.

3. The principal does not want to attend the convention.
   The teachers do not want to attend the convention.

4. George will repair the tractor and plow the field.
   He will hire Thomas to do the plowing.

5. Judy will not give Ben a job.
   Judy will not lend Ben any money.

Lesson 54

Sentence Editing

A quick review of all the lessons you have completed to this point will show you that you have learned effective ways to express your ideas in sentences, and techniques for examining and revising sentences that do not express your ideas clearly. With continued practice you should be able to achieve variety, economy, unity, and coherence in your sentences by combining some and revising others.

VARIETY

In studying sentence combining, you may have begun to think that long sentences are better than short sentences. In some cases they are better because they may be able to show the relationship of ideas more clearly than several short, choppy sentences; however, several sentences of the same length can be dull and monotonous, as you can see in the first half of the following example, but the revised sentences in the second half create reader interest because they vary in length:

NOT: Wendy arrived at the cabin. She unlocked the door. She entered the deserted cabin. She looked carefully into each dark corner of the room.
BUT: Wendy arrived. She unlocked the door. As she entered the deserted cabin, she looked carefully into each dark corner of the room.

Then vary the patterns within sentences. Some may begin with the subject, others with the predicate, a dependent clause, or a verbal phrase:

V-ing phrase:	Running to catch the bus, Mr. Watson slipped and fell on the sidewalk.
Compound sentence:	His briefcase flew open, and a brisk wind scattered his papers over the street.
Dependent clause:	After he had arrived at the office, he could not find the contract that he needed for the ten o'clock meeting.
Predicate first:	On the desk lay a stack of papers.
Adverb:	Fortunately he found another copy of the contract among them.

ECONOMY

After you write or combine sentences, you should go over them carefully and take out any unnecessary words to keep clear focus on what you are saying. Endless repetition bores readers and, in some cases, may interfere with the readers' understanding of the

sentences. The following sentences give examples of the kinds of words and phrases you probably should eliminate to achieve economy in writing.

Redundancy is the unnecessary repetition of words similar in meaning. Improve the sentence by eliminating one word or word group:

NOT: **As a rule** he is **usually** on time.
BUT: **As a rule** he is on time.

NOT: He expects to arrive tomorrow **evening** about **midnight.**
BUT: He expects to arrive tomorrow about **midnight.**

Padding is the use of vague, general words like *line, element, factor, situation, aspect,* and many others:

NOT: The important **factor** to consider in the news writing **situation** is the human interest **element.**
BUT: We should consider human interest in writing news stories.

Forms of the verb *be* and expressions like *who was* or *which is* sometimes can be eliminated:

NOT: The coat **which is blue** is ten years old.
BUT: The **blue** coat is ten years old.

Wordy transitions take up space but say very little:

NOT: **It goes without saying,** nevertheless, that they are unwilling to cooperate.
BUT: Nevertheless, they are unwilling to cooperate.

NOT: **Taking this factor into consideration,** they concluded that his findings were incomplete.
BUT: Therefore, they concluded that his findings were incomplete.

Pretentious words do not give elegance to writing:

NOT: I can say with genuine veracity that my intentions to attain the pinnacle of success are of the most praiseworthy caliber.
BUT: Truthfully, I intend to succeed.

EXERCISE 54A

Rewrite the following sentences to remove colorless, unnecessary, and uninformative words. First, cross out unnecessary words and add needed words. Then arrange the remaining words into an effective sentence.

1. The purpose of his lecture was to explain how one goes about giving artificial respiration to a person who has almost drowned.

2. The fact of the matter is that news which appears in newspapers is old by the time readers get their papers because television can give a report at the scene as it is happening.

3. It goes without saying that there are many reasons why the rules committee refuses to listen to Dwight Huston's grievances.

4. The man who was wearing a blue shirt made every attempt possible to rescue the dog which was small and brown and white as it perched precariously on a log in the river which was raging.

5. The different fields of occupation have intrigued me since I was in high school, and I am still contemplating carefully what course my future program of study will take.

6. The evidence at hand seems to point to the fact that Tim Elliott was not present at the time of the demise of the victim who had been put to rest by a bullet which penetrated his skull.

7. In all the careful considerations given to the problem at hand, Laura Richards has maintained an air of complete control and calm which is certainly admirable, to say the least.

8. There appears to be from time to time the expression of the feeling that there could be more efficiency in turning out products which are assembled on our assembly line.

UNITY

When you combine sentences, you carefully relate ideas to one another to achieve unity. If unrelated ideas creep in, they turn your readers' attention away from the main point. The following example may be slightly exaggerated, but the words in bold type show unnecessary information that intrudes in the sentence. The repair of the car obviously has nothing to do with the addition of rooms to the house, and the information could be deleted without loss of meaning:

> NOT: The retired couple decided to enlarge their house by adding three new rooms, **and they had their car repaired the next day.** They consulted an architect, who drew plans for them.
> BUT: The retired couple decided to enlarge their house by adding three new rooms. They consulted an architect, who drew plans for them.

EXERCISE 54B

Rewrite the following sentences to eliminate any ideas not directly related to the main thought in the sentence.

1. On his way home from work Dave crashed into an oncoming car, but he did not have time to get his homework done.

2. Mary Cummings, who operates the beauty shop and whose mother lives in Nebraska, won the award this year for an original hairstyle.

3. If you like seafood, you will like Harvey's Haven, which serves delicious hamburgers.

4. The reference book John is using contains helpful information for three of his classes, but he finds he has little time to play baseball.

5. Because Ellis dislikes working out details of a research project, he hired Ross, who is a star athlete.

COHERENCE

Also of great importance is achieving coherence (a holding together) by maintaining consistent point of view in tone, person, number, and tense (Lesson 50); repeating necessary terms; using transitions (Lesson 29); and keeping structures parallel (Lesson 53).

Study the following set of sentences:

1. All his keys were accidentally locked in the house by Matt.
2. He was leaving for work.
3. He could not get back into his house.
4. He cannot drive his car.
5. He feels like throwing in the towel.
6. He feels like going fishing.
7. He cannot get his fishing gear out of the garage.
8. The garage is locked too.

Notice that these sentences lack coherence for the following reasons:
a. The first sentence fails to focus on Matt, the person who is experiencing several problems, because the verb is passive *(were lost).*
b. Verbs needlessly shift from past tense to present tense, beginning with the third sentence, thus distorting the time sequence.
c. The series of sentences lacks connectors and transitions to show the relationship of ideas clearly.
d. The tone changes unnecessarily with the informal expression *throwing in the towel.*

But the sentences are coherent for these reasons:
a. Sentences two through seven repeat the subject *he,* thus maintaining focus on the subject.
b. Sentences two through seven are parallel.

Now compare the single sentences on the left with the sentences on the right, which have been combined and revised to achieve coherence:

SINGLE SENTENCES	COMBINED SENTENCES
All his keys were accidentally locked in the house by Matt. He was leaving for work. He could not get back into his house. He cannot drive his car. He feels like throwing in the towel. He feels like going fishing. He cannot get his fishing gear out of the garage. The garage is locked too.	Matt accidentally locked all his keys in the house as he was leaving for work; as a result, he could not get back into his house or drive his car. He felt like escaping his problems by going fishing, but he could not get his fishing gear out of the garage because it was locked too.

EXERCISE 54C

Revise and combine the following sets of sentences to achieve coherence. Review the examples in this unit if you need help.

1. Many mistakes are made by new drivers.
   The experienced driver could make just as many if they were not careful.

2. Many well-constructed homes were built by the Johnson brothers.
   They also erect flimsy houses.
   The flimsy houses probably can fall down in a strong breeze.

3. Jim was wearing a real sharp suit for the contest.
   He feels sick.
   Nan meets him at the door.
   She is dressed in jeans and a shirt.

4. Ted Owen and myself organized the football parade.
   You never realize the amount of work.
   You become involved in a project like that.

5. The movie is super. It was produced by the old movie producer Clyde Thornton. He sure knew what he was doing when he did that.

6. It's a good thing for a person to be an excellent marksman if they're going hunting for big game in Africa. You never know when one of the enraged beasts might attack you.

EDITING CHECKLIST

After you have written a paragraph or essay, your instructor might use the following correction symbols to indicate the kinds of changes you should make to improve your paper:

AWK *Awkward sentence or awkward phrasing.* AWK indicates that a sentence does not follow the usual pattern of sentences in English. Sometimes the awkwardness comes from grammatical problems, sometimes from the change of thought in the middle of a sentence. The following sentence is awkward and confusing because the writer attached a new idea before completing the first idea. By breaking this sentence apart and writing each idea in a separate sentence, you can examine the relationship of ideas. Then you can combine the sentences with connectors into a single logical sentence:

> NOT: Mathematics is a complex subject that many people are afraid to study mathematics because they think they will fail.
>
>   a. Mathematics is a complex subject /b/.
> **/that/** b. Many people are afraid to study /c/.
> **/because/** c. They think they will fail.
>
> BUT: Mathematics is a complex subject that many people are afraid to study because they think they will fail.

The next sentence might also be labeled *Awkward* because the writer has strung vague, general ideas together, probably because he did not have enough information about the topic. First, the relationship of ideas—the relationship of the body to the person—is distorted because the writer seems to be separating the body from the person when they belong together. Second, the term *factor,* like *situation* and *thing,* indicates vagueness:

> NOT: The human body is a major factor of a person's life, if it stays healthy, the person will also stay healthy. The blood in the body is also an important factor.

Satisfactory revision of the sentences above would depend on the writer's deciding precisely what he wants to say. If he cannot decide, he should read about his topic to get specific information, or he should choose a topic that he understands thoroughly.

C *Connector (Lessons 28–35).* The connector you have used does not provide a logical link between sentences or word groups because the meaning of the connector does not fit with the meaning of the sentences or word groups.

CS *Comma splice (Lesson 28).* You have used only a comma between two independent clauses. You need either a comma and coordinating conjunction or a semicolon alone.

DM *Dangling modifier (Lesson 42).* The modifier, usually a verbal phrase, has no noun in the sentence to modify.

Frag *Fragment (Lesson 45).* You have written only a part of a sentence. You may have to add a subject or a verb, or you may attach the fragment to the sentence before or after it.

MM *Misplaced modifier (Lesson 42).* The modifier should be moved next to the noun that it modifies.

P *Punctuation.* (Refer to Lessons 46–48 and the index in this book for a list of punctuation with various structures.)

P Agr *Pronoun-antecedent agreement (Lesson 26).* Pronouns should be the same person (first, second, third) and number (singular, plural) as the noun or pronoun they refer to or replace.

Paral *Parallelism (Lesson 53).* Two or more words, phrases, or clauses connected by coordinating conjunctions should be the same grammatical constructions—two or more nouns, adjectives, infinitives, dependent clauses, and so on.

Pass	*Passive verb (Lesson 39).* Change the verb from passive to active. In other words, make the actor the subject of the sentence.
Ref	*Pronoun Reference (Lesson 26).* The pronoun does not refer to a particular noun before it. Rewrite by including a noun that the pronoun can refer to, or change the pronoun to a noun.
R	*Run-on (Lesson 28).* You have not used any punctuation between two independent clauses. Add either a comma and a coordinating conjunction or a semicolon alone.
Shift	*Shift in point of view, person, number, tense (Lesson 50).* You may have begun writing in third person and shifted to second person. You may have begun writing in third person singular and shifted to third person plural. You may have shifted verb tenses without reason.
SV Agr	*Subject-verb agreement (Lesson 27).* You have used a singular noun with a verb form that belongs with a plural noun or vice versa.
Tense	*Verb tense (Lessons 7–12).* You must use verb tenses that indicate the time that the events you are discussing took place. In addition, you must determine, for example, whether one event happened in the past before another time in the past, or whether an event began in the past and continues to the present.
Trans	*Transition needed (Lesson 29).* You should show the relationship of ideas by using a transitional word or expression between or within sentences.

EXERCISE 54D

The following paragraph, written by a student, has been marked with correction symbols to indicate the parts of the paragraph that should be revised. Read the entire paragraph so that you understand what it is about. Then revise it to eliminate the problems. Rewrite the entire paragraph on another sheet of paper.

Home builders are meeting buyers' needs with houses that are small, well-

Paral   Tense

designed, and *they can afford*. Although both adults work, they *preferred* a small house

Frag   Shift

of 700 to 1,000 square feet. *(With two bedrooms instead of three or four.) You* also want

Run-on

a small lot for less yard upkeep they may choose a condominium with yard service pro-

SV Agr

vided. Though the house *are* small, "frills" such as fireplaces, air conditioning, dish-

Ref

washers, clothes dryers, and other conveniences that save *them* work and keep them

Pass   P

comfortable *are wanted by home buyers.* To give the appearance of roominess; design-

Tense   wrong connector

ers *will provide* high ceilings; *however,* vertical space costs only half as much as

CS Ref

horizontal space,   *they* also include many built-in cabinets. Perhaps of greatest im-

Shift   Pass

portance is building houses that *you* can afford to buy. The price *is kept down* by small

houses built on small lots.

Unit Eleven Review

Practice Test

PART I

A. Make point of view consistent in the following passage by changing pronouns and verbs to appropriate forms. Pronoun reference, pronoun-antecedent agreement, or verb tenses may be faulty. Cross out words to be changed and write revisions above them.

(20 points—2 points each)   (Lessons 50, 53)   Score _____

Students who begin college sometimes does not realize how much time he will

need to complete all the work he has to do to accomplish the goals of each of his

courses. As a result, you sometimes take too many courses the first semester. Or

you may think that you can work full time and also carry a full load in college. As we

fall behind in completing assignments, we realized that we had to cut down the

number of hours we worked; or, if that was not possible, we had to take fewer

courses. You have to realize that very few people can work forty hours a week, at-

tend class twelve or fifteen hours, and study twenty-five to thirty hours all in one

week. They have to develop a realistic work schedule if they are to succeed in

college.

B. Make tone consistent by changing informal expressions to those preferred in Standard English.

(8 points—2 points each)   (Lesson 51)   Score _____

1. This is all the farther he can travel.

2. The man suspicioned he was being followed.

3. Did Jan receive an invite to the party?

4. She seems to be pretty well informed.

C. Revise any faulty comparison you find in the following sentences. If the comparison is satisfactory, place X in the blank.
(10 points—2 points each)   (Lesson 52)   Score _____

1. Jim likes Paul better than Bob.   _____

2. Mr. Wayne drives the youngest of his two daughters to school.   _____

3. Evelyn is beautifuler than Sue.   _____

4. This is a most unique tool.   _____

5. The Hawkinses' house is much more elaborate than Dale Smith.   _____

D. Rewrite each of these sentences to make structures within them parallel. Begin by labeling the subject and verb. Then identify the structures to be made parallel.
(12 points—3 points each)   (Lesson 53)   Score _____

1. Brent will either catch some fish, or he will buy them at the fish market.

2. The bank messenger is conscientious, careful, and can be trusted.

3. The old woman neither could speak nor walk.

4. The townspeople waited quietly and with patience for the jury's verdict.

E. Combine the following sentences by placing ideas in their proper relationship to one another by using phrases, clauses, and transitional expressions. Also revise the sentences by eliminating unnecessary words or adding needed words. Add punctuation only where it is needed. Try to make each set of senteces just one sentence—no more than two.
(50 points—10 points each)   (Lessons 50–54)   Score _____

1. /After/   The freighter had dropped anchor in the harbor.
              The customs inspector went aboard. /and/
              He inspected the entire ship.

2.   The train crossed the prairie.
       It carried a large shipment (V-ing)
       The shipment was gold.
       It was guarded by armed men. (V-ed)
       There were at least twenty-five armed men.

3.   Two men rode horseback.
       Two men raced through the dry, brown hills.
       They were followed by fifty horsemen.
       The horsemen shot at them.

4.   The bank opened in the morning. The people came in to deposit money.
       They came to make loan payments. They came to buy traveler's checks.
       They came to cash checks.

5.   The little burro tried to cross the river. It stepped into a large hole in the
       riverbed. It sank beneath the water. Then it bobbed to the surface. It strug-
       gled to get to the other side.

PART II

The following paragraph has been marked with correction symbols to indicate the parts
of the paragraph that should be revised. Read the entire paragraph so that you understand what it is about. Then revise it to eliminate the problems. Rewrite the entire
paragraph on another sheet of paper.
(100 points—Use point system of Unit Eleven Practice Writing Test)   Score _____

Tense

Before 1964 the gates of Yellowstone National Park *are closed* to automobile traf-

P

fic when snow fell; but since then visitors can participate in snowmobile expeditions.

Shift   Shift

Visitors can hire a local guide, or *you* can tour by *yourself* on well-marked trails that

SV Agr   Shift   P

is maintained by a volunteer group. *You* could rent snowmobiles, and clothing designed

Frag

especially for withstanding a below-zero wind chill factor. *(Since snowmobiles can*

P

reach speeds of up to 45 miles an hour.) Visitors can easily take a one-day-75-mile

SV Agr   P   P   Shift

round trip that *include* a stop at Old Faithful time for lunch and a few side trips. *You*

Run-on

can see steaming geysers blow and mud pots bubble you can watch animals such as

elk and buffalo roam over the snow. The atmosphere of the park is very different from

Frag

summertime. *(When crowds of people fill the park every day.)*

Unit Eleven

Practice Writing Test

(These are the instructions you will receive when you take the Unit Eleven Writing Test. Write your paragraph on a separate sheet of paper.)

Write six to eight sentences (approximately 100 to 150 words) about a SINGLE topic. Try to write sentences of different lengths for variety. WRITE AT LEAST TWO COMPOUND SENTENCES AND TWO SENTENCES WITH DEPENDENT CLAUSES. Use connectors such as *but, or, as a result, however, if, although, when, who, which,* and *that.* Your sentences will be evaluated on their content, form, grammar, and punctuation.

You may use another sheet of paper to write your first and final drafts of the sentences. Be sure to attach your extra sheets to this test. Do all your writing during the class period. DO NOT TAKE THE TEST HOME.

Your instructor may assign a topic. Or you may write about any of the following topics: an accident, a disagreement or conflict, observations about current events, housing, social customs and folklore, working conditions, entertainment, recreation, alternative life styles, computers, energy, hazards, or any other topic that YOUR INSTRUCTOR APPROVES. Choose a topic that you understand well. Base it on your own experience, but write it in THIRD PERSON.

EVALUATION

Content—all sentences about one subject	50 points _____	
Form—variety of length; 2 compound, 2 with dependent clauses	50 points _____	
		Total _____

Points taken off for the following:

Fragments, run-ons, commas splices	Minus 20 each _____	
Misused semicolon or comma	Minus 5 each _____	
Sentence style errors, awkward wording, PA agr, Ref, SV agr, DM, MM, Shift, Tense	Minus 3 each _____	
Spelling, comma omitted, capitalization	Minus 1 each _____	
		Total _____
		TOTAL _____

Show your paragraph to your instructor.

Spelling Appendix

NOUN PLURALS

As you learned in Lesson 15, most nouns form their plurals by adding -s or -es: house/houses, dish/dishes, box/boxes, toy/toys. However, some nouns in English have special ways of forming their plurals:

1. Some nouns ending in an -f sound form their plurals by adding -s and make a spelling change within the word as well:

    wife / wives   thief / thieves   knife / knives

    Other nouns ending in an -f sound add only -s:

    belief / beliefs   chief / chiefs   roof / roofs

    Some have two forms:

    elf / elves OR elfs   scarf / scarves OR scarfs

2. The suffixes -en and -ren are added to form the plural of these nouns:

    ox / oxen   child / children

3. The following nouns change the spelling within to form the plural:

    man / men   foot / feet   goose / geese
    woman / women   mouse / mice   tooth / teeth

4. Plurals of figures, words, and letters are usually formed by adding -s:

    He misdialed the 2's.   She mispronounced   Tom uses too many
                             r's.   so's.

5. Compound nouns usually form their plurals by adding -s or -es at the end of the group or unit:

    schoolhouse / schoolhouses   cupful / cupfuls

    However, in hyphenated words, the main word in the unit takes the plural suffix:

    mother-in-law / mothers-in-law   man-of-war / men-of-war

Words that come from Latin and Greek frequently have two plural forms: They may retain their Latin or Greek plural form, especially in scientific or technical writing, or they may end in -s or -es in everyday usage:

1. Latin words ending in *-us* in the singular end in *-i* in the plural:

        fungus / fungi (funguses)   alumnus / alumni
        nucleus / nuclei (nucleuses)

2. Latin words ending in *-a* in the singular end in *-ae* in the plural:

        vertebra / vertebrae (vertebras)   formula / formulae (formulas)
        antenna / antennae (antennas)   alga / algae

3. Latin words ending in *-um* in the singular end in *-a* in the plural:

        curriculum / curricula (curriculums)   datum / data
        medium / media (mediums)

4. Latin words ending in *-ix* or *-ex* in the singular end in *-ices* in the plural:

        index / indices (indexes)   appendix / appendices (appendixes)
        apex / apices (apexes)

5. Greek words ending in *-is* in the singular end in *-es* in the plural:

        analysis / analyses   thesis / theses
        parenthesis / parentheses   basis / bases

6. Greek words ending in *-on* in the singular end in *-a* in the plural:

        phenomenon / phenomena   ganglion / ganglia (ganglions)
         (phenomenons)   criterion / criteria (criterions)

Answer Key

EXERCISE 1

1. a. subject   b. predicate
2. a. noun   b. pronoun
3. a. verb

EXERCISE 2A

1. V	4. V	7. V
2. V	5.	8.
3. V	6.	9.

10.	13.	16.
11. V	14.	17. V
12. V	15. V	18. V

EXERCISE 2B

1. arrive   5. ends
2. starts   6. wins
3. hits   7. leave
4. cheer

EXERCISE 3A

1. N	4.	7.
2. N	5. N	8. N
3.	6. N	9.

10. N	13.	16. N
11. N	14.	17.
12. N	15. N	18. N

EXERCISE 3B

1. Linda, arm
2. friend, Linda, hospital
3. doctor, arm
4. Linda, arm
5. doctor, cast, arm

EXERCISE 3C

1. V N	5. V N
2. V N	6. N
3. V	7. V N
4. V N	8. V N

EXERCISE 3D

1. N	3. N	5. V	7. N
2. V	4. N	6. V	8. V

EXERCISE 3F

1. Candles lighted the room.
   (N   V   N)
2. Their friends heard the wind.
   (N   V   N)
3. Betty served the drinks.
   (N   V   N)
4. Ted cooked sausages.
   (N   V   N)
5. Karen screamed.
   (N   V)
6. She rubbed her leg.
   (V   N)
7. A cat meowed.
   (N   V)
8. Everyone laughed.
   (V)

EXERCISE 4A

1. The carpenter bought lumber.
   (NS   Vt   Ndo)
2. He built a cabin.
   (NS Vt   Ndo)
3. He sawed the wood and hammered nails.
   (NS Vt   Ndo   C   Vt   Ndo)
4. The carpenter smashed his thumb.
   (NS   Vt   Ndo)
5. He yelled.
   (NS Vi)
6. He called his doctor.
   (NS Vt   Ndo)
7. The doctor used a splint and bandages.
   (NS   Vt Ndo   C   Ndo)
8. The carpenter rested.
   (NS   Vi)

EXERCISE 4B

	SUBJECT	PREDICATE
	NS	Vi
1.	Lucy	rides
	NS	Vi
2.	engine	runs
	NS	Vt Ndo
3.	senator	won the election

<table>
<tr><td></td><td>NS</td><td>Vi</td></tr>
<tr><td>4.</td><td>Matt</td><td>draws</td></tr>
</table>

    NS   Vt   Ndo
5. Lucy   rides her bicycle

    NS   Vt   Ndo
6. Steve   runs the engine

    NS   Vi
7. senator   won

EXERCISE 5A

	SUBJECT	PREDICATE
	NS	LV Nsc
1.	dog	is a collie
	NS	LV Nsc C
2.	Walt	is a reporter and Nsc photographer
	NS————	LV Nsc
3.	Mr. Watson	is the teacher
	NS————	LV Nsc
4.	Mary Ryan	became the chair-person
	NS	LV Nsc
5.	He	remained a super-visor
	NS	LV Nsc Nsc————
6.	desserts	are cake, ice cream, C Nsc and pie
	NS	LV Nsc
7.	Tiger	is a cat
	NS————————	LV Nsc
8.	Haynes Institute	is a college

EXERCISE 5B

    NS LV   Nsc
1. Jean is an artist.

    NS Vt   Ndo
2. She designs greeting cards.

        NS   LV Nsc
3. Her husband is Mike.

    NS C NS Vi
4. Jean and Mike moved.

    NS Vt   Ndo
5. Jean called the movers.

    NS Vt   Ndo   Ndo
6. Mike packed the suitcases and boxes.

        NS   Vt   Ndo
7. The movers carried the furniture.

        NS   Vt   Ndo
8. The movers loaded the van.

    NS C NS   Vt   Ndo
9. Boxes and furniture filled the van.

    NS C NS   Vt   Ndo
10. Jean and Mike left the apartment.

       NS Vt   Ndo
11. They cleaned the house.

         NS Vi
12. The van arrived.

         NS   Vt   Ndo
13. The movers arranged the furniture.

        NS   Vt   Ndo
14. Jean unpacked several boxes.

        NS   Vt   Ndo
15. Mike found his tools.

        NS C NS Vt   Ndo
16. Jean and Mike bought food.

        NS Vt Ndo
17. They ate dinner.

        NS Vt   Ndo
18. They read the newspaper.

        NS Vt   Ndo
19. They watched television.

         NS Vi
20. The day ended.

UNIT ONE REVIEW
Practice Test

Part I
A.

1.	V	N	5.	V	
2.	V	N	6.	V	N
3.	V	N	7.		N
4.	V	N	8.	V	N

B.

	SUBJECT	PREDICATE
	NS	Vt Ndo C
1.	plane	carried passengers and Ndo cargo
	NS	LV Nsc
2.	plane	was a jumbo jet
	NS	Vt Ndo
3.	Darkness	covered the land
	NS NS	Vi
4.	stars, moon	shone
	NS	Vt Ndo C
5.	plane	passed Chicago and Ndo Milwaukee
	NS	Vt Ndo
6.	Passengers	saw the lights

C.
1. Darkness covered the land.
2. The plane passed Chicago and Milwaukee.
3. Passengers saw the lights.

D.
Show these sentences to your instructor or tutor.

Part II
Show these sentences to your instructor or tutor.

EXERCISE 6A

    NS   NS   Vt   Ndo
1. Joann and Tom spend their weekends
   Adv————————————
   at an open-air market.
   Adv——————— NS   Vt   Ndo
2. During the week Joann finds rocks
   Adv———— C Adv———
   on the beach and in fields.
   Adv NS Adv   Vt   Ndo
3. Later she carefully polishes the rocks
   C Vt Ndo Adv———
   and drills holes into them.
   NS Vi Adv   Adv———— C
4. She sits outside under a tree and
   Vt   Ndo
   makes jewelry.
   NS   Adv   Vt   Ndo Adv———
5. Tom skillfully shapes clay into plates,

   ————————————
   jars, and bowls.
   Adv NS Adv   Vt   Ndo Adv———
6. Next, he carefully places them into a
   ———— C Vt   Ndo Adv
   furnace and bakes them hard.
   Adv   NS Vt   Ndo   Ndo
7. Sometimes he paints the plates, bowls,
      Ndo C Vt   Ndo Adv
   and jars and bakes them again.
   NS   Adv   Vt   Ndo   C
8. People eagerly buy the pottery and
   Ndo   Adv———
   jewelry at the market.

EXERCISE 7A

   NS   NS   V
1. Kara and John own a motor
   home.   P
   NS V
2. They plan trips every
   summer.   P
   NS   V
3. A friend sometimes goes
   with them.   S
        NS   V
4. Their children enjoy the
   outdoors.   P

        NS   NS
5. Even the dog and the cat
   V
   like traveling.   P
   NS V
6. They explore new territory.   P
   NS   V
7. Cooking sometimes creates   S
   problems.
       NS   NS
8. Sleeping bags and blankets
   V
   protect the children at night.   P

EXERCISE 7B

          NS
1. Each bird <u>occupies</u> . . .
      NS   NS   NS
2. A robin, a sparrow, and an oriole
   <u>live</u> . . .
         NS
3. Each one <u>needs</u> . . .
        NS
4. Two robins <u>live</u> . . .
        NS
5. Each male <u>warns</u> . . .
   NS
6. He <u>keeps</u> . . .
   NS
7. He also <u>attracts</u> . . .
        NS   NS
8. The male and female <u>build</u> . . .
   NS
9. They <u>feed</u> . . .
        NS
10. Later they <u>fly</u> . . .

EXERCISE 7C

            V   Adv———
1. Stewart travels to Miami every week.
      Adv   V
2. He usually has business appointments
   in the morning.
   Adv————————   V
3. Once a month he buys new clothes or
   books.
                  Adv   V
4. Stewart and his friends frequently have
   dinner together.
   Adv   V
5. Sometimes he stays in Miami for the
   weekend.

EXERCISE 7D

       NS   V
1. Susan ~~reserve~~ <u>reserves</u> . . .
           NS   V
2. She usually ~~make~~ <u>makes</u> . . .
       NS   NS   V
3. Jerry and Bob ~~buys~~ <u>buy</u> . . .
           NS   V
4. Each couple ~~bring~~ <u>brings</u> . . .
       NS   V
5. Betty ~~are~~ <u>is</u> . . .
       NS   V
6. She ~~make~~ <u>makes</u> . . .
           NS   V
7. One day they ~~hikes~~ <u>hike</u> . . .
            NS   V
8. Another day they ~~swims~~ <u>swim</u> . . .
           NS   V
9. Each evening they ~~eats~~ <u>eat</u> . . .
           NS   V
10. Afterwards they ~~sings~~ <u>sing</u> . . . and
    V
    ~~tells~~ <u>tell</u> . . .

EXERCISE 8A

1.	R	dragged	6.	R	replied
2.	R	rewarded	7.	I	shook
3.	R	accepted	8.	I	built
4.	I	sank	9.	I	swam
5.	I	forgot	10.	I	drank

EXERCISE 8B

1.	left	6.	lived
2.	visited	7.	drove
3.	stopped	8.	wound
4.	saw	9.	stalled
5.	was	10.	needed

EXERCISE 8C

   Adv——
1. Last year Rita sold jeans and tops.
   <u>Past</u>
                Adv——
2. She made a profit each week. <u>Past</u>
   Adv——
3. In June she hired Mark and Megan.
   <u>Past</u>
   Adv
4. Now she has a successful business.
   <u>Present</u>

   Adv——
5. Once a month they travel to buyers'
   meetings. <u>Present</u>

EXERCISE 8D

   Adv——
1. Last year Ray <u>raced</u> his horse.
                 Adv——
2. The horse <u>won</u> prizes frequently.
3. Ray and a friend <u>exercise</u> (exercised)
           Adv——
   the horse every day.
                  Adv——
4. Ray <u>feeds</u> (fed) the horse every day.
   Adv——
5. Once a day the friend <u>brushes</u> (brushed)
   the horse's coat and mane.

EXERCISE 8E

           write
Jennifer and Steve ~~wrote~~ magazine
       interviews
articles. Jennifer ~~interviewed~~ famous people.
  is   are
One ~~was~~ a baseball player. Two ~~were~~ novel-
      tells
ists. She ~~told~~ about their lives and their in-
         discusses
terests. Steve ~~discussed~~ photography. He
takes   makes
~~took~~ photographs. He ~~made~~ drawings.
                  work
Jennifer and Steve sometimes ~~worked~~ to-
     interviews
gether. She ~~interviewed~~ people. Steve
photographs
~~photographed~~ them.

EXERCISE 9A

   NS   Vt   Ndo   Adv
1. Linda begins working next week.

Linda		begins

   NS   Vi——   Adv.
2. Steve will stay home.

Steve	will	stay

   NS LV——   Nsc
3. He will be a "househusband."

He	will	be

   NS Vt——   Ndo   C   Vt
4. He will clean the house and wash
Ndo
clothes.

He	will	clean, wash

NS Vt—— Ndo C Vi
5. Linda will buy groceries and help
Adv————
in the kitchen.

Linda	will	buy, help

NS Vt—— Ndo
6. The children will clean their rooms.

children	will	clean

NS Vt———— Ndo
7. The family is going to try the experiment
Adv——
for a year.

family	is going to	try

NS Vt————
8. Other families are going to try the
Ndo Adv
experiment also.

families	are going to	try

EXERCISE 9B

1. rides	6. is going to spend
2. travels	7. will buy
3. needs	8. are going to entertain
4. will have	9. will enjoy
5. will earn	

UNIT TWO REVIEW
Practice Test

Part I
A.
Show these sentences to your instructor or tutor.

B.

1.	R	studied	6.	I	clung
2.	R	rolled	7.	R	dropped
3.	R	chased	8.	I	went
4.	I	bore	9.	I	froze
5.	I	bent	10.	I	knew

C.
NS V
1. Seagulls ~~circles~~ circle . . .
NS V
2. Charlie ~~are~~ is . . .
NS V
3. The tiger ~~catched~~ caught . . .
NS V
4. Maggie ~~buyed~~ bought . . .
NS V————
5. The fence ~~are going to keep~~ is going to keep . . .
NS V
6. Three squirrels ~~runned~~ ran . . .
NS V
7. The tire ~~bursted~~ burst . . .
NS V
8. The dog ~~snuck~~ sneaked . . .
NS V
9. Bells ~~ringed~~ rang . . .
NS V
10. Swans ~~swimmed~~ swam . . .

D.

	SUBJECT	AUXILIARY	MAIN VERB
1.	Donna	is going to	buy
2.	Amy, Ted	will	work
3.	(You)		Sit
4.	rain		fell
5.	Don Johnson		is

E.
1. examined
2. will plant
3. swims OR swam OR will swim
4. won
5. fly OR flew OR will fly

Part II
A, B, and C
Show these sentences to your instructor or tutor.

EXERCISE 10A

1. Aux	4. Aux
2. Main	5. Main
3. Main	6. Aux

EXERCISE 10B

Show these sentences to your instructor or tutor.

EXERCISE 10C

Adv————
1. In recent years people have learned. . .
2. They have tried . . .
Adv————
3. Before the energy crises people had received . . .
4. Homeowners had heated . . .
5. Gas companies had encouraged . . .
Adv————
6. But for the past few years the gas companies have changed . . .
7. They have shown . . .

EXERCISE 10D

```
          NS   V————
1. The ship h̶a̶v̶e̶ ̶s̶a̶i̶l̶e̶d̶ has sailed . . .
       NS   V————
2. Nancy h̶a̶s̶ ̶d̶r̶o̶v̶e̶ has driven . . .
      NS   V————
3. Bob h̶a̶d̶ ̶d̶r̶a̶n̶k̶ had drunk . . .
      NS   V
4. Mark s̶e̶e̶n̶ saw OR had seen . . .
          NS   V————————
5. The people h̶a̶s̶ ̶d̶i̶s̶c̶u̶s̶s̶e̶d̶ have dis-
   cussed . . .
       NS   V
6. Fred d̶o̶n̶e̶ did OR had done . . .
           NS   V————
7. The plumber h̶a̶v̶e̶ ̶b̶o̶u̶g̶h̶t̶ has
   bought . . .
        NS   V————
8. David h̶a̶d̶ ̶c̶h̶o̶o̶s̶e̶d̶ had chosen . . .
   NS————   V————
9. Susan Miller h̶a̶s̶ ̶w̶r̶o̶t̶e̶ has written . . .
           NS   V————
10. The choir h̶a̶d̶ ̶s̶a̶n̶g̶ had sung . . .
```

EXERCISE 10E

Show these sentences to your instructor or tutor.

EXERCISE 10F

1. caused
2. needed OR need
3. had organized
4. had met
5. had organized
6. had bought
7. had held
8. helped
9. have made OR are making
10. have bought OR are buying
11. will train
12. will have prepared

EXERCISE 11A

	SUBJECT	AUXILIARY	MAIN VERB
1.	storm	was	coming
2.	rain	was	pounding
3.	dam	had	cracked and released
4.	Water	was	rushing
5.	People	were	running and screaming
6.	water		flooded and crushed
7.	Mud	was	covering
8.	Water		hid

EXERCISE 11B

1. are working
2. have been studying
3. will be flying
4. was running
5. am helping
6. is walking
7. had been enjoying
8. has been writing
9. were stopping
10. is riding
11. will be taping

EXERCISE 11C

1. sit, sits, sat, sat, sitting
   sit
2. play, plays, played, played, playing
   plays
3. ride, rides, rode, ridden, riding
   rode
4. ski, skis, skied, skied, skiing
   skied
   had been skiing
5. hit, hits, hit, hit, hitting
   hit
6. hurt, hurts, hurt, hurt, hurting
   hurt
7. carry, carries, carried, carried, carrying
   carried
8. break, breaks, broke, broken, breaking
   had broken
9. plan, plans, planned, planned, planning
   had been planning
10. change, changes, changed, changed, changing
    changed
11. entertain, entertains, entertained, entertained, entertaining
    are OR were entertaining
12. sign, signs, signed, signed, signing
    signed
13. visit, visits, visited, visited, visiting
    visited

EXERCISE 11E

```
   NS   C  NS   Vt      Ndo
1. Sarah and Ruth pack their suitcases.
```

```
      NS     Vt──── Ndo      Ndo    C
```
2. They are taking blouses, jeans, and
```
Ndo
```
swimsuits.
```
   NS     VI──── Adv────
```
3. They are going to Door County, Wisconsin.
```
   NS     C    NS    Vt    Ndo
```
4. Working and relaxing please them.
```
         NS   Vt       Ndo
```
5. The train leaves the station.
```
   NS           Vt──── Ndo
```
6. Passengers are waving their hands.
```
   NS   VI   Adv────
```
7. They smile at their friends.
```
   NS   C    NS   Vt──── Ndo
```
8. Sarah and Ruth are enjoying the ride.
```
   NS   Vt   Ndo    Adv────
```
9. They like looking out the window.
```
   NS      LV      Nsc
```
10. Traveling is a wonderful experience.

EXERCISE 12A

```
   NS   LV   Nsc
```
1. Jim is an attorney.
```
   NS  Vt────   Ndo    Adv────
```
2. He may spend the holiday at home.
```
   NS  Vt────   Ndo  Adv────
```
3. He would prefer a trip to San Francisco.
```
   NS  Vt──────── Ndo   C
```
4. He should be mowing the lawn and
```
Vt       Ndo
```
painting the fence.
```
   NS  VI──── Adv────  C   VI
```
5. He might work in the morning and rest
```
Adv────
```
in the afternoon.
```
   NS  Vt   Adv  Vt   Ndo   Adv────
```
6. He could also play tennis in the afternoon.
```
   NS  Vt────     Ndo
```
7. He does enjoy the game.
```
   NS  Vt──── Ndo  Adv  Adv────
```
8. He will make plans early next time.

EXERCISE 13A

1. Snow does not fall.
2. Tree branches do not break.
3. Animals do not hide.
4. The car does not skid.
5. The car does not crash.
6. The driver does not escape.
7. The baby did not crawl.

8. Her brother did not run.
9. The dog did not bark.
10. The cat did not hide.

EXERCISE 13B

1. The singer is not Tana Lee.
2. She has never performed . . .
3. Sometimes she does not wear . . .
4. She does not use . . .
5. Her performance never pleases . . .

EXERCISE 13C

1. should not
2. cannot
3. will not
4. did not
5. he is
6. I will
7. they would
8. you have

EXERCISE 13D

1. Animals can hardly live . . .
2. The rocket would hardly fly . . .
3. Mary won't ever leave . . . OR
   Mary will never leave . . .
4. She doesn't ever want . . . OR
   She never wants . . .

EXERCISE 13E

1. Does Rick drive race cars?
2. Does he own three cars?
3. Do his friends attend the races?
4. Do they cheer loudly?
5. Does Rick win?
6. Did Maggie buy a novel?
7. Did she enjoy the story?
8. Did Betty also read the novel?
9. Did she like the hero?

EXERCISE 13F

1. a. Do children and adults fly kites for
      fun?
   b. Who fly kites for fun?
2. a. Do kite builders usually use colorful
      paper and thin wood for kites?
   b. What do kite builders usually use
      for kites?
3. a. Do they build kites carefully?
   b. How do they build kites?
4. a. Did workers once take a line across
      Niagara Falls with a kite?
   b. Where did workers take a line with
      a kite?

5. a. Did they first carry a thin line with the kite?
   b. What did they first carry with the kite?
6. a. Did they then pull a rope across the Falls with the thin line?
   b. How did they pull a rope across the Falls?
7. a. Finally, did they pull a cable across with the rope?
   b. Finally, what did they pull across with the rope?

EXERCISE 14

1.   NS   Vi   Adv——
   The seasick sailor ~~laid~~ lay in his bunk
   Adv——
   all day.

2.   NS   Vi———   Adv——
   The sun ~~had rose~~ had risen at six
   o'clock.

3.   NS   C   NS   Vi   Adv——
   Squashes and pumpkins lay in the
   field. A

4. Vt   Ndo   Adv———
   Set the suitcase on the rack. A

5.   NS   Vi———
   The exhausted man ~~had laid~~ had lain
   Adv   Adv———
   there for two hours.

6.   NS   Vi———   Adv   Adv——
   Bob ~~had set~~ had sat down in the
   broken rocker.

7. Vt   Ndo   Adv———
   ~~Lie~~ Lay the baby in her crib.

8. NS   Vt   Ndo
   Divers raised the sunken treasure. A

9.   NS   Vi———   Adv——
   The fishing net had risen to the surface. A

10.   NS   Vi   Adv———   Adv——
    The cat lay on the soft pillow in the
    sun. A

UNIT THREE REVIEW
Practice Test

A.
1. drags, dragged, dragged, dragging
   dragged
2. falls, fell, fallen, falling
   fall

3. travels, traveled, traveled, traveling
   were traveling OR are traveling
4. speaks, spoke, spoken, speaking
   has spoken OR had spoken OR will have spoken
5. swims, swam, swum, swimming
   swims

B.

1.   NS   Adv   V———
   The student never had to write an essay.
2.   NS V   Adv V
   He did not select a topic easily.
3.   NS V   Adv V
   He did not write the essay carefully.

C.
1. can't   cannot
2. won't   will not
3. They're   They are
4. He's   He is

D.
1. a. Did the flight last five hours?
   b. What lasted five hours?
2. a. Did the travelers arrive in Hawaii?
   b. Who arrived in Hawaii?
3. a. Did friends meet them in the terminal?
   b. Where did friends meet them?

E.
1. built
2. had wanted
3. need
4. will build
5. will have decorated

F.
1. lies, lay, lain, lying
   were lying OR had been lying OR have been lying
2. raises, raised, raised, raising
   raised
3. sets, set, set, setting
   had set OR has set

PART II
A.
1. stands, stood, stood, standing
2. runs, ran, run, running
3. says, said, said, saying
4. turns, turned, turned, turning
5. speaks, spoke, spoken, speaking

Show your sentences to your instructor or tutor.

B.
Show these sentences to your instructor or tutor.

EXERCISE 15A

1. fires	apartments
2. bosses	windows
3. boys	fishes
4. travelers	valleys
5. grandmothers	toys

EXERCISE 15B

1. bread, meat, fruit, vegetables
2. box, bottle, cup, bag
3. pine, maple, poplar, fir
4. Chicago, Atlanta, Cleveland, Boston
5. shoes, socks, shirt, blouse

EXERCISE 15C

1. furniture
2. states
3. cars (automobiles)
4. flowers
5. meat

EXERCISE 16A

1. Adj	6. Adj
2. Adj	7. Adj
3. Adj	8. Adj
4. N	
5. Adj	

EXERCISE 16B

1. NO DETERMINER, the
   Candy filled the jars.
2. That, some
   That woman took some candy.
3. This, both
   This kind pleases both people.
4. All, their
   All employees offered their assistance.
5. The, several
   The information pleased several people.
6. Five, No DETERMINER
   Five elephants carried equipment.

EXERCISE 16C

___X___ Electronics manufacturers organized ___a___ convention. ___X OR The___ Members set ___the___ date for early in ___X___ November. Two members sent ___X OR the___ invitations to ___X___ business representatives in ___the___ United States, ___the___ British Isles, ___X___ Japan, ___X___ China, ___the___ Philippines, and ___the___ Netherlands. ___The___ president Thomas Wilson offered ___a___ prize of ___a___ hundred dollars for ___a___ well-designed program. ___The___ meeting place was ___the___ Convention Center in ___X___ Los Angeles. On ___the___ last day ___the___ manufacturers met for ___X___ dinner in ___a___ hotel banquet room. ___The___ dinner included ___X___ appetizers, ___X___ steak, ___X___ vegetables, ___X___ dessert, and ___X___ tea, or ___X___ coffee. ___The___ coffee was imported from ___X___ Brazil. Sheri Patton, ___the OR a___ singer, provided ___the OR X___ entertainment after ___the OR X___ dinner.

EXERCISE 17

1. Jay's sister and Susan's brother.
2. Bert Jones's OR Bert Jones' house
3. Burton and Washborn's store
4. many children's dreams
5. the editor's response
6. his father-in-law's boat
7. the professors' conference

EXERCISE 18B

	HOW MANY	WHICH ONE
1.	Several	pine, the, old
2.		The, smiling, its, tiny
3.	Ten	red, the, smallest
4.	twenty-five	The, black-and-white, running
5.	Three	frightened, the, creaking, cabin

EXERCISE 18C

1. five muscular truck drivers
2. the magnificent, snow-covered fir trees OR the fir trees, magnificent and snow-covered
3. small, peaceful, quiet American town OR small American town, peaceful and quiet
4. a sunny, warm, inviting, secluded Hawaiian beach OR a secluded Hawaiian beach, sunny, warm, and inviting

(You may arrange the adjectives above in a number of ways. Ask your instructor or tutor to check the exercise if you have questions.)

EXERCISE 18D

1.   NS   Vt   Adj Adj   Adj
   Peggy bought an old-fashioned sewing
   Ndo
   machine. (NO COMMAS)
2.   Adj NS   Vt   Adj Adj   Adj
   The group praised the dedicated, reli-
         Ndo
   able teacher.
3.   Adj Adj   NS   Adj C Adj
   The young witness, upset and nervous,
     Vt   Adj Adj   Ndo
   described the automobile accident.
4.   Adj Adj   NS   Adj   Adj
   Three small children, hungry, frightened,
     C Adj   Vi Adv————
   and crying, sat on the step.
5.   Adj   Adj   Adj   Adj   NS Vt
   The brilliant, flashing street sign at-
        Ndo
   tracted attention.

EXERCISE 19A

1.   Adv-when NS Vt   Adj Adj Ndo
   Yesterday Paul began a new job.
2.   Adv-when——— NS Vt   Adj
   In the morning he attended two
   Ndo
   classes.
3.   NS Vi   Adv-how C Vt Ndo
   He listened closely and took notes
   Adv-how
   constantly.
4.   Adv-when——— NS Adv-how Vt   Adj
   After lunch he carefully read company
   Ndo
   rules.

5.   Adv-when——— NS Vi   Adv-where C
   That evening he went home   and
     Vt   Adj Ndo   Adv-how
   studied his notes thoroughly.
6.   NS Vt————   Ndo   Adv-how
   He had prepared himself well.
7.   Adv-when——— NS Vt   Adj Ndo
   The next day he understood the lec-
        Adv-how
   tures easily.
8.   Adj   Adj NS   Vt Adv Vt
   Other new employees had not studied
     Adj   Ndo Adv-how
   their notes completely.
9.   NS   Adv-how Vt   Adj Ndo
   Paul willingly helped two others
   Adv-when
   after class.
10. NS   Adv-how Vt   Adj Ndo
   They greatly appreciated his help.

EXERCISE 19D

1. real   very, really
2. real good   very well, extremely well
3. fine   well
4. sure   very, surely
5. sure   surely, certainly
6. bad   badly
7. bad   badly
8. good   well

EXERCISE 20A

1.   Pr   Nop
   The cat climbed up the tree.
2. Pr   Nop
   Into the lake leaped the dog.
3.   Adv
   The lamp suddenly fell down.
4.   Pr————   Nop
   Dale succeeds in spite of her problems.
5.   Pr
   Their grandparents arrived home after
   Nop
   dark.
6.   Pr   Nop
   How can you study in the family room?
7.   Pr   Nop
   The baby looks like him.
8.   Pr   Nop
   I will meet you at the drive-in.
9.   Pr Nop
   Come to my house tonight.
10.   Adv
   I never saw him before.

EXERCISE 20B

1. Late Friday the temperature dropped
   — NS, Vi
   suddenly to zero. **dropped** — Adv-where
2. Snow fell during the night. **fell**
   — NS, Vi, Adv-when
3. The lake froze within a few hours.
   froze — NS, Vi, Adv-when
4. The next day skaters glided over the
   lake. **glided** — NS, Vi, Adv-where
5. Three people built a huge fire
   near the lake. **built** — NS, Vt, Ndo, Adv-where
6. Some went into the warm lodge. **went** — NS, Vi, Adv-where
7. They sat around the fireplace. **sat** — NS, Vi, Adv-where
8. Outside the lodge more snow fell. **fell** — Adv-where, NS, Vi

EXERCISE 20C

1. of the house   outside
2. of his sons   Two
3. of the rooms   all
4. on the third floor   room
5. of his children   Each
6. off the kitchen   room
7. of their meals   rest
8. of the living room   wall
9. of hot chocolate   cup
10. at the top   room

EXERCISE 20D

1. The girl with the dog fell down. — Adj
2. The girl fell down with the dog. — Adv-how
3. Tom backed his car down the steep
   driveway and ran into the fence. — Adv-where, Adv-where
4. Two of the chairs in the kitchen
   needed a coat of paint. — Adj, Adj, Adj
5. By nightfall most of the hunters had
   returned to camp. — Adv-when, Adj, Adv-where

6. The flock of geese flew in formation
   over the quiet forest. — Adj, Adv-how, Adv-where
7. Tons of concrete filled the forms
   for the bridge pillars. — Adj, Adj
8. Dana waited anxiously at home
   for a telephone call. — Adv-where, Adv-why
9. At the end of the play the actors
   greeted members of the audience. — Adv-when, Adj, Adj
10. Dave moved the piano from one
    corner of the room to the other. — Adv-where, Adj, Adv-where

EXERCISE 20E

1. on the back porch   fell
2. on a scrap of paper   letter
3. with great fury   broke
4. in a small boat   transferred
5. with carved legs   piano
6. with a knowlege of furniture people
7. with one broken leg   table

UNIT FOUR REVIEW
Practice Test

Part I
A.
1. teachers   lessons
2. fathers   cars
3. chiefs   guns
4. monkeys   jungles
5. girls   blouses

B.
1. students C   Europe P
2. Sara P   mother C

C.
1. flower   rose
2. city   Paris
3. coin   penny
4. bird   robin
5. food   apple

D.
1. Adj   5. Adj
2. Adj   6. Adv
3. Adj   7. Adj
4. N   8. Adv

E.
1. the guards' signals
2. the driver's radio
3. the child's toothbrush
4. the boys' parents
5. the women's team

F.
Show this exercise to your instructor or tutor.

G.
1. damp, foggy day
2. tall, narrow cupboard
3. No comma
4. powerful, muscular football player
5. soft, flowered paper towel

H.
Show this exercise to your instructor or tutor.

I.
1. <u>good</u>   well
2. <u>real</u>   really OR very
3. <u>bad</u>   badly

J.
1. on the fence   rooster
2. Into the burning hotel ran
3.   X
4. with the red beard   man
5. on the T-shirt   picture
6.   X
7. in the water   found

K.
1. During the heavy storm a man in a plastic raincoat and boots fed the hungry pig.
2. A young man slipped on some oil in his garage and was severely injured.

Part II
A, B, and C.
Show these exercises to your instructor or tutor.

EXERCISE 21A

  NS LV Adj Nsc Adj———
1. Dale was the leader of the band.
  Adj NS LV Adj-c Adv
2. The music sounds pleasant tonight.
  Adj NS LV Adj-c C Adj-c
3. The fabric feels soft and warm.

  Adj Adj NS LV Adj Nsc
4. The three bottles are plastic containers.
  NS C NS   LV Adj
5. Ted and Richard became volunteer
  Nsc
  firefighters.
  NS LV——— Adj-c Adv———
6. Burt has been active in the ski club.
  NS C NS   LV Nsc
7. Tom and Margery are pianists.
  Adj NS LV Adj-c   Adv———
8. The sky looks threatening in the west.
  NS——— LV   Adj Nsc
9. Mrs. Wilson remained the director
  Adj———
  of the company.
  Adj NS LV Adj-c
10. The story proved false.

EXERCISE 21B

  Adj NS Vi——— Adv———
1. The cart is standing in the hall.
  Adj NS LV Adj-c
2. The paintings look restful.
  Adj NS Vt Adj Ndo
3. The kitten tasted the milk.
  NS——— LV   Nsc
4. Mr. Danton became a counselor.
  Adj NS LV Adj-c
5. The runner appeared exhausted
  Adv———
  after the race.
  Adj NS Vi   Adv
6. The watchman appeared suddenly.
  Adj NS Vt Adj Ndo
7. The firefighters sounded the alarm.
  Adj NS LV Adj-c
8. The crowd became silent.
  Adj Adj NS LV Adj-c
9. The delivery boy proved unreliable.
  Adj NS LV——— Adj Nsc
10. Don's parents will be camp super-
    Adv———
  visors next month.

EXERCISE 21C

1. Two thirsty, hungry men sailed to the small, deserted island.
2. A sudden, violent storm had damaged their small, unsafe boat.
3. They gathered large and small pieces of wood for a huge fire.

4. They waited through the long, dark, stormy night for help.
5. A freighter sent a small boat for them the next morning.

EXERCISE 22A

```
     NS   Vt     Nio    Ndo
```
1. Sid wrote Tony a letter.
```
   NS————— Vt   Nio  C  Adj Nio
```
2. Mr. Richards sold June and her mother
```
   Adj Adj Ndo
```
an old farmhouse.
```
   NS   Vt  Adj Nio  Ndo
```
3. Steve built his dog a house.
```
   Adj NS  Vt   Adj Nio    Adj
```
4. The twins gave their father a bright-
```
          Ndo Adv—————
```
colored tie for his birthday.
```
   Adj NS   Vt   Nio   Ndo
```
5. The director found Terry a position.

EXERCISE 22B

```
    NS    LV Adj   Nsc
```
1. Trudy is Tom's boss.
```
   NS   C  NS    Nio————— Ndo
```
2. Trudy and Tom sold Mr. Hirsch a computer.
```
   NS   Vt  Nio————— Adj
```
3. Tom gave Mr. Hirsch some additional
```
   Ndo
```
instruction.
```
   NS   Vt  Nio  Ndo
```
4. Trudy gave Tom a bonus.
```
   Adv————— NS  Vi  Adv—————
```
5. After the trip they returned to Chicago
```
   C   Vt       Ndo
```
and reported their success.

EXERCISE 23A

```
   S————— P—————
```
1. The one dog worked all day.
```
   S  P—————
```
2. He kept the sheep in one part of the

grassy meadow.
```
   S————— P—————
```
3. The other dog chased rabbits and

gophers.
```
              S————— P—————
```
4. At night the shepherd cooked his meal

and fed the dogs.

```
              S  P—————
```
5. Sometimes he sat outside and watched

the stars in the black sky.

EXERCISE 23B

```
        NS      Vt
```
1. The weary pioneers made frequent
```
   Ndo
```
stops along the route.   NS Vt Ndo
```
       NS     Vt    Ndo  C  Ndo
```
2. Many people prefer steak and potatoes
for dinner.   NS Vt Ndo
```
   NS       LV        Nsc
```
3. Autumn is a relaxing season.
NS LV Nsc
```
        NS      Vt
```
4. The modern camera takes remark-
```
   Ndo
```
able pictures.   NS Vt Ndo
```
   NS————— LV       Nsc
```
5. Bruce Bennett is an amateur photographer.   NS LV Nsc
```
   NS LV       Adj-c
```
6. He is extremely talented.
NS LV Adj-c
```
       NS     Vt    Nio
```
7. The skydivers awarded Elaine the
```
   Ndo
```
trophy.   NS Vt Nio Ndo
```
      NS   Vi
```
8. Last year Tom traveled extensively
in Africa.   NS Vi
```
   NS————— Vt      Ndo
```
9. Dan Baker appointed a new chairperson of the board.   NS Vt Ndo
```
   NS    Vi————— Adv—————
```
10. Karen has been resting since her

car accident.   NS Vi Adv
```
       NS     Vt    Nio
```
11. The college president gave gradu-
```
   Ndo
```
ates their diplomas.   NS Vt Nio Ndo
```
      NS   Vt    Ndo
```
12. The pilot flew the plane for the first
time yesterday.   NS Vt Ndo

EXERCISE 23C

```
   Adj     NS     Vt   Adj Ndo
```
1. Careful research revealed the reason
```
   Adj—————
```
for the widespread illness.   Research
revealed the reason.

      Adv   Adj   NS   C   NS

2. Thoroughly cleaned kettles and pans
   Vt⎯⎯⎯⎯⎯⎯ Adj Ndo   Adj⎯⎯⎯

   should prevent the spread of the dis-

   ease.   Kettles and pans should prevent
   the spread.
   Adv Adj NS   Vt   Adj   Adj

3. Very few people know Mark's last
   Ndo

   name. People know name.
   Adj Adj   C   Adj   Adj   NS

4. The hungry and thirsty two-year-old boy
   Adv   Vi   Adv

   eagerly ran home. The boy ran.
   Adj Adj   Adv   Adj NS

5. The captain's privately owned plane,
   Adj   C   Adj   Vi   Adv

   damaged and scorched, landed safely.
   The plane landed.

EXERCISE 23D

1.	Subject	4.	Subject
2.	Modifiers	5.	Predicate
3.	Modifiers		

UNIT FIVE REVIEW
Practice Test

Part I

A.

	SIMPLE SUBJECT (NOUNS)	SIMPLE PREDICATE (VERBS)
1.	Linda Thompson	had been developing
2.	she	demonstrated
3.	John Holt	had listened
4.	He	had spoken, praised
5.	John	was asking
6.	she	arranged, flew
7.	She	smiled, extended
8.	She	pulled
9.	She	talked, could make
10.	She	hurried

B.

1. Linda Thompson demonstrated new selling techniques for sportswear.
2. Linda arranged to meet John Holt at his office in Chicago.
3. She had a boring, disappointing meeting with John Holt.

C.

1.	Modifiers	4.	Predicate
2.	Subject	5.	Predicate
3.	Subject	6.	Modifier

D.

1.	NS Vi	4.	NS Vt Ndo
2.	NS Vt Nio Ndo	5.	NS LV Adj-c
3.	NS LV Nsc		

E.

1. The huge, circular lamp hung from the carved, wooden ceiling.
2. The tanned, muscular swimmer rapidly crossed the Olympic-sized pool.
3. The injured bricklayer placed his bleeding hand on the white examining table.

F.

Show these sentences to your instructor or tutor.

Part II
A. and B.
Show these exercises to your instructor or tutor.

EXERCISE 24A

1.	me	Nio	7.	She	NS
2.	them	Nio		him	Nio
	their	Adj		mine	Nop
3.	He	NS	8.	his	Nop
	your	Adj		you	Nop
4.	They	NS	9.	his	Adj
	us	Nio	10.	I	NS
5.	you	NS		I	Nsc
6.	We	NS			
	our	Adj			

EXERCISE 24B

1.	him	he
2.	I	me
3.	Us	We
4.	I	me
5.	I	me
6.	myself	I
7.	theirselves	themselves
8.	them	they
9.	Me	I
10.	I	me

EXERCISE 25A

1.	Each one	S	6.	anybody	S
2.	Few	P	7.	Neither	S
3.	Several	P	8.	some	P
4.	Anything	S	9.	All	S
5.	both	P			

EXERCISE 26A

	PERSONAL PRONOUN AND POSSESSIVE	PER-SON	NUMBER	GENDER
1.	it/its	3	singular	neuter
2.	he/him/his OR she/her/hers	3	singular	masc. or fem.
3.	they/them/their/theirs	3	plural	masc., fem., or neuter
4.	she/her/hers	3	singular	feminine
5.	they/them/their/theirs	3	plural	masc., fem., or neuter
6.	they/them/their/theirs	3	plural	neuter
7.	he/him/his	3	singular	masculine
8.	your/yours	2	sing. or pl.	masc. or fem.
9.	me/my/mine	1	singular	masc. or fem.
10.	us/our/ours	1	plural	masc. or fem.

EXERCISE 26B

They————————them
1. Virginia and Sam grew many vegetables.
He   them————————
2. Sam liked beets and carrots.
She   them
3. Virginia preferred tomatoes.
They————————   it
4. Virginia and Sam prepared a salad for
them————
Barry and Jean.
He   them————————————
5. Sam brought lettuce, cucumbers, and
————————   it
peppers from the garden.
They————————————————
6. Virginia, Sam, Jean, and Barry ate the
it
salad.

EXERCISE 26C

	ANTECEDENT	PRONOUN
1.	bird	its
2.	piece	its
3.	car	it
4.	someone	him/her
5.	Renee and Bob	themselves
6.	team	It
7.	one	his/her
8.	Frank	him
9.	children	They
10.	mothers	their

EXERCISE 26D

1. notification
2. operation
3. clerk
4. break OR breakage
5. gratification
6. removal
7. thickness
8. value

EXERCISE 26E

These are possible revisions. Show your sentences to your instructor or tutor if you have questions.

1. The manager and his secretary drove him to the airport.
2. His misfortune made him unhappy.
3. The treasurer bought all the supplies.
4. His anger bothered Jane.
5. Thieves stole Judy's watch.
6. Bob studies engineering in order to become an engineer.
7. The neighbors say the house is haunted.
8. Meg is learning to speak French in order to visit France.
9. Their dating (or courtship) goes on and on.
10. Her dislike of school upsets her parents.

EXERCISE 27

	SUBJECT	VERB
1.	Each	has
2.	You and Meg	are
3.	Bill or John	is coming
4.	group	intends
5.	None	has read OR have read
6.	Peggy and Anne	conduct
7.	Neither the man nor his son	has
8.	surgeon	attends
9.	*The Skyfighters*	is

10.	team	go
11.	One	has registered
12.	Either Janice or her parents	drive
13.	Ten dollars	seems
14.	Mathematics	is
15.	treasures	are
16.	dog	makes
17.	Dick, Bob, and Barb	are
18.	Nobody	likes
19.	rooms	need
20.	Any	is OR are

UNIT SIX REVIEW
Practice Test

Part I
A.

	PERSONAL PRONOUN OR POSSESSIVE	PER-SON	NUM-BER	GENDER
1.	they/them/ their/theirs	3	plural	neuter
2.	he/him/his OR she/ her/hers	3	singular	masc. or fem.
3.	we/us/our/ ours	1	plural	masc. or fem.
4.	they/them/ their/theirs	3	plural	masc., fem., or neuter
5.	he/him/his OR she/ her/hers	3	singular	masc. or fem.

B.
1.	me	I
2.	I	me
3.	I	me
4.	hisself	himself
5.	Us	We

C.
1.	Many	P
2.	Everyone	S
3.	One	S
4.	several	P
5.	all	S

D.
1.	guest	his or her
2.	miner	his
3.	carpenter	he/her
4.	child	his
5.	Carla and Jane	their

E.
These are suggested revisions. Show your sentences to your instructor or tutor if you have questions.

1. Her unhappiness concerned her husband.
2. The sales pleased the authors (editors, publishers, dealers).
3. She plans to become a dentist herself.
4. His schooling (education) does not end.
5. Art critics (friends, art lovers) all praised her paintings.

F.
	SUBJECT	VERB
1.	results	are described
2.	collection	needs
3.	Warren and Peggy	are
4.	family	eats
5.	Each	wants

Part II
Show these sentences to your instructor or tutor.

EXERCISE 28A

1. . . . ways of living, but some still . . .
2. . . . along paved roads, and they wear cotton and woolen clothes.
3. . . . in the future, and they will not use . . . OR . . . in the future, nor will they use . . .
4. . . . from walrus tusks, and the art . . .
5. . . . and other animals; now they are . . .

EXERCISE 28B

1. Run-on
2. CS
3. Run-on
4. CS

EXERCISE 29A

1. . . . with the typing pool supervisors; as a result, they were not . . .
2. The office manager, nevertheless, arranged . . .
3. The supervisors still wanted no part of Tom's plan or equipment.

4. . . . discussed every aspect; however, they could see . . .
5. Finally, the office manager called Tom in for a conference.
6. Tom refused; consequently, the supervisors cancelled . . .
7. Tom, as a result, lost the contract.

EXERCISE 29B

1. . . . several concerts last season; for the first time . . .
2. . . . medical school next fall; as a result, (consequently,) she has to . . .
3. . . . give a dinner party; only their best friends. . .
4. . . . on a bus, but he found the trip . . .
5. . . . engineering course; however, (nevertheless,) it seemed wise . . .
6. . . . through the forest, but he always watches . . .
7. . . . as her brother; nevertheless, (however,) she would not . . .
8. . . . hunt, and hike; in addition, (moreover,) he likes to read . . .

EXERCISE 30A

1. Margery and Janet visited the science museum. compound subject
2. Tom visits his family and neighbors on weekends. compound direct object
3. Mr. Stevens fired the bookkeeper last week and hired a new bookkeeper and typist this week. compound predicate and compound direct object
4. At the picnic people barbecued hamburgers and toasted marshmallows. compound predicate
5. Dr. Stone, his partner, and another doctor flew to New York for a medical conference. compound subject
6. Neil attends movies, rock concerts, and motorcycle races. compound direct object
7. Last Saturday the hardworking gardener pruned the fruit trees, raked the leaves, and mowed the lawn. compound predicate
8. The kindly, careful dentist filled Susan's tooth quickly and painlessly. compound adjectives and compound adverbs
9. The young, well-trained pilot flew a twin-engine plane from San Francisco to Reno and returned the same day. compound adjectives and compound predicate.

EXERCISE 31A

1. Mrs. Martin, our next-door neighbor, gives . . .
2. The athletes—tennis players, golfers, and swimmers—gathered . . .
3. The actor Bruce Manning has appeared . . . (NO COMMAS)
4. . . . a huge cave, a hiding place . . .
5. The *Concorde*, a supersonic jet, flew . . .
6. The Blakes' house, a Victorian mansion, burned . . .
7. The names of George Washington and Abraham Lincoln, presidents of the United States, appear . . .
8. The knight Sir Gawain charged . . . (NO COMMAS)
9. The third speaker at the conference, the State Water Resources representative, outlined . . .
10. . . . the old house, first the residence of a wealthy manufacturer, then the hideout for jewel thieves.

EXERCISE 32

1. Temporary workers can sometimes help large and small companies reduce their payrolls.
2. The companies hire the temporary workers for special projects during peak seasons and later dismiss them (the temporary workers).
3. Temporary workers experience certain disadvantages; (:) they lack the security of full-time employment, and they cannot receive fringe benefits and collect unemployment insurance.
4. Clerical workers and secretaries make up the largest number of temporary workers.
5. Technically skilled personnel—data and word processors, engineers, accountants, and health care workers—are finding increasing opportunities for temporary employment.

UNIT SEVEN REVIEW
Practice Test

Part I
A.

1.	g	5.	j	9.	e
2.	i	6.	b	10.	h
3.	c	7.	k		
4.	f	8.	a		

B.

1. napkins and tablecloths <u>compound direct object</u>
2. <u>rode the ski lift to the top of the mountain and enjoyed the spectacular view</u> compound predicate
3. <u>Barbara accepted Carol's offer, but Dan refused.</u>   compound sentence
4. The bank <u>and the title company</u> compound subject
5. <u>The guard stopped the nervous young woman at the gate, and later he received praise for his action.</u> compound sentence

C.

1. . . . of ten; consequently, he . . .
2. . . . colleges, attended a convention, and talked . . .
3. . . . parents' house, but they . . .
4. . . . amplifier, a tuner, and two speakers; it was installed . . .
5. First, the pilot . . . crew; second, he . . . plane; third, he . . .
6. Furthermore, Martin . . .
7. . . . was uncomfortable; in addition, the furniture . . .
8. . . . Gary's eye; however, the doctor . . .
9. . . . found, moreover, the solution . . .
10. . . . mountains; as a result, rivers and . . .

D.

1. Sandra Holmes, the author of children's mystery stories, left . . .
2. The boat *Sea Squirt* needs . . .
3. . . . two former presidents of the United States, George Washington and Abraham Lincoln.

E.

1. Passengers on a cruise in the western Mediterranean visited nine ports in a two-week period; they traveled almost four thousand miles.
2. Two hostesses on the Greek ship planned programs for the passengers; they spoke with individual passengers in English, French, German, Spanish, and Italian.
3. One afternoon about a hundred passengers in the lunge played Bingo, the hostesses gave directions and called numbers in the five languages.
4. The stewards and the waiters on the ship spoke Greek and several of the other languages; as a result, they were able to speak to most of the passengers.

5. . . . passengers took guided tours at each **of** the ports, and some of them **bought souvenirs**; later they returned to their "floating hotel."

Part II
Show these sentences to your instructor or tutor.

EXERCISE 33A

1. condition
2. time
3. manner
4. cause
5. condition
6. concession
7. place
8. concession
9. purpose
10. time

EXERCISE 33B

1. The Wilsons, <u>after they had traveled all night</u>, found . . .
2. <u>Although Peter was engaged to Nan</u>, he . . .
3. . . . a lot of comment <u>because each person sees it differently</u>.   (NO COMMA)
4. <u>While the young woman was waiting for the test results</u>, she . . .
5. . . . window, <u>because it had a crack in it</u>, leaked . . .
6. <u>As soon as Celia saves enough money</u>, she . . .
7. The toolbox stayed <u>where the carpenter had placed it two years before</u>.   (NO COMMA)
8. <u>After Jed Walker retired</u>, the town's one taxi . . .
9. <u>If the accountant goes to the office early</u>, she . . .

EXERCISE 33C

1. When Tom was sixteen, he decided to study medicine because he wanted to help people.
2. After he graduated from high school, he attended a four-year college.
3. He studied hard the whole time because (while) he took biology, chemistry, physics, and other required courses.
4. In addition, he worked as an orderly in a small hospital because he wanted to get some practical experience and earn money.
5. After Tom had sent applications to several medical schools, he waited for the mail each day.

6. He faced disappointment several times because the medical schools could not accept him.
7. Although he became discouraged, he did not give up hope.
8. After he finally received a letter of acceptance, he packed his belongings, moved to a large city, and found an apartment.
9. When (after) medical school classes began, he studied harder than ever.
10. After he graduated from medical school, he spent a year as an intern and four years as a resident in radiology.

EXERCISE 34A

1. that he bought two months ago — radio
2. who was lost in the department store — child
3. that would bring the contract — letter
4. whom he despised — people
5. (that) Sue showed at school — puppy
6. which arrived after a long delay — furniture
7. who viewed it — those
8. whose fiancée cried at their engagement party — man

EXERCISE 34B

1. that pet owners choose — Adj
2. Although finches are about the same size as canaries — Adv
3. that many people enjoy — Adj
4. which are very affectionate — Adj
5. which sometimes live twenty years — Adj
6. because they require a lot of attention — Adv
7. Although most birds eat seeds — Adv
8. If owners let their birds exercise by flying about a room — Adv
9. when they need food and rest — Adv

EXERCISE 34C

1. Jeff Brown, who owns the big yacht, is . . .
2. NO COMMAS
3. NO COMMAS
4. NO COMMAS
5. Janet Oakes' new play, which began last week, has received . . .

6. Warren Hill, who owns the bakery, is . . .
7. . . . the mayor's speech, which lasted two hours.
8. Blake, who constantly repairs his house, fell . . .

EXERCISE 34D

1. Five people who had known one another since high school days devoted a year to organizing a new bank.
2. Carrie Willett, who had worked as a bank manager for five years, became president of the bank.
3. Tom Fields, whose real estate business had been extremely successful for twelve years, became the head of the loan department.
4. Linda Carson, who gave up her position as personnel manager of a large department store, took charge of the bank's hiring and supervising of employees.
5. The directors wanted Bryce Sutton, whose wife had inherited a large fortune, as treasurer.
6. Ted Weber, whom people seemed to admire and trust, handled public relations and advertising.
7. During the year the bank directors, who kept working at their regular jobs, rented a small building, moved furniture in, and hired the banking staff.
8. Ted Weber placed advertisements that attracted widespread attention in newspapers in the surrounding area.
9. He also developed radio and television announcements that proved to be effective.
10. During the first week the bank was crowded with customers who wanted to open accounts and arrange for loans.
11. The bank directors, who had been slightly apprehensive before opening day, were exhilarated by the response.

EXERCISE 34E

1. Some people avoid mowing their lawns for two or three weeks, an attitude that irritates their neighbors. OR Their indifference (lack of responsibility) irritates their neighbors.
2. The promotion which she had earned came after many years.

3. Maria was disappointed because the trip to Australia cost much more than she had expected.
4. The *No Smoking* signs that had been placed on the classroom walls were fluorescent red.
5. The newsmagazine that contained depressing reports lay on the living room table.
6. Ken offered to lend Tom some money. Ken's offer (or thoughtfulness) made Tom happy.
7. Everyone bet Barbara would marry Bill, not Ben. The betting (speculation) made Bill nervous.
8. Mr. Hopkins had a toothache all night. The dentist pulled the decayed (aching) tooth the next day.

EXERCISE 35A

1.		X
2.	(that) he would operate the mill next year	Ndo
3.	Why the accident happened	NS
4.		X
5.	whoever signed it	Nop
6.		X
7.	that he has no time for sleep	Ndo
8.	that unexpected guests arrived last night	Nsc
9.	whoever calls	Nio
10.	that he cannot dissect frogs	Appos

EXERCISE 35B

1. Mark decided when he would fly to Europe.
2. Why Glenn refused the promotion is a mystery.
3. Millie knows that she will want a larger apartment soon.
4. The committee knows who will receive the award.
5. The well-trained athlete asked whether he qualifies for the football team.

EXERCISE 35D

1. who fly from California across the Pacific (Adj)
2. As they fly southwest toward the equator (Adv)
3. how the pilot can find the international airports on Oahu and Hawaii, two dots of land in the West Pacific (N)

4. which reaches across 1,600 miles of ocean (Adj)
   that began erupting 25 million years ago (Adj)
5. If the water of the Pacific Ocean were drained (Adv)
   because it stands almost 33,500 feet above the ocean floor (Adv)
6. that Polynesians from other Pacific Islands migrated to the Hawaiian Islands (N)
7. as they sailed northwest toward the Hawaiian Islands (Adv)

EXERCISE 36A

1. Dennis, who attends a private school, told his parents that he will not go back when the fall semester begins; he will look for a job instead.
2. After Cleo had finished her father's portrait, she decided (that) she would paint a picture of a mountain cabin that she remembered; later she would paint portraits of her children.
3. Because the moon was full that night, it cast bright light on the mirror-smooth lake that lay at the edge of town, but no one knew that a swimmer with scuba gear was crossing the lake under water.
4. The weight lifter raised the three-hundred-pound weights to his shoulders; with a tremendous push he raised them above his head where he held them for a moment before he dropped them to the floor.

EXERCISE 37A

1. P	5. D	9. D	13. P
2. D	6. P	10. D	14. P
3. D	7. D	11. P	15. P
4. I	8. I	12. P	16. I

UNIT EIGHT REVIEW
Practice Test

Part I
A.

1. X	5.	9. X
2.	6.	10.
3. X	7.	11. X
4. X	8. X	12.

B.
1. who owns the tailor shop   Adj
2. because the movie has not begun   Adv
3. while he was eating lunch   Adv
4. Whoever buys a car today   N
5. after the play had ended   Adv
6. who spend time in Paris   Adj
   which was built for a world exposition in the early 1900's   Adj
7. As slowly moving elevators carry tourists to the top of the Eiffel Tower   Adv
   until spectators can see the whole city   Adv

C.
1. P   3. P   5. I
2. D   4. D

D.
1. NO COMMAS   (Which window?)
2. NO COMMAS   (Which man?)
3. NO COMMAS   (Which newspaper?)
4. Tracy Watson, who lives in Oakland, flew . . .
5. Cheryl's house, which needs a coat of paint, could be . . .

E.
1. The artist contributed several paintings that he had completed in Europe to the museum.
2. The museum director accepted the paintings enthusiastically. His enthusiasm (approval, acceptance) pleased the artist.
3. The board of directors, who valued the artist's contribution, sent a letter of appreciation.

F.
1. Tourists who plan a trip to California during the summer may wonder what kinds of clothes they should take with them.
2. Tourists discover that a daytime temperature of 95 degrees in the inland valleys is hot; however, the heat is not extremely uncomfortable because it is dry.
3. As the tourists travel west from the valleys to the coast, the temperature drops; in fact, they may feel uncomfortably cool at 60 degrees, and they may reach for a sweater or a jacket.
4. Tourists who travel south along the Pacific Ocean find the mornings cool and foggy until about 10 A.M. when the sun finally emerges.

5. Tourists can enjoy a pleasant day most of the summer because almost no rain falls between May and September and the days are sunny and warm; as a result, they enjoy their vacation in California.

Part II
Show these sentences to your instructor or tutor.

EXERCISE 38A

VERB	VERBAL
1. is going	fishing
2. was holding	crying
3. have been swarming	flying
4. are beginning	
5. had been going	shopping

EXERCISE 38B

1. The college student, gazing at the towering mountain before her, wanted an exciting adventure.
2. The college student tried climbing the mountain.
3. Carrying heavy equipment tired her quickly.
4. She rested occasionally, sitting on a ledge.   OR   By sitting on a ledge,
5. She spent her resting time looking out over the green valley below.
6. Feeling hungry, she ate a granola bar and drank hot chocolate.
7. Her goals were trying to reach the top before noon and to return to the valley before nightfall.

EXERCISE 38C

1. However, Alan's supervisor, Celeste, refused because Alan had been a valuable employee for several years.
2. After Celeste had attended a conference about employee-assistance programs, she believed that Alan could be helped.
   After attending a conference about employee-assistance programs, Celeste . . .
3. After Celeste had prepared a proposal for an employee-assistance program, she talked with the company manager.
   After preparing a proposal for an employee-assistance program, Celeste . . .

4. Celeste pointed out that the program would save the company money but training a new employee would cost more than helping Alan.
5. After the company manager talked with other managers and supervisors, he tried the program.
   After talking with other managers and supervisors, the company manager . . .

EXERCISE 38D

1. Bathing was an important ritual among early Egyptians and other ancient peoples; ancient Greeks, for example, provided heated water.
2. Bathing was also popular among early Romans who built luxurious baths where people could talk with others, enjoy works of art, and listen to music while bathing.
3. The Romans brought water by aqueducts and stored it in reservoirs; later they heated the water to various temperatures and distributed it by pipes to bathing areas.
4. In later centuries some people took very few baths because they believed baths were bad for them.
5. They used perfumes (to try) to cover up unpleasant odors.
6. By the 1700s doctors were encouraging people to bathe and telling them that cleanliness promoted good health.
7. People today provide relaxation for themselves by soaking in hot tubs, enjoying the massaging action of water in spas, and swimming in heated indoor and outdoor pools.

EXERCISE 39A

1.	gives	A
2.	must be trained	P
3.	are offered	P
4.	sell	A
5.	provide	A
6.	was taught	P
7.	are emphasized	P
8.	must have	A
9.	plunges	A
10.	travels	A

EXERCISE 39B

1. Mount Everest was conquered in 1953 by Edmund Hillary and Tensing Norgay.

2. The climbers were surrounded by towers of ice.
3. Goggles, padded clothes, and oxygen masks were worn by the men.
4. Camps were set up by the climbers on the way up the mountain.
5. The last camp was erected at 25,850 feet by Hillary, Norgay, and other men.
6. A stormy night was spent in a tent 1,200 feet from the peak by Hillary and Norgay.
7. In the morning the steep slopes were climbed by them.
8. At one point they were stopped completely by a ridge of ice.
9. Fortunately a passage to the top was found by them.
10. The top was finally reached by them just before noon.

EXERCISE 39C

1. Thousands of children and adults play video games.
2. The games no longer challenge many players who play regularly.
3. In another five years designers will make games more realistic and complex.
4. Videodiscs may provide scenery for war games and adventures.
5. A player in one city may challenge a player in another city by using computers connected with telephone lines or cable television.
6. Complex war games may pit people in several locations against one another.

EXERCISE 40A

	VERB	V-ED VERBAL
1.	is required	
2.	was carried	injured
3.	had been fractured	bruised
4.	had been asked	authorized
5.	has been located	hidden

EXERCISE 40B

1. Irradiated potatoes, for example, have been stored for seven months in Japan.
2. In experiments meats, fish, and poultry, which appear to be fresh, have been stored for up to fourteen months.

3. Irradiation, praised by scientists, is an effective weapon against insect infestation such as the Medfly.
4. Irradiation can replace chemicals currently used to fumigate food.
5. These chemicals, suspected of causing cancer, may be harmful to humans.

EXERCISE 41A

	VERB	INFINITIVE VERBAL
1.	urged	to buy
2.	decided	to travel
3.	was	to please
4.	heard	(to) cry
5.	appeared	to sign
6.	made	(to) follow
7.	told	to cancel

EXERCISE 41B

1. The old lady pretended to be a cousin of the president.
2. The teacher hopes to convince the principal to add more basic writing classes.
3. Melody told her fiancé to find an apartment downtown.
4. The doctor needed a small car to drive around town.
5. Elaine's plan is to buy several acres of land near her home.

EXERCISE 41C

1. Giovanni worked hard all day to complete the concrete sidewalks.
2. The interior decorator helped Theo (to) choose wallpaper and upholstery fabric for his apartment.
3. The author was disappointed to receive a rejection slip from the editor.
4. The company president expected to open a new plant in Georgia and to spend six months there herself.
5. The new owners of the house immediately painted all the walls to cover fingerprints, crayon marks, and splotches of paint.
6. Craig Hudson was eager to show everyone his completed house plans and to begin building immediately.

EXERCISE 42

1. Looking out the window, three curious people saw the mysterious object.
2. Joan's uncle waited for the thirsty dog, lapping water eagerly from the mud puddle.
3. Upset by the decision, the woman decided to look for another job.
4. The tall, blonde woman wearing a red bikini held a small poodle.
5. Standing on the beach, frightened swimmers watched three sharks not far from shore.
6. While painting the wall, Jane fell to the floor when the ladder slipped.
7. Running to catch the train, Ted dropped his suitcase, and his clothes scattered everywhere.
8. The sun, shining brightly through the window, lighted the room.
9. Sitting in the doctor's office for an hour, the patient read the magazine from cover to cover.
10. After opening the package, the cook should place the frozen vegetables in boiling water for four minutes.
11. The boy carrying a BB gun gently stroked the soft, fluffy kitten.

EXERCISE 43

1. The young woman prepared the dinner automatically, her mind fixed on the events of the day.
2. The mission having been accomplished, the astronauts were able to return to earth.
3. He relaxed in his large chair, the fire blazing in the fireplace and the wind blasting the trees and shrubs outside.
4. The new owners moved eagerly into the old house, its rooms newly painted and carpeted.
5. The heir having been located, the attorney was able to settle the old man's estate.
6. The best-selling novel lay in the rubbish, its cover badly stained, its pages torn.

EXERCISE 44A

1. Barbara's aunt, a little old lady, puffed nervously on the cigarette, trying hard to look sophisticated.

2. The airplane, overloaded with cargo, barely missed the treetops at the end of the runway.
3. Wanting to appear well informed, the young man used words he could scarcely pronounce.
4. The girl combing her hair is Dave's friend.
5. Sobbing uncontrollably, Barbara paid no attention to the strolling musicians singing beneath her window.
6. Michael awoke suddenly in his hotel room and saw two men looking out the door and down the hall.
7. Many students have been able to pay college tuition with scholarships donated by business people in the community.
8. Marcia, efficient and well trained, typed the letters rapidly, her fingers moving quickly over the keys.

EXERCISE 44B

1. The young, blond man sat at the desk, typing a letter to the mayor very rapidly.
2. He burned with anger because of the damage done to his new green sports car the night before.
3. Lying in bed about midnight, he heard a car racing wildly down the street; it sideswiped the left side of his car, denting the door and fender badly.
4. The letter completed, he read it once again, then corrected two typing errors.
5. He asked the mayor why the police did not patrol the streets more closely.
6. Driving to the post office, he stopped to the right of a late model black sedan waiting for the traffic light to change.
7. He immediately noticed long scratches and dents along the right side of the car, matching those on his car.
8. The light having changed, the black car raced across the intersection down the crowded street.
9. The young man pursued the black car as closely as he could, hoping to catch a glimpse of the license plate.
10. Managing to see three numbers, he repeated them over and over to himself as he followed the car.
11. The black car turned a corner and disappeared down a side street.

12. Hearing a siren behind him, the young man pulled over to the curb and stopped.
13. The police officer, noting the dents on the side of the young man's car, said the police had been looking for the person who had sideswiped the mayor's car the night before.
14. The officer was pleased that he had found the person.

EXERCISE 45A

1.	S	5.	F	9.	F
2.	F	6.	S	10.	S
3.	S	7.	S		
4.	S	8.	F		

EXERCISE 45B

The duckbill platypus, a strange creature that lives in Australia and Tasmania, seems to be both a waterfowl and animal.

Although the platypus is a mammal, its young hatch from eggs.

Its body looks like that of an otter; yet it has a ducklike bill, used for finding worms in the mud and feeding on tadpoles and small fish; and it has broadly webbed feet, used for swimming.

The male platypus has a poisonous spur on his hind foot for self-defense.

UNIT NINE REVIEW
Practice Test

Part I
A.
```
      NS      Vt          Ndo
1. The mayor dedicated the auditorium
   Adv————
   last Sunday.
```

```
                          NS      Vt
2. Several hundred ceiling lights illumin-
        Ndo
   ated the building.
```

B.
```
      NS        PV————— Adv—————
1. The furniture was carried into the new
   —————
   apartment by the movers.
        NS——— PV————— Adv———
2. The test tubes were placed in the incu-
   ————
   bator by the biologist.
```

C.
1. <u>recovered</u> <u>from</u> <u>their</u> <u>sea-</u>
   <u>sickness</u>   V-ed
2. <u>carrying</u> <u>the</u> <u>furniture</u> <u>into</u>
   <u>the</u> <u>apartment</u>   V-ing
3. <u>The</u> <u>prizewinner</u> <u>having</u> <u>ar-</u>
   <u>rived</u>   Absolute
4. <u>to</u> <u>take</u> <u>the</u> <u>history</u> <u>exam</u>   Inf
5. <u>to</u> <u>pass</u> <u>the</u> <u>tax</u> <u>relief</u>
   <u>legislation</u>   Inf
6. <u>Holding</u> <u>a</u> <u>job</u> <u>and</u> <u>taking</u>
   <u>five</u> <u>courses</u>   V-ing
7. <u>writing</u> <u>essays</u> <u>to</u> <u>be</u> <u>a</u>
   <u>challenge</u>   V-ing
8. <u>To</u> <u>hope</u> <u>for</u> <u>success</u>   Inf
9. <u>Opening</u> <u>the</u> <u>refrigerator</u>
   <u>door</u>   V-ing
10. <u>working</u> <u>twelve</u> <u>hours</u> <u>a</u> <u>day</u>
    <u>for</u> <u>two</u> <u>weeks</u>   V-ing

D.
These are suggested revisions. Show your sentences to your instructor or tutor if you have questions.

1. While washing the car, Steve knocked over the bucket accidentally.
2. Unhappy with the apartment, the couple agreed to find another place.
3. Sam filled with vegetables the copper kettle, which he kept polished.
4. Reaching the amusement park, they took a ride on the roller coaster.
5. Sitting on his perch, the parrot amused Bob.

E.
1. The restaurant manager works constantly to provide appetizing menus and a relaxed atmosphere.
2. Brett Weaver, who represented the Star Corporation, could scarcely lift his heavy brown leather suitcase filled with samples of attractive upholstery material.
3. The woman, fearing everyone who approached, waited apprehensively for her friend to arrive.
4. Helping physically disabled people gives Wayne great satisfaction.
5. Having examined her odd assortment of clothes, the news reporter decided she would throw everything away and invest in a few coordinated skirts, blouses, and jackets.

Part II
A. and B.
Show these exercises to your instructor or tutor.

EXERCISE 46A

1.	comma	4a
2.	X	4b
3.	X	4a
4.	comma	4a
5.	semicolon	7b
6.	semicolon	7b
7.	colon	5b
8.	comma	4a
9.	semicolon	5a
10.	semicolon	5a
11.	X	4a
12.	semicolon	5a
13.	comma	6a

EXERCISE 46B

1.	X	8b
2.	X	9b
3.	X	12b
4.	X	9b
5.	comma	12a
6.	X	8b
7.	X	9b
8.	X	9b
9.	comma	10a
10.	comma	10a
11.	comma	13

EXERCISE 47A

A.
1.	comma	1a
2.	comma	1a
3.	X	9c
4.	X	1b
5.	X	1b
6.	X	2b
7.	X	2b
8.	X	9c
9.	dash	12a
10.	dash	12a
11.	comma	8b
12.	comma	8b

B.
1.	X	9c
2.	X	3b
3.	comma	1a
4.	comma	1a
5.	X	9c
6.	comma	5a

C.
| 1. | dash | 1c |
| 2. | comma | 6 |

3.	comma	6
4.	dash	1c
5.	X	2b
6.	comma	8b
7.	comma	8b
8.	comma	8a
9.	comma	8b
10.	comma	8b
11.	parenthesis	12b

23. dash OR parenthesis
24. dash OR parenthesis
25. question mark
26. double quotation mark
27. italics
28. question mark
29. double quotation mark
30. italics
31. italics

EXERCISE 48A

A.
1. comma
2. X
3. comma
4. double quotation mark
5. comma
6. comma
7. comma
8. comma
9. period OR exclamation point
10. double quotation mark
11. X
12. X
13. X
14. comma
15. comma
16. double quotation mark
17. comma
18. comma
19. comma
20. question mark
21. comma

B.
1. italics
2. comma OR colon
3. double quotation mark
4. double quotation mark
5. dash
6. dash
7. italics
8. italics
9. comma OR colon
10. double quotation mark
11. bracket
12. comma
13. bracket
14. double quotation mark
15. single quotation mark
16. double quotation mark
17. comma
18. double quotation mark
19. single quotation mark
20. single quotation mark
21. X
22. double quotation mark

EXERCISE 49

1. Juan Garcia, Spanish
2. Harold Radcliff, *Car Repair Is a Challenge*
3. Last, Sunday, Bob
4. His, Wild Oak Street
5. People, New York City, Lake Tahoe
6. Last, March, Terry, Eugene, Oregon
7. Jeff, Life Science 2a
8. Martha, English
9. The, French
10. Judge Walters

UNIT TEN REVIEW
Practice Test

Part I
A.
1. capital
2. comma
3. double quotation mark
4. comma
5. comma
6. X
7. comma
8. comma
9. semicolon
10. X

B.
1. semicolon
2. comma
3. dash OR colon
4. period
5. comma OR question mark
6. X
7. X
8. semicolon
9. comma
10. X

C.
1. comma OR exclamation point
2. question mark
3. comma
4. X

5. comma
6. semicolon
7. colon
8. period
9. period
10. question mark

D.
1. X
2. double quotation mark
3. double quotation mark
4. X
5. italics
6. italics
7. X
8. X
9. dash OR parenthesis
10. dash OR parenthesis

E.
1. X
2. comma
3. double quotation mark
4. double quotation mark
5. double quotation mark
6. italics
7. italics
8. comma
9. comma
10. capital

Part II
Show these sentences to your instructor or tutor.

EXERCISE 50A

1. The artist should clean his brushes each time he finishes painting. *He* will find the brushes ready to use the next time *he decides* to paint.
2. Americans must vote for the people they want to run their government. *They* have no one to blame but *themselves* if *they* get officials whom *they do not* want.
3. When preparing to write an essay, I try to select a topic which I understand thoroughly. If *I* have only general information, *I cannot* write a convincing paper.
4. The newspaper is sometimes considered to be the voice of the people. But when *it contains* news stories against the best interests of the people, *one begins* to wonder whether *it speaks* for the people or for *its* own personal interests.

5. If everyone wants to do *his or her* part to help others, *he or she* should work with volunteer service organizations and not expect to get paid for every minute *he or she spends* working.   OR   If *people* . . .
6. A person who buys this car receives a guarantee which says *the owner* will not be charged for parts which have to be replaced, but *he* or *she* will be charged only for the labor for replacing them.
7. When a person fills out an application for a position, *he or she* should try to fill out every blank to indicate to the interviewer that *he or she has* tried to give all the information requested.   OR   When people . . .

EXERCISE 50B

1. Quite unexpectedly the homeowners returned to their house and *found* someone searching through their belongings for valuable items.
2. There *were* at least thirty people at the intersection when the two cars collided.
3. A person may enjoy eating olives, but *he may refuse* to try snails.
4. The photograph of the bride's aunts and uncles *was* copied and sent to each of them.
5. Travelers in several countries in Europe *see* storks' nests built on top of chimneys.
6. As the clumsy waitress *served* the four-course meal, she *dropped* bits of food on each of the diners.

EXERCISE 50C

Show this exercise to your instructor or tutor.

EXERCISE 51A

1. Because the chairman is sick, the meeting has been canceled.
2. They were enthusiastic about the invitation they had received from William.
3. Jim could have done a great deal of work with help.
4. Ted Jones was angry because his son had involved himself in a serious predicament.
5. Jane should decide what is best and not wait for Tom to help her.

6. The manager would like to be released from the contract, but he has nearly given up hope of getting approval.
7. The football player was too ill to play in the game and did not appear that day.
8. He believed that she had forgotten their date.
9. This is as far as the bus goes.

EXERCISE 51B

1.	leave	let
2.	plan on	plan to do
3.	quite	quiet
4.	liable	likely
5.	less	fewer
6.		A
7.	alright	all right
8.	affect	effect
9.	amount	number
10.	formally	formerly
11.	further	farther

EXERCISE 52

1. Dick is the taller of my two sons.
2. Mrs. Smith hates weddings more than her husband does.
3. A light blue dress is more becoming than a yellow one.
4. Martha says that her frog can jump farther than mine.
5. Jim is a more powerful weight lifter than any other man in the neighborhood.
6. Jerry already weighs more than he (weighs).
7. Brad's camping equipment is more complete than Tom's (equipment).
8. Mr. Hollis says that Meg is the best musician of his four piano students.
9. I do believe that this new armchair is more (less) comfortable than the old one.
10. Does a pound of potatoes weigh more than a pound of feathers?

EXERCISE 53A

1.	having a conversation	conversing OR talking
2.	Mary can either	Either Mary can OR Mary can either wash the car or repair the window.

3.	who writes stories	a writer OR a story writer
4.		A
5.	to paint	painting
6.	which John built	built by John
7.	to read three novels	reading three novels
8.	an intellectual	intellectual (Omit "an")
9.	without meaning	meaningless
10.	will work	workable

EXERCISE 53B

1. Either Sarah and Tom will buy . . . or they will consider . . .
Sarah and Tom will either buy . . . or consider . . . (No punctuation)
Sarah and Tom either will buy . . . or will consider . . . (No punctuation)
2. He is both a karate expert and an excellent wrestler.
He is not only a karate expert but also an excellent wrestler.
3. Neither the principal nor teachers want to attend the convention.
4. Either George will repair . . . , or he will hire . . .
George will either repair . . . or hire . . . (No punctuation)
5. Judy will neither give Ben a job nor lend him any money.

EXERCISE 54A

These are suggested revisions. Show your sentences to your instructor or tutor if you have questions.

1. He explained how to give artificial respiration to a drowning victim.
2. Because television can give on-the-spot coverage, newspaper stories by comparison are old when readers receive their papers.
3. The rules committee refuses to listen to Dwight Huston's grievances for many reasons.
4. The man in the blue shirt tried valiantly to rescue the small brown-and-white dog perched precariously on a log in the raging river.
5. I still cannot decide what job I would like to have.
6. Evidence suggests that Tim Elliott was not present when the man was shot through the head.

7. Laura Richards is to be admired for her control and calm in handling the problem.
8. Our assembly line efficiency could be increased.

EXERCISE 54B

These are suggested revisions. Show your sentences to your instructor or tutor if you have questions.

1. On his way home from work Dave crashed into an oncoming car.
2. Mary Cummings, who operates the beauty shop, won the award this year for an original hairstyle.
3. You will like Harvey's Haven, which serves delicious hamburgers.   OR   If you like seafood, you will like Harvey's Haven.
4. The reference book John is using contains helpful information for three of his classes.
5. Because Ellis dislikes working out details of a research project, he hired Ross.

EXERCISE 54C

These are suggested revisions. Show your sentences to your instructor or tutor if you have questions.

1. New drivers make many mistakes, but experienced drivers can make just as many if they are not careful.
2. The Johnson brothers had built many well-constructed homes, but they had also erected flimsy houses, which looked as if they would fall down in a strong breeze.
3. Jim, neatly dressed in a new suit, felt disgusted when he saw Nan wearing jeans and a shirt for the contest.
4. Ted Owen and I never realized how much work we would have when we agreed to organize the football parade.
5. Veteran producer Clyde Thornton demonstrated his ability and talent when he produced that movie.
6. Because a big game hunter in Africa never knows when an enraged beast might attack him, he should be an excellent marksman.

EXERCISE 54D

Home builders are meeting buyers' needs with houses that are small, well-designed, and affordable. Although both adults work, they prefer a small house of 700 to 1,000 square feet with two bedrooms instead of three or four. They also want a small lot for less yard upkeep. They may choose a condominium with yard service provided. Though the house is small, home buyers want "frills" such as fireplaces, air conditioning, dishwashers, clothes dryers, and other conveniences that save the buyers work and keep them comfortable. To give the appearance of roominess, designers provide high ceilings because vertical space costs only half as much as horizontal space. The designers also include many built-in cabinets. Perhaps of greatest importance is building houses that people can afford to buy. Small houses built on small lots keep the prices down.

UNIT ELEVEN REVIEW
Practice Test

Part I
A.
Show this exercise to your instructor or tutor.

B.
1. This is as far as he can travel.
2. The man suspected that he was being followed.
3. Did Jan receive an invitation to the party?
4. She seems to be fairly well informed.

C.
1. Jim likes Paul better than Bob does.   OR   Jim likes Paul better than he likes Bob.
2. Mr. Wayne drives the younger of his two daughters to school.
3. Evelyn is more beautiful than Sue.
4. This is a unique tool.
5. The Hawkinses' house is much more elaborate than Dale Smith's (house).

D.
1. Either Brent will catch some fish, or he will buy them at the fish market.   OR   Brent will either catch some fish or buy them at the fish market.

2. The bank messenger is conscientious, careful, and trustworthy.
3. The old woman could neither speak nor walk.
4. The townspeople waited quietly and patiently for the jury's verdict.

E.

These are suggested revisions. Show your sentences to your instructor or tutor if you have questions.

1. After the freighter had dropped anchor in the harbor, the customs inspector went aboard and inspected the entire ship.
2. Carrying a large gold shipment guarded by at least twenty-five armed men, the train crossed the prairie.
3. Two men on horseback, followed by fifty horsemen shooting at them, raced through the dry, brown hills.
4. When the bank opened in the morning, people came in to deposit money, make loan payments, buy traveler's checks, and cash checks.
5. As the little burro tried to cross the river, it stepped into a large hole in the riverbed and sank beneath the water; then it bobbed to the surface and struggled to get to the other side.

Part II

Before 1964 the gates of Yellowstone National Park were closed to automobile traffic when snow fell, but since then visitors can participate in snowmobile expeditions. Visitors can hire a local guide, or they can tour by themselves on well-marked trails that are maintained by a volunteer group. They can rent snowmobiles and clothing designed especially for withstanding a below-zero wind chill factor. Since snowmobiles can reach speeds of up to 45 miles an hour, visitors can easily take a one-day 75-mile round trip that includes a stop at Old Faithful, time for lunch, and a few side trips. They can see steaming geysers blow and mud pots bubble. They can watch animals such as elk and buffalo roam over the snow. The atmosphere of the park is very different from summertime when crowds of people fill the park every day.

Index

A, an, 90-92
Absolute phrases, 269, 289
Active verb, 252-53, 260
Adjective (Adj), 96-99
  Comparison, 326-28
  Complement (Adj-c), 124-26
  Dangling, 266-67
  Descriptive, 98
  Determiner, 87-92, 154
  Nominal, 98
  Position, 99
  Possessive, 94-95
  Prepositional phrase, 112-15
  Punctuation, 99
  Subject complement, 124-26
  Verbals, 245, 261
Adjective clause, 214-22, 236
Adjective Test, 97
Adverb, 25-26, 34, 39, 102-6
  Position, 104-5
  Prepositional phrase, 108-11
  Verbals, 247, 261
Adverbial clause, 206-11, 216, 235, 291
Adverb Test, 27, 102
Antecedent, 157-63
Apostrophe, 94-95
Appositive, 193-94, 226, 235, 291
Articles, 90-92
Auxiliary verbs, 4, 39, 48, 51, 65, 67

Be, 17-18, 29, 57-58
Brackets, 294

Capitalization, 305-7
Clause (definition), 235
Clauses
  Adjective, 214-22, 236
  Adverbial, 206-11, 216, 236, 291
  Dependent, 206-11, 214-22, 225-28
  Independent, 174-76, 205, 235, 284-86
  Noun, 225-28
  Subordinate, 206-11
  within clauses, 231-32
  within verbals, 231-32
Coherence, 337-38
Colon, 288, 300
Combining sentences, 127-28, 174-75, 189, 197, 206-8, 210-11, 218-20, 227-28, 245-47, 257-58, 269
Comma with
  Absolute phrases, 269, 289
  Addresses, 299
  Adjective clause, 217-18
  Adjectives, 289
  Adverbial clause, 291
  Appositive, 291

Comma with
  Compound predicate, 288
  Compound sentence, 285
  Compound subject, 288
  Coordinating conjunction, 285
  Dates, 299
  Degrees and titles, 299
  Noun of direct address, 293
  Prepositional phrase, 293
  Quotation marks, 298-99
  Salutation, 300
  Series, 288
  Transitional words, 293
  Verbal phrase, 291-92
Comma fault or splice, 177
Command, 32
Comparative degree, 326-27
Comparison, 326-27
Complete subject and predicate, 133
Complex sentences, 206-28, 236
Compound-complex sentences, 232
Compound predicate, 188-89, 191
Compound sentence, 174-76, 179-80, 191, 235
Compound subject, 187-88
Compound words, 345
Conjunctions (C)
  Coordinating, 2, 175, 235
  Correlative, 331-32
  Subordinating, 181-82, 208, 236
Conjunctive adverbs, 179-83
Contractions, 69-70
Correction symbols, 339-40

Dangling modifier, 266-67
Dash, 289, 291, 294
Demonstrative pronouns, 154
Dependent clause, 205, 235
Determiner, 87-92
Direct object (Ndo), 11-12, 130, 135, 226, 245, 261

Ellipsis, 300
Exclamation point, 284

Fragment, 276-77
Fused sentence, 177
Future perfect tense, 49, 50-54
Future tense, 39-42, 48-49

Gerund, 245-47
Greek plurals, 345-46

Hyphen, 301, 345

Idioms, 325
Indefinite pronouns, 152-53
Independent clause, 174-76, 205, 235, 284-86

Indirect object (Nio), 130-31, 226
Infinitive, 33
  Phrase, 260-62
Informal English, 315, 319-22
Intensive pronouns, 150
Interrogative pronouns, 155
Intransitive verb, 11-13, 18, 135
Irregular verbs, 34-36, 48, 50-51, 76-78
Italics, 297-301

Latin plurals, 345
Linking verb (LV), 17-19, 124-26

Main verb, 39, 48, 65
Modals, 64-65
Modifiers, 83, 136-37
  Adjective, 2, 136-37
  Adverb, 25-26, 83, 136-37
  Clause, 206-11, 214-22
  Complement, 124-26
  Dangling, 267-68
  Misplaced, 265-66
  Misused, 106
  Prepositional phrase, 108-15, 208, 235
  Verbals, 235, 244, 247

Negatives (not, never), 67-68
Noun, 2, 7, 8, 62, 184-85
  Antecedent, 157-63
  Capitalization, 305-8
  Clause, 225-28, 236, 291
  Collective, 167
  Common, 85
  Count, 89-90
  Direct address, 293
  General, 85
  Noncount (mass), 89-90
  Plural, 84, 345-46
  Proper, 85
  Singular and plural, 84
  Specific, 85
  Subject, 2-3, 11, 20-21
  Third person, 146
  Verbal, 247, 256, 261
Noun Test, 7
Number, singular-plural, 345-46

Object complement, 134-35, 261

Padding, 335
Paired connectors, 331-32
Parallelism, 330-32
Parentheses, 297
Passive verb (PV), 252-53, 265
Past participle, 256-57
Past perfect tense, 48, 49, 50-54
Past tense, 34-35, 48, 49, 52

Period, 284, 299
Person (nouns, pronouns), 146
Phrase (definition), 235
Phrases
    Absolute, 269, 289
    Appositive, 193–94, 226, 235, 291
    Prepositional, 108–15
    Verb, 39–40, 235
    Verbal, 235, 244, 247
Point of view, 314–17
    Number, 316
    Person, 316
    Tense, 316–17
    Tone, 314–15
Positive degree, 326–27
Possessives, 7, 94–95, 147–48
Predicate (P), 2–3, 11, 133, 187–89
Preposition (Pr)
    Object of, 108, 226, 245
    Phrase, 108–15, 208, 235
    Punctuation, 293
Present participle, 245–47
Present perfect tense, 48–49, 50–54
Present tense, 21, 28–29, 30–31, 48, 49
Progressive tenses, 49, 57–59
Pronouns, 2, 145–63
    Demonstrative, 154
    Gender, 147
    Indefinite, 152–53
    Intensive, 150
    Interrogative, 155
    Person, 146
    Personal, 146–47
    Point of view, 314–17
    Possessives, 147–48
    Reflexive, 150
    Relative, 214–15
Pronoun-antecedent agreement
    (P Agr), 156–62
Pronoun reference, 156–63
Punctuation with
    Absolute phrase, 289
    Adjective clause, 217–18
    Adjectives, 99

Punctuation with
    Adverbial clause, 209
    Appositives, 194
    Compound structures, 175, 182–84, 189
    Conjunction, 175
    Dates, 299
    Dependent clause, 232
    Prepositional phrase, 293
    Quotation marks, 298–99
    Titles and degrees, 299
    Transitional expressions, 179–83, 235, 293
    Verbal phrase, 247–58

Question, 71–73
Question mark, 71–73, 284
Quotation marks, 298–99

Reflexive pronoun, 150
Regular verbs, 34, 48, 50–51
Relative pronouns, 214–15
Run-on sentences, 177

Second person, 146
Semicolon, 175, 288
Sentence combining
    Absolute phrase, 269
    Adjective clause, 218–20
    Adjective complement, 127–28
    Adverbial clause, 206–8, 210–11
    Appositive, 193
    Compound sentence, 174–75
    Compound subject or predicate, 189
    Noun clause, 227–28
    Verbal phrase, 245–47, 257–58, 263
Sentence Keys, 12–13, 18–19, 126, 131, 133–36
Sentence patterns, 11–13, 18–19, 124–26, 130–31, 133–36, 175
Simple sentence, 176, 235
Simple subject and predicate, 133
Spelling, 30, 35, 84, 345–46
Subject (S), 2–3, 11, 20, 133, 166–67, 187–89, 245

Subject complement (Nsc), 17–19, 124–26, 135, 226
Subject-verb agreement, 30, 165–67
Subordinating conjunction (Sr), 181–82, 208, 236
Superlative degree, 326–27

Tense, 29, 316
The, 90–92
To be, 17, 29, 57–58
Tone, 314–15
Transitional expressions, 179–83, 235, 293
Transitive verb, 11–13, 135

Unity, 336

Verb (Vi, Vt, LV, PV)
    Active, 252–53, 260
    Auxiliary, 4, 39, 48, 51, 65, 67
    Base, 29–30, 39
    Intransitive (Vi), 11–13, 18, 135
    Irregular, 34–36, 48, 50–51, 76–78
    Linking, 17–19, 124–26
    Main, 39, 48, 65
    Modal, 64–65
    Passive (PV), 252–53, 265
    Phrase, 39–40, 235
    Principal parts, 29, 51, 76–78
    Regular, 34, 48, 50–51
    Tense, 29, 31, 47–48, 316
    Transitive (Vt), 11–13, 135
Verbal, 244
Verbal phrase, 235, 244, 247
Verb Test, 4
Voice, active and passive, 252–53, 265

When, where, why, how—adverbs, 25–26, 34, 39, 102–6
Which one, 97
Who, which, that, 214–15
Word usage, 322–25